THE RELIGION OF
AYAHUASCA

THE RELIGION OF AYAHUASCA

The Teachings of the Church of Santo Daime

ALEX POLARI DE ALVERGA

Translated from the Portuguese
by Rosana Workman

Park Street Press
Rochester, Vermont • Toronto, Canada

Park Street Press
One Park Street
Rochester, Vermont 05767
www.ParkStPress.com

Park Street Press is a division of Inner Traditions International

Originally published in 1999 by Park Street Press under the title *Forest of Visions: Ayahuasca, Amazonian Spirituality, and the Santo Daime Tradition*

Library of Congress Cataloging-in-Publication Data

Alverga, Alex Polari de.
 [Guia da foresta. English]
 The religion of Ayahuasca : the teachings of the Church of Santo Daime / Alex Polari de Alverga.
     p. cm.
 Includes bibliographical references.
 Summary: "An insider's experience and personal transformation with ayahuasca and the religious philosophy surrounding it"—Provided by publisher.
 ISBN 978-1-59477-398-3 (pbk.)
 1. Santo Daime (Cult) 2. Ayahuasca. 3. Hallucinogenic drugs and religious experience. 4. Alverga, Alex Polari de. I. Title.
 BL2592.S25A5813 2010
 299'.93—dc22

                                                              2010026897

Printed and bound in the United States by Lake Book Manufacturing

10   9   8   7   6   5   4   3   2   1

Text design and layout by Virginia Scott Bowman
This book was typeset in Garamond Premier Pro with Goudy Oldstyle and Gill Sans as display typefaces

To Madrinha Rita, Padrinho Alfredo, and Padrinho Waldete for sharing their teachings that represent Padrinho Sebastião's doctrine so well.

To Pedro, Ze, Neves, Nonata, Isabel, Marlene, other sons and daughters, and all the people of Céu do Mapiá, because it is with them that Padrinho's memories stay alive and accessible to all of us.

To all Padrinhos and Madrinhas, brothers, sisters, and friends. To everyone who graciously gave me pieces of recorded material or helped clarify parts of Padrinho Sebastião's life.

My thanks also to Gustavo for the support in the realization of this project; to Ana for her help and dedication in transcribing the tapes; and to Nelso for his enthusiasm during the writing of this book.

Contents

Foreword

• • •

Stephen Larsen

IN 1992 A mysterious visitor arrived at our little personal growth center in the Shawangunk Mountains of New York State. He was an Andean shaman, a Quechua-speaking *Yachag*. He told us in his fluent Spanish that he was an appointed spokesman from the traditional peoples of the Andean high plateaus, and he delivered a message that gave us goosebumps!

Exactly five hundred years had passed since the coming of the European conquerors to the New World, and an Incan prophecy was asking for fulfillment. The white men's arrival had been prophecied before they ever set foot on this continent. The white brother, forgetful of many things, would enact awful cruelties on the native peoples during the first five hundred years. There would be disrespect of the most fundamental rules of the proper human relationship to the earth, and the resulting catastrophes would affect *Pachamama,* the Great Earth Mother.

But after five hundred years, a great turnabout would occur. The white brother would awaken, like a sleepwalker, from his violent trance. There would be an amazing healing that would affect the entire world, helping with the purging catastrophes that were coming. The spirit of the Condor (South America) was asking to dance with the Eagle (North America). From their flight would emerge great joy and brotherhood between the peoples of North and South America and a new understanding between the children of the white brother and of the traditional peoples. A new relationship between the earth and all of humanity would ensue.

Not long after the Andean shaman had appeared, a flow of visitors from South America began to come to our center and into our lives. I began to realize our own inevitable participation in a great story, the prophecy of which the shaman spoke. He was the messenger for a living process already underway. We began to find Spanish and Portuguese mingling in our conversations. When two mother-saints from Bahia, Brazil, came and divined the living, loving presence of Oshun—the *orisha** who rules beauty, love, and abundance—in our waterfall and enacted a ceremony of thanksgiving, gifting her with fruits and flowers, we knew that the dance of the eagle and the condor had begun.

In 1995 I was asked by the International Transpersonal Association (ITA) to help design a journey that would follow a conference to be held in the Amazon the next year, for participants interested in shamanic practices. I wanted to find an experience that was both authentic and relatively safe for the group we had in mind: about forty physicians, psychologists, social workers, and corporate executives. After considerable research and a helpful connection with Guilherme Barcellos, a Brazilian participant in one of our shamanism workshops, a possibility opened to bring our group to the legendary community of Mapiá in the heart of the Amazon. I read an article in *The Shaman's Drum* about one of the leaders of the village, Alex Polari de Alverga, a former political activist who had spent years in jail under the military junta in Brazil. Purged by torture, brutality, and deprivation, Polari found a new spiritual path after his release, the Santo Daime, an Amazonian religion born out of jungle entheogens, mediumship, and healing. Its unique and potent combination of Christianity and indigenous practices offered a way of spiritual opening that appealed to Polari's questing soul.

It is a classic story: a battered and disillusioned young man embarks on a spiritual search. He encounters a forest saint with luminous eyes and a great white beard, who opens his spiritual eyes and heals his soul. He passes through many trials and tribulations, not the least of which is the illness and death of his teacher. Ultimately, he becomes the *Padrinho* with the long white beard himself—the wise forest guide for a new generation of seekers. This story is, in fact, the substance of this book. The meeting of Alex Polari with Padrinho Sebastião Mota de Melo, one of the two founders of the tradition called Santo Daime, is a spiritual encounter comparable to the search of the Tibetan saint Milarepa for his teacher Marpa, the translator.

---

*God or goddess. In the Yoruba tradition each orisha has a specific domain.

It is a story close to the bone of our contemporary soul-quest; the modern search for initiation: Castaneda to Don Juan, Kyriakos Markides to Daskalos. An educated seeker from the modern world humbles himself before an illiterate man of the working class who nonetheless opens him to a spiritual knowledge deeper than anything in his university education. It is in the details of such a dialogue that we all may be brought further on our own journey, our own quest for rediscovery of an ancient wisdom to help with the trials of modern living. This book is rich in such dialogue. If Polari's considerable scholarship and political savvy did not provide the answers he needed when he first encountered the Padrinho, they seem to have helped him frame important questions. He was able to recognize the eloquent simplicity of the answers he received and to write them down for posterity. The experiences, setbacks, and lessons of his initiation can instruct our own journey.

I finally met Alex Polari in 1996 at the scheduled ITA conference in the Amazonian rubber trade town of Manaus. There he was, a bearded man with luminous eyes and a quietness about him. Polari had prepared a scholarly paper on the psychological, cultural, and spiritual dimensions of the Daime's use as an entheogen. He seemed quite at home in the intellectual ambiance of the conference. He had brought a group of Daime singers and musicians with him to Manaus, so we were able to bring attendees of the conference to some Daime works* that he led nearby. After our papers had been presented and the conference closed, Alex traveled with our group the thousand miles or so by plane, then smaller plane, then motorboat, then a dugout canoe fitted to ply the *igarapé,* the tortuous winding streams that course through the untouched rain forest. It was a journey of almost mythic proportions for most of us, as we penetrated farther and farther into the great natural wonder that is the Amazonian rain forest.

Our group had a twofold interest. One was the astonishing existence of a real-life utopia in the jungle. The community of about six hundred, which constitutes the village of Mapiá, was said to live in harmony with nature, using the forest sustainably (they called it their "extractionist"

---

*A Daime works is a sacred ceremony involving special preparation prayers and hymns in which the Daime (ayahuasca) is taken as a sacrament—often several times. A typical Daime works lasts three to six hours and is attended by anywhere from three to over three hundred people.

philosophy), and to have an effective community health program relying largely on naturally occurring plant remedies and homeopathy. We also knew that the center of their communal life is a developed tradition involving the sacred use of entheogens.

Santo Daime is an essentially Christian religion but is also profoundly ecumenical and syncretic, incorporating Native (South) American, African, and Espiritismo* elements. *Mestre* (master) Raimundo Serra Irineu, the original founder of the religion and the teacher of Sebastião Mota, was of African extraction. This majestic, seven-foot-tall black man learned the power of the drink known as *ayahuasca,* made from the leaves *Psychotria viridis* and the vines *Banisteriopsis caapi* from the indigenous people of the forest. It was he who adapted that ancient technology of the sacred to the specifically Christian inflection it receives in Daime. Mestre Irineu generated the first *Hinario,* the book of sacred channeled hymns that are sung in Daime services, and laid down many of the ethical guidelines that are observed in Daime practice.

What would an entire community organized on such spiritual and ritual bases be like? In our alienated, mechanized societies, the possibilities cry out to every sensitive heart. It would be the realization of peaceful community life in harmony with the natural and even the spiritual ecology—the devas of the plant world and the near-regions of what Theosophy calls the Astral, the World of Spirits.

I had become excited by the existence of such psychologically sophisticated visionary utopias through reading Kilton Stewart's legendary article on the Malaysian Senoi, "Dream Theory in Malaya."[1] It described a peaceful people living in harmony and social cooperation through the daily interpretation of dreams and using dream lore for inspiration for their songs and community rituals. Is it possible? A community in which dreams weave minds and hearts together in harmonious ways? Aldous Huxley had touched on this mythos in his visionary book *Island,* in which altered states are integrated into personal and communal life. Now we would enter a real-life experiment based on principles that many of us held dear; but we wondered about their practical efficacy.

---

*Espiritismo, a widespread Brazilian tradition, is based on the work of the European esotericist Allain Kardec, which has enjoyed immense popularity in Brazil. It continues to flourish in our time.

I know I was in a mythic landscape when the hummingbird appeared. I had read that the *beija-flor,* the "one who kisses flowers," was an important spiritual messenger who greeted people on their arrival in the jungle. We had been on the igarapé for many hours now. Fallen branches and sometimes the great boles of the jungle hardwoods lying across the river made the going treacherous. At times we were in the rapid swirling water as often as in the canoe. Sometimes we slithered over the slimy boughs, sometimes under. Now, in a calmer section, I was riding along, hypnotized by the greenish filtered light that penetrated the forest canopy. Then suddenly the hummingbird made its exquisitely brief, magical appearance. My amazement was so great, my heart seemed to be fluttering at the same blurry speed as its wings. The creature was larger than any hummingbird I had ever seen and multicolored, hovering in that vibratory nimbus made of woven energy. In some wordless place where shamanic lore works its magic, I knew I had been greeted. I had met the messenger of the forest! We were in the energy field of Mapiá. The canoes arrived at the village a half-hour later.

Joseph Campbell always said that if you want to read what is important in a culture or a community, look for the largest building.[2] In Mapiá there could be no doubt: there it was, a virtual cathedral, made of teak, ebony, and mahogany, shaped in the form of a six-pointed star. It sits back from the river, toward the crest of a gently sloping hill above a small brook, which flows down through the village. One climbs many stairs to reach it, and as I climbed these stairs that stretched up the Amazonian hillside, I remembered a dozen cathedrals and shrines all over the world where one must climb for blessings, in some cases on hands and knees, kissing every step and praying. I found myself doing that silently in my mind as I mounted the long ascent.

To enter the church, one passes by a smaller building that glows with lit candles—even in the daytime. It is the shrine where the remains of Padrinho Sebastião, Alex's great teacher, have been placed in honor. The main way into the church passes this shrine. Large enough to house the entire community, the church is where the great Daime works of Mapiá are celebrated, and people come from miles around, through the forest and on the igarapés. In the center of the church is a star-shaped hardwood altar. Rising from the altar into central high peak of the building is a beautiful carving: the Tree of Life, with a vine wrapped around it. Listen, says the Daime: Christ has returned to Earth in the form of this vine, *I am the Vine, ye are the branches.* In a sacred marriage of two plants, the *jagube,* the vine, is combined with the *chacruna,* the leaf, to make the sacred tea of the Daime ceremonies.

We jaded postmodern types tend to look with a jaundiced eye on any would-be utopia, and we had dwelt among poverty, filth, and degradation in adjacent Brazilian communities. But in Mapiá we found homes and public spaces such as the canteen almost excruciatingly clean. Knowing what it must have taken to get them that way, without modern cleaning agents or tools, we were amazed.

There is a neat, efficient looking little medical clinic, where we saw a boy with advanced leprosy who had come in from a jungle community some distance away. The twelve physicians on our expedition were impressed with what they saw: a mixture of contemporary "allopathic" medicine used as needed—they happily received the satchels of antibiotics, antiseptics, bandages, and supplies from us—alongside the herbal-homeopathic modes of healing. I met with one of the jungle pharmacists, a woman who makes potent preparations from indigenous wild plants. In an amazing conversation hampered by my limited Portuguese, I learned how elemental spirits of the rain forest appeared to her, sometimes even before the physical plant was discovered, and helped her understand the pharmaceutical uses of their plant. "Yes, but do they really work?" I heard myself asking, half hating myself for the skeptic's question. "Yes," she said simply, "they work." Here in the jungle, I realized, there is not much room for placebos or double-blind studies—or for remedies that don't work! Life seems precarious and precious. Healers need to heal well, shamans to be able to cast out demons of the same vigor as all the vital, tenacious tropical species!

Near the center of the village is a school that seems fit for hobbit children, with fairy landscapes and mushroom houses painted on the building. Little bright-eyed students come and go happily. Although resources are limited, there is an attempt to present a modern education, a glimpse of what lies beyond the seemingly endless forest. These children will have to learn to live simultaneously in the world of the forest and the vast global village, our world with its intricacies and deceptions. Literacy and even erudition are highly prized in Mapiá, though *caboclos* (the illiterate natives of the forest) are not scorned.

It was in Mapiá that Padrinho Sebastião's visionary journey came to fruition. Mapiá is the true proving-ground, the place on earth where the spiritual principles that (the tradition believes) will inform the next millennium are to be tested and validated. Padrinho Sebastião said, "All your ideas and insight matter little unless you put them into practice every day in community—and with your brothers and sisters."

One of my personal goals in visiting Mapiá was to experience a community based on a mythos close to my heart: the idea of the "New Jerusalem," a community actually modeling itself on the archetype of the holy city. The religion my family converted to when I was about eight years old was called The Church of the New Jerusalem, sometimes referred to as "Swedenborgian." This movement was more well known in nineteenth-century America when its principles informed much of the New England Transcendentalism and Utopian Movement in nineteenth-century America.[3] Though in the whole community, only Alex Polari had read the works of Emanuel Swedenborg (1688–1772), the great Swedish scientist and visionary, I was amazed to find resonances of a philosophical and spiritual sort on every side.[4]

Swedenborg postulated a world of spirits adjacent to and in intimate contact with this one. We may be consciously or unconsciously in the presence of spirits all the time; and they may influence us for good or evil, depending on their natures. This belief also seems to permeate the Daime tradition. Careful ritual protections accompany the Daime works and ceremonies, so that contact with the "good" spirits is maximized, and interference from the "bad" spirits is warded away. "No evil may enter this sanctuary" is usually said at the beginning and throughout the Daime services. However, the protection is in essence more religious than magical (although in the Amazon magic never seems far).* In the context of the Daime ceremony, the prayers to Christ and the Virgin, the blessing of the space, the uniforms, the men and women separated but dancing in harmony and sending love, all help protect the psyche in its open, vulnerable state produced by the entheogen.

Swedenborg saw authentic human spiritual life as combining two

---

*In a nutshell, magic aims at direct spiritual effect by a ritual of some kind, whereas religion enacts a ritual of propitiation to a higher power for protection.

fundamental principles, which he referred to as Love and Truth. In the Daime conception, all beings owe their lives to *"Pai Eterno,"* the Divine source (mediated and guided by a feminine aspect, the *Virgem Maria,* or the Rainha [queen].* In both traditions there is an idea of sin, not so much as invitation of divine wrath as an erroneous understanding. Enterprises that fail to inquire into divine intentions are doomed to failure—not through divine displeasure but through estrangement from the flowing source of all life, and failure to acknowledge the interconnectedness of all things. (The official name of the Daime church is The Church of the Universal Flowing Light.) Swedenborg called this same principle *influx,* and maintained that the Divine flows into all things as into a vessel, that humankind is merely the recipient of an overflowing of the Divine. The real goal of spiritual practice, therefore, is to prepare a place—to use truth and love to cleanse and chasten oneself to receive more adequately the Divine. As Padrinho Sebastião said, *Examine a conscientia, examine direitino*, meaning examine your consciousness well, and assess your worthiness to receive the Bridegroom. If you don't do it voluntarily, the *passagem,* and the *apuração* (the passages and the cleansing of your own energies) will come upon you like punishments. (In the Daime ceremonies these cleansing responses are never far away, and one hears one's brothers and sisters purging explosively or weeping softly all around.)

If creation, as Sri Ramakrishna would say, is a ceaseless streaming forth of the Divine into all things for both systems, then "all things must be God things." Swedenborg saw nature as a book that instructed us in spiritual things by analogy, what he called *correspondences* (everything in nature corresponds to something in spirit). Padrinho Sebastião regarded nature, and *la floresta,* the forest, as an inexhaustible book of lessons for humanity. That is why the Christ came again in the form of a vine, so that humanity might "humble itself before a plant," and receive high spiritual instruction through bowing at the shrine of nature.†

Rainha in Portuguese means "queen." Here it refers to the Virgin Mary, who is addressed as the Queen of the Forest, Sky, and Sea. *Rainha* is also the name given to the feminine plant of the two used in Daime (*Psychotria viridis*).

†For Swedenborg, the Second Coming took place in the world of spirits in 1757. For Padrinho, it is now and into the eschaton, with the Daime as the literal embodiment of the Christ.

Probably the single most important agreement of the two systems is the notion that all the good intentions and profound meditations—even the transformative events of the *miraçao,* Divine revelations that come very personally in the Daime work, often after the passagem, are useless unless brought into daily practice. Swedenborg called them *uses*: the effects, small or great, that we exert on others and on all of creation by extension. As the Padrinho emphasizes in the text that follows, "Everything I have said is useless, unless you can realize it in community practice—in actions embodying these principles toward your brothers and sisters." Swedenborg placed in importance loving one's neighbor after loving the Lord. Practical and charitable expressions of one's affections allow love, an inexhaustible source of renewal of Divine origin, to flow through one's life into the community. And lastly Daime and the Swedenborgian path complement each other in providing a daily and intimate spirituality and a praxis, a way of working on oneself, to the Christian tradition.*

Mapiá inhabitants, and the Daime community generally, seem to walk their spiritual talk. One sophisticated pilgrim to world spiritual communities gave high praise to the levels of daily work and discipline, community contribution, and charity that he saw in Mapiá. He said only in the most disciplined Zen and Theravada temples had he seen a comparable work ethic and impeccable community spirit. When disaster or flood strikes neighboring communities, refugees stream into Mapiá because they associate the place with cleanliness, compassion, and charity.

When one attends Daime works in other Brazilian locations and in American and European cities, warmth overflows. The strictest *fardadoes,* (also called "star-people") who maintain order and group cohesion during the ceremonies, seem friendly after the works are concluded. There is a feeling of commonality, of having worked together on an eternal project and having done a good job.

My wife, Robin, and I later attended an unforgettable Daime Works in Rio de Janeiro at Ceú do Mar (Sky of the Sea), a church plastered to the side of a granite monolith that looks down over the city, surrounded by riotous

---

*It would seem that Christianity is lacking in these regards, certainly compared to the eastern and shamanic traditions, except in certain monastic practices, such as those of the Greek Hesychasts and the practices of Saint Ignatius of Loyola.

subtropical vegetation.* As is usual in Daime churches, the men's and the women's groups were on opposite sides of the church. This was the largest men's group we had witnessed, but the men were also the toughest-looking bunch I have ever seen anywhere. Knife scars and other wounds, all the grim imprints of urban Brazilian existence, marked their faces; they looked laughably incongruous, like pirates wearing white shirts and ties; and with silver stars on their breasts. But when the works began and they started to sing, an extraordinary transfiguration occurred. Robin and I each independently felt the same thing: the Daime had saved these men from the streets and from themselves. They were radiant with life and love.

They sang like rough-hewn angels with their deep voices and even threatened to drown out the women, who often dominate the singing. The authenticity of the transformation was unmistakable to our heightened senses and with the Spirit of Truth in the room. Addiction, violence, perverse passions had all been touched by the Universal Flowing Light. These men were not only in recovery, they were in ecstasy. (Having begun my career as a mental health professional many years ago in tough urban settings such as New York City, I know a miracle when I see one.) These people's lives were touched by the Spirit! There was an enormous outpouring of love and fellowship at the end of the session, as the men hugged each other and said farewell until next time.

Mestre Irineu and Padrinho Sebastião, illiterate men from the lowest socioeconomic classes, seem to have discovered and established a religion that offers much of value to its participants. A humble religion of the *caboclos,* the native men of the forest, the Daime works well on even harder cases—university intellectuals, professionals, and politicians. When CONFEN, the official Brazilian regulatory agency, came to Mapiá to investigate the Daime as a drug (see chapter 12) they experienced the Daime and most important, according to reports, left as brothers who had shared a sacrament and an ineffable experience together. Thus the church demonstrated its legitimacy, and its sacrament, the Daime, is legal in Brazil.

Our group left Mapiá not so much converts as witnesses to an extraordinary human experiment performed with integrity and compassion. Many held a little special something—insight or experience—close to their hearts.

---

*Padrinho himself had come to Rio and deplored the ethos of materialism, acquisition, and violence that he saw.

And none can forget the beautiful simplicity of the hymns, rising above the forest and momentarily hushing the chatter of monkeys and the cries of the birds. This remarkable human community sings and dances its heart out for the love of God and Goddess deep in the deepest forest of the world. Theirs is a song of universal brotherhood and compassion, respect for nature, and good will toward all creatures. When Earth reaches up so joyfully, we can feel Heaven touching Earth.

Not a convert, at least as yet, I feel I have a fairly objective eye to Santo Daime's struggles and limitations. As in any human community, there are conflicts and ego trips. The problems they face are not dissimilar to the rest of the world's travails—economic, social, personal. Yet, as Padrinho says in the pages that follow, humanity needs religion to form communities. We are not yet able to create paradise out of our own wits and resources. But if we can live with an awareness of the presence of the Divine in our lives, a blessedness starts to attend our doings and flows through the community, touching with the light of compassion the very atmosphere we live in.

Ultimately, Alex Polari grew to be that which he respected, a great *Padrinho,* with his own *Hinario* to be sung on special occasions. For me, listening to his Hinario is an uplifting experience, as if I were ascending a spiral Jacob's ladder into the Bright World. He continues to live in Mapiá, surrounded by a living family: his wife Sonia, whom he first met in prison so long ago as a ministering angel and who has come to receive her own beautiful hymns, and their grown children Joanna, Thiago, and Paula, all accomplished musicians and singers. They are individuals, yet they live gracefully in community. When we find ourselves among them, there is always a genial, pleasant warmth. Song and laughter are frequent.

The Religion of Ayahuasca is more than a saga, it is an epic journey of becoming, right at the genesis of an important religious tradition that may yet, especially if its own prophecies are true, play a part in the age that is to come. The eagle and the condor are in dancing flight, north learns from south, south from north. All are once again learning to honor the sacred earth and the spirits that guide human destiny. May we gradually learn how to undo five-hundred years of hard lessons with a renewed appreciation of ancient wisdom and the sacrament of love for our brothers and sisters of whatever people, continent, or culture!

Preface

• • •

Jonathan Goldman

THE FIRST TIME I drank Daime was on January 5, 1988, in a ritual led by Alex Polari de Alverga on a mountaintop in the countryside of Brazil. When I walked through the door of Alex's church, I embarked upon an adventure that has taken me into places—literally and figuratively—that I never even dreamed existed. Since that time I have entered onto a spiritual path, the Santo (Holy) Daime, that has brought me personal healing and evolution, positively transformed my relationships and professional life, and given me an opportunity to serve others in a real and deeply satisfying way. So I write this introduction with a sense of honor and excitement that comes with knowing that you who read this book will soon encounter truthful information about an extraordinary man, Sebastião Mota de Melo, and an extraordinary path to God.

This book is the first in the English language written about the Daime by someone who knows his subject matter intimately. I have read many articles on the Internet and in several books by people who, in typical American style, drink Daime a few times and decide they understand enough to tell others about it. I often cringe at the descriptions and explanations offered by these writers, and find myself praying that no one else reads them. My prayer is the opposite for the book you hold in your hands. It is time for the Daime to step out of the shadows, and we are most blessed to have Alex Polari to reveal the light for us.

Because I first met Alex in the context of spiritual ritual, I knew his higher self before I knew him as the brother and friend he is to me today. I have been deeply impressed by both of these aspects of Alex. He is a man of extraordinary courage, wisdom, and compassion, who works harder than anybody I have ever met, traveling many months of the year to lead rituals all over the world as part of his duties as one of the leaders of the Daime Path. These rituals are powerful beyond my ability to describe them, but Alex projects a sense of calmness, strength, dignity, and an exquisite focus that allows those attending the rituals to enter into new depths of their own being.

When I was last in Céu do Mapiá, the center of the Daime religion located a two-day's canoe ride up a river in the Brazilian Amazon, I stayed with Alex and his wife, Sonia, and their four children in a three bedroom house. I slept in Alex's library and the range of books I saw on the shelves, and the knowledge that Alex had not only read them all, but studied most of them, added to my already enormous respect for him. I saw books in English, Portuguese, and Spanish. I saw books written by and about Hindu saints, Buddhist lamas, and Christian mystics. Political histories sat next to medical texts that sat next to the verse of poets throughout the ages that sat next to explorations of spiritual, political, and economic systems from a wide variety of viewpoints. Alex has the ability to expound on any number of subjects in a manner that teaches ways of thinking that I never considered. His intellect is extraordinary.

But Alex is also an activist. He is presently involved in a project to bring nutritious food to the region of the Amazon in which he lives, one of the poorest regions in the world and one beset by disease—much of which could be prevented by better nutrition and sanitation. He is a living example of the teachings of his guide and teacher, Sebastião Mota de Melo, about whom much of this book concerns. He puts theory into practice, and then he writes about it beautifully.

The Holy Daime is a syncretic religion whose origins and center are in the Amazon rain forest of Brazil. Its historical antecedents date back at least to the Inca Indians, who are known to have employed a sacredly prepared admixture of jungle plants to aid them in their spiritual life. According to legend, when the Spanish conquerors came to South America looking for gold, the low level of their spiritual evolution led them to seek and take the golden metal in abundance in that region. What they failed to grasp was that the true gold, the golden realms of nonphysical reality that Inca initiates could enter into through their religious practices, was accessed by the drinking of a sacred tea. In the face of invasion many of the Incas abandoned their cities and found refuge in the depths of the jungle, taking with them the key to the golden realm, the tea that became known as *ayahuasca,* named after one of the priests who had led his people to safety.

Whatever the historical facts of the matter, we know for certain that many Indian tribes all over the Amazon basin, who are separated geographically by thousands of miles of jungle and who have had no physical means of communicating with each other, have extremely similar spiritual practices that center around the drinking of an almost identical sacred brew. Until the early part of this century these practices were exclusively the province of the Indian tribes.

Late in the second decade of this century, a young Brazilian man by the name of Raimundo Irineu Serra was invited by a friend to journey into Peru to participate in the ceremonies of a local tribe. He joined in a number of ceremonies, in between which he worked as a border guard in the Amazon region of Brazil. During one such ritual he received a vision that was to lead him to the formation of the Santo Daime religion. He saw a woman in the Moon who identified herself as the Queen of the Forest. She told him to go into the jungle by himself for a week to fast, pray, and drink the sacred tea. When he did this he was informed, to his total surprise, that he had a spiritual mission: He was to establish a new spiritual path to be called the Santo (Holy) Daime. He came to understand that the woman with whom he was communicating was in fact an embodiment of the Divine Feminine in one of Her aspects, the Queen of the Forest. He came to directly meet her and re-remember his relationship with Her in another of Her aspects, the Virgin Mary, and learned that the Lady of Conception was offering herself as his patroness, guide, and protector. He also came to understand that she was instructing him to create a religion that would center around the direct experience of the divine forces contained both in the forest and in the astral plane. Access to these subtle realms would be facilitated by the drinking of the sacramental tea that, in its new context, was to be called Daime.

One of the central mysteries of the Daime, and one that clearly shows Daime's uniqueness, concerns the nonphysical beings to which the religion is dedicated. These beings, some familiar to westerners from a Judeo-Christian background, are not merely archetypes and symbols. It is the experience of most people who become initiates within the Daime Path, and of many who drink Daime but do not join the Path, that Jesus Christ, the Virgin Mother, and other beings not necessarily traditionally connected with Christianity, are palpable, seeable, heard, and, in some cases, touchable entities. It is not unusual for a person to directly experience teaching and healing within the *miração,* the living visions that the Daime often brings. The experience of those who participate in such direct communication is that they are not seeing visions, which implies a relationship to the experience similar to watching a movie. The experience of the miração is one of being taken within one's own consciousness into the dimensions inhabited by these beings, or, conversely, experiencing them actually entering the room itself where the ceremony is being conducted. The descriptions of these experiences are not unlike the descriptions of spiritual revelations and life-transforming visions reported by people throughout history.

It is most important to note that this experience of direct contact with spiritual beings, spiritual teachings, and the Divinity both within oneself and outside oneself is not in any way reserved for an elite. There are no human intermediaries in the Daime. It was one of Padrinho Sebastião's main teachings that the purpose of religious practice is the direct experience of each participant with the Divine. A central mystery of the Daime is that of the nature of the sacrament itself. It is the experience of Daime practitioners that there is a vastly intelligent Divine Being embodied in the tea. It is simultaneously a Being and a gateway to other dimensions where other Beings reside. The physical tea is made in a ceremony in which an alchemical process takes place. There is a combining of elements in an intensely focused and sacredly held space that results in the incarnation, the embodying of a Divine Being into a liquid body. This is only strange to imagine until we consider that we incarnate by the same process. We, too, are divine beings in physical (chemical) bodies who are born for a purpose that we grow to discover. The being of the Daime incarnates to provide teaching, comfort, healing, and spiritual evolution to those who join it. This Being in tea form is a true, living sacrament. When we drink it we enter into the most intimate communion possible. We take it into the interior of our bodies. It enters our bloodstream. By joining physically, body to body, we allow the spiritual joining that facilitates such rapid, yet real, growth.

The purpose of the ritual that takes place around the drinking of the sacrament is to create and hold a space for direct contact between the participant and the Divine. The role of the leaders of the ritual is never to interpret experience, but simply to be the human aspect of the center pole of the spiritual atmosphere. In this the Daime is true to the original teaching of Jesus, who never sought to establish an elite class of priests to intercede between people and the Divine. Rather he taught that direct experience of God was the birthright of all humans. The Daime Path is laid out for each of us who is drawn to it, to walk and evolve as we go, at an accelerated, but distinctly individual, pace. The rituals are extremely organized and disciplined. A great emphasis is put on leaving expression of the individual ego out of the ritual. This creates a climate of inner freedom that allows participants deep, individual communion.

As Irineu Serra, who would become known throughout the Amazon region and eventually the world as Master Irineu, began to remember who he was, he came to understand that he had come into this life with a clear mission. Simply put, it was to "replant" the Doctrine of Jesus Christ on Earth. *Doctrine* is a very important word in the Holy Daime. It does not signify a set of rigid rules or an orthodox set of ideas. The Doctrine spoken of in many hymns of the Daime is a living matrix of consciousness. Jesus Christ implanted a conscious seed in this world by his life and death. This was his mission: to initiate the vast change in human consciousness that is now beginning to come to fruition. The Doctrine, which is the organizing principle of humanity's awakening, is seen within the Daime to possess an active intelligence of it's own. Legend has it that when Jesus died, the Doctrine saw the distortions being made to Jesus' teachings, and It knew the necessary darkness ahead for humanity. It left the world at large, entering the deep forest. There It secreted Itself in the jagube vine and the rainha leaf. It waited with It's guardians, the native peoples of the Amazon, for the day when humanity would be ready to reembrace It. When the time arrived It called Master Irineu, who had been part of the original mission of Jesus, to his new mission of replanting the Doctrine in greater humanity. Through the Holy Daime, It is calling to Itself, one by one, the many souls who are ready to rapidly awaken the seed that Jesus planted, the Christ Consciousness, in themselves. It calls us, not only for ourselves, but also to accept responsibility for helping to secure the Doctrine on Earth in these delicate times. The meaning of "these times" is captured in the symbols of the Holy Daime, the six-pointed star and the cross with two cross beams.

The six-pointed star is an ancient symbol that predates the Jewish people.

It symbolizes the joining of Heaven and Earth—male and female Divinity—and the creation of humanity as the result of this union. The symbol of the cross predates Christianity by millennium. It also symbolizes the male and female principles of heaven and earth meeting in the place of androgyny: the heart. The particular cross given to Master Irineu for use in the Daime symbolizes the mission of Jesus Christ. The lower crossbeam, which it shares with other Christian religions as well as with many ancient peoples, symbolizes the first part of the mission of Jesus, which was to plant the seed of compassion in humanity and to call us to direct, conscious connection with the Divine. The second crossbeam represents the Second Coming of Christ, which is the birth of that seed—the Christ—in the hearts of all humanity. It is in this context that the religion of the Holy Daime is best understood. It has been delivered to earth at this particular time to play It's particular part, along with many other paths and sacred technologies, in this "Second Coming."

On another level, the uniting of these symbols within a single religion, and the subsequent act of singing and dancing around them, symbolically reunites Christians and Jews. We were originally one people and the separation of this group into two religions, and the subsequent horrors of the past two thousand years, are entirely the distorted creation of misguided siblings. It was an immensely liberating moment for me when I was shown this and was moved to declare peace within myself.

Master Irineu proceeded to do as he was instructed and began conducting rituals, or "works," in his hometown of Rio Branco. By 1930 a core of people had gathered around him and out of this group the Santo Daime religion was born. Many of these early followers were poor and uneducated. Some came for the healing of serious illness, a motivation that is still a main entrance point for people coming to the Daime. The rituals Master Irineu was guided to lead, which are still performed today, involved the singing of and dancing to a series of songs, or hymns, that had been delivered to him and to others of his followers from Divine sources. This re-created, halfway around the world and almost two thousand years later, a main form of worship practiced by the followers of Jesus at the time of the early Christian communities.

It is a unique aspect of the Daime doctrine that all the teachings of the religion are delivered through songs. The songs are sung in a form that allows them to be learned in a call and response form. In one voice the whole community prays and praises God together musically.

The region of Brazil that Mestre Irineu lived in was, and still remains, the poorest in a poor country. I find it most interesting and extremely comforting that this mission was given to a very black man in the center of one of the poorest, and most important (from a global point of view) regions on earth. It points a divine finger, dramatically and symbolically, to help reorient us to what is important in these times. Salvation will not come from those countries and religions that have herded us to the cliff's edge. It is coming from a return to mystery, a surrender to the Divine in and around us, and a new alliance with nature. The Amazon is a mystery and from it has come a key to entering the great mystery.

Interwoven with this impulse to praise God, in community and in total direct participation of all members of the community, were the influences and ritual forms drawn from the Indians of that region and from the religions of Africa brought to Brazil by Master Irineu's forebears. The resulting eclectic, yet highly organized and spiritually aligned ritual form, is centered around the drinking of the sacred tea that became known as the Daime, which in Portuguese means "give me," as in "give me strength, give me love, give me light." Over time the Daime became known as a "short cut," a very intense, demanding path to which people whose souls are ready to take a huge evolutionary leap are drawn, people who require a very deep cleansing and healing to take this leap, and who have the motivation to find the courage to follow their soul's urging.

People came to the Daime from many backgrounds. One who came in the early 1960s was a man named Sebastião Mota de Melo. By trade he was a canoe maker, but by predilection he was a mediumistic healer of the first order. Before coming to the Daime he spent many years leading and training groups of mediums in the healing and service of souls in need, incarnate and disincarnate. In the course of his life he became deathly ill. He came to Master Irineu, as did many people, in the hope of being healed from the liver ailment that was killing him. In the course of his healing, which was a complete recovery, he became an initiate and close follower of Master Irineu.

Master Irineu died in 1971. Upon his death, three branches of the Holy Daime formed, one of them led by Sebastião Mota de Melo, who became known as Padrinho (Godfather) Sebastião. Padrinho Sebastião, through his own awakening, came to understand that his mission was to lead his followers to a new life in the center of the jungle itself, to bring his people into the heart of the life force of the planet, and to build a sustainable community. This book is the story of this great man, this true spiritual teacher, who discovered for himself and was discovered by the tradition to be the reincarnation of John the Baptist, the harbinger of the mission of the Master Jesus.

Although they had almost no material resources, Padrinho Sebastião and his people entered the jungle and established a village at a place called Rio do Ouro (River of Gold). They endured sickness and hardship that would have stopped people with even slightly less faith. After having lived there for a few years, they discovered that the land on which they were living was owned by an absentee owner.

Padrinho Sebastião declared that he "would not live on another man's land." And so he and his followers moved to another location. It took one year to move their possessions by canoe and by hand. Eventually they arrived at a site that became known as Céu do Mapiá, or "Heaven of Mapiá," where they began the task of establishing a viable community in the heart of the rain forest. Their commitment from the first was to live in a harmonious relationship with nature, according to the principles of the doctrine they were living. They knew they were there under the auspices of the Divine Beings who guided their life and work, and that those beings were "replanting" a way of life to serve as a center for a religion and as a model of a sustainable, harmonious, spiritually alive community.

To understand the significance of the existence of Céu do Mapiá, despite its small size, consider the fact that almost all settlements begun in the Amazon rain forest have taken one of two roads: They have become either ecological dominators, carving a "civilized" area out of the forest and destroying the ecological system of the area, or so many of the inhabitants of them have died of disease that the rest become discouraged and the projects have been abandoned. Sebastião Mota de Melo's dream was different. His people are successfully living in harmony with nature and yet gradually adding those technological advances that make their lives sustainable. Every resident, except for children born there, has consciously and freely chosen to follow their spiritual calling to live in that community. They are living there because they want to, which makes a huge difference on all levels to the health of the community. Mapiá is surviving and growing in spite of social and economic questions that are sometimes of a life-and-death nature. It is a living laboratory for an ecologically harmonious, spiritually alive community organized around an intimate relationship with the forces of nature and the universe. This town is worth knowing about and supporting, whatever one's own path. At present it is beginning to serve as a model for the reorganization of other villages in the Amazon region.

In the early 1980s Daime communities formed in the large cities in southeastern Brazil and the Holy Daime became a national movement. Also during the '80s, the tea that is drunk in the Daime rituals, and is also still being drunk in Indian ceremonies and by other religious groups in Brazil, was declared to be protected in perpetuity by the Brazilian government. After long, careful investigation it was understood that by its nature Daime, or ayahuasca, or hoasca, as it is variously named, opens a gateway to spiritual realms of existence and does not lend itself to abuse even if there were those interested in doing so. This was a huge step for the Daime and other groups whose mission is to provide this gateway for those called to enter. It provides a model for the other countries that the Daime has entered.

During this initial phase of expansion of the Daime within Brazil, Alex Polari was released from the prison in which he had been incarcerated by the dictatorship. He has, as we all do, his own story of how he was led to the Daime, which involves his thinking he was making a film. Like many of us who arrive at a life that it had never even occurred to us to dream about, he discovered that there existed a plan for him that his conscious mind learned of only long after it was well into effect. He and his wife, Sonia Palhares, founded the community of Céu da Montanha with some of the new generation of Daimistas, people raised in the cities of southern Brazil who were discovering in Padrinho Sebastião and the Daime the direct experience of spiritual awakening, authentic transformation, and the potential for conscious community that their previous enterprises had spoken of and dreamed about, but never delivered. Alex developed a deep and multidimensional relationship with Padrinho Sebastião. He clearly was blessed by that relationship.

In January 1990 Padrinho Sebastião died. He was succeeded by his son, Alfredo Gregorio de Melo, who currently presides over a new stage in the evolution of this most unique religion. When Padrinho Sebastião died, there were only a dozen Daime communities in Brazil. At this moment the Holy Daime resides in over fifty locations, including almost twenty in Europe. There are even churches in Japan. The Holy Daime has spread from being the vision of a man in the heart of the Amazon forest, to being an authentic worldwide movement that attracts a growing number of people in many parts of the world. The possibilities of powerful and rapid spiritual awakening, deep healing, social relations based on respect, love, and mutual support, the model of a sustainable and supportable community in the jungle, and the perceived urgency of this moment on earth are drawing people from all levels of society and all backgrounds.

The Daime is by no means a panacea. It is a powerful spiritual path, a shortcut that I think will never be a mass religion. It is too demanding. Most people would not consciously choose to engage in a long, demanding ritual in which they have a good chance of being shown, up close, that which they have falsely created in their own consciousness and their living a life that separates them from their own Divine nature. And then have it cleaned out. With no excuses accepted. And no whining allowed.

But for those who feel called, the Daime often provides healing in the truest sense, the healing of our false perception of separation. It leads the way, not only to improved health on all levels, but to the freedom that comes from knowing who we are, and that we are completely loved, and from the step-by-step surrender to the will of the Divine. As with everything else in the Daime, this knowledge and the experience of freedom is a palpable thing.

One of the most important teachings offered by Padrinho Sebastião, and embodied most beautifully in Alex Polari, is that our salvation must be rooted in work. The Daime is not a path of transcendence, it is a path of transformation. We bring Spirit to bear upon matter in our own bodies and in our lives. The result is that we are engaged in a dynamic process of constant discovery and in evolving relationships, both earthly and divine. We are called to work on earth, to interact directly with nature. We are called upon to fulfill our earthly responsibilities. We are called to support our families and to raise our children to be grounded, truthful, spiritual people. Whether or not the Daime is their path is a discovery and a negotiation between themselves and God. Some children of Daimistas join the path of their own accord when they reach an age of decision. Some do not.

Not everybody comes to the Daime to become an initiate, a member of the religion. It is strictly forbidden to proselytize or to in any way entice someone to participate in the rituals of the Daime. I have the right to tell you about my experience, as Alex Polari tells you about his with Padrinho Sebastião. Whether or not you drink Daime, and what you do with that relationship with that Divine Being, is between you and that Being. People come to the Daime because they are called from inside themselves. The motivation to hear the call may be an illness, or it may be a conscious search for awakening. It can also come by way of intuition, or dreams, or by retrospectively viewed Divine orchestration. It may come to you from reading this book.

Whatever the initial motivation, those who arrive at the doorway soon understand they are entering a serious, demanding work whose rewards far exceed its demands, but whose demands include attention, humility, courage, and a willingness to undergo a deep transformative process that is oftentimes uncomfortable.

The rituals are called "works." And they are. Those who enter the Daime wanting a path that is both a shortcut and an easy shortcut are quickly disabused. They don't stay around long. Or they "change their opinion," as a hymn of Padrinho counsels us to do and do again.

The Holy Daime Path is an authentic mystery school. There are levels of knowledge, stages of initiation that one passes through in one's program of rapid evolution. Unlike some other paths and schools, the stages are not externally regulated. There are not specific programs or practices that an initiate follows, nor are there specific ceremonies to mark one's progress. The job of the initiate is to show up, drink Daime, work on the earth to live the teachings of the doctrine: love God, love the earth, love all beings in God's creation, including yourself, love and respect your brothers and sisters, accept the truth of your own divinity and of your own faults, learn to embody forgiveness and mercy, and gain the hard won humility that comes from meeting a Divine force head on. Each new doorway is marked by a significant deepening of one's relationship with the Divine. It also usually is marked by a difficult passage, a facing up to another level of unconscious separation.

The Holy Daime is not for everyone. The rituals of the Daime are not meant to be an "experience," but rather to provide a chance to interact intimately with a Divine Being of unimaginable intelligence, compassion, clarity, and spiritual power. They require us to bring our whole selves to the work. They provide an opportunity for seeing truth, gaining knowledge, and to transform oneself, one's health, and one's life. What we get out of them depends on our level of readiness and our willingness to surrender our ideas of separation and enter into a new relationship with ourselves and with the Divine. As one of Padrinho Sebastião's hymns says:

> *I live in the Forest*
> *I have my teachings*
> *I don't call myself Daime*
> *I am a Divine Being*
>
> *I am a Divine Being*
> *I came here to teach you*
> *The more you ask of me*
> *The more I have to give to you.*

For those who are called to the Daime by an inner voice, this Divine Being offers a chance to awaken to spiritual reality in a way unique in all this world. Those who come looking to get high in an interesting spiritual context are quickly disabused of their expectations.

The Daime is, in actuality, a simple path. When you read the words of Padrinho Sebastião you will see that he was a simple man. It will help you to let go of false ideas about the relationship of complication and depth. His words will also show you that to be awake is not to be removed from living in the world, but to engage in it on God's terms, teaching by the example of your life. Padrinho is a man whose teachings have value to anyone who wants to know what a life totally surrendered to the will of God is like.

In October 1989 I had the indescribable privilege of spending a month with Padrinho Sebastião in Céu do Mapiá. I arrived to find I had been designated to be Padrinho's acupuncturist. He was suffering from congestive heart failure in the middle of the jungle, with no doctors, medication, or hospitals for hundreds of miles. He was dying, and it fell to my friend and teacher Jose Rosa, an M.D., and myself to keep him on earth long enough for medication and a helicopter to arrive. Immediately I found myself over my head. My training and experience in Chinese medicine were useless except in that they provided a grounding that facilitated the necessary surrender to Divine guidance that then allowed me to let go of my head and to become available as an instrument for Padrinho's healing. I was forced to take a quantum leap in my own spiritual process and in my healership to help this man who was so beloved of his people, and who would become so to me.

I remember clearly the moment I came to know the being who is Padrinho Sebastião and my relationship to him. Sitting upon his bed, propped up with pillows, he was having constant difficulty breathing. I was in the middle of giving him an acupuncture treatment when I looked up and our eyes met. He had the eyes of an enlightened hawk. In that moment, I knew with utmost certainty that Padrinho saw everything about me. He saw my higher self, which at that time was a distant mystery to me. He saw my lower self, which I thought I was pretty adept at hiding. He saw my fears and my potential. He saw God in me and he saw everything I had done to hide God from myself. He saw me for real. And with all he saw he loved me totally and completely. He accepted all I was and all I wasn't, with truthfulness and yet without judgment. In that moment something in my heart eased and opened. Some veil of despair I had set there as a protection was pushed aside and I looked out through new eyes. In that moment I came to the spiritual life.

Padrinho showed me his love, but he also gave me something else just as important. He showed me a model, in himself, of how I could be. He showed me that an awake human being sees on all levels—but with compassion. He showed me that truth and love are married to each other, eternally. He showed me that I had divorced them, and then created a story about how they couldn't live together any more. In his presence they began a new courtship inside me.

I was once told how to recognize a teacher of light from a teacher of darkness, and it has helped me immensely in my own discernment. It sometimes can be difficult to tell merely from the words a teacher speaks or the way they appear. To use the vernacular, everybody has a good rap. Many teachers are charismatic and exciting. Many can do various kinds of healing, various kinds of magic. Universal power is, after all, neutral. In the short run, the students of many teachers feel expanded and liberated. But it can be useful to look at the students and ask yourself if the students are, over time, becoming more or less empowered in themselves? Is the relationship leading to more or less spiritual and practical maturity? Are the students becoming more or less independent in their thinking? Is everybody being energetically fed by the relationship or is the teacher feeding off the students?

As you meet Padrinho Sebastião Mota de Melo in these pages through the clear, loving eyes and beautiful writing of Alex Polari, you will be meeting the real thing, the genuine article. You will meet not only Padrinho but also some of his disciples, not the least of which is Alex himself. These are people who have been guided, in some cases saved from a destructive life, by their relationship with the man called Saint Sebastião. But they have also grown and evolved themselves, discovering their own higher nature that Padrinho saw long before they did. Some, like Alex and Sonia, have become spiritual and civic leaders in their own right.

Céu do Mapiá has five hundred inhabitants that have come of their own free, uncoerced will to live out the dream of Padrinho Sebastião. There are thousands of people around the world discovering the path begun by a black rubber tapper turned soldier and that was continued by a canoe maker from the Amazon. People from literally every walk of life, every social class, every race, and every background are, one by one, coming to study with the teacher that is the Daime.

The Daime Path and the life of Padrinho Sebastião are, if nothing else, extremely interesting because they are both so unusual and so real. In reading this book, you have one advantage over me when I met Padrinho. Through Alex Polari's extraordinary writing ability and the beauty of this translation by Rosana Workman, you will understand what Padrinho is saying. So you can, if you wish to use the book in this way, study the words and learn the biography of a true teacher, a unique leader of a new religion. You can gain the inspiration that comes from witnessing the courage of a person who lived utterly true to his guidance and triumphed. That would be time well spent with any book. But there is another option if you wish to take it. If you choose to go beyond the story and the words of Padrinho, you can enter into a relationship with the Being who is still Sebastião Mota de Melo. He left his body behind, but he is as alive as he was in Céu do Mapiá and at the River Jordan.

Introduction

. . .

AMAZON: A MAGICAL word with so many meanings. To this day it evokes legends and awakens fascination—El Dorado for greedy adventurers and yet a sanctuary for human beings who understand the future of our planet. It was once called the "Green Hell" by the Spanish conquistadores, the same who brought about the Incas' apocalypse. As they climbed the mountains with their horses and arquebuses, they encountered a people who were highly spiritual, gifted with great wisdom, with their own technology, as well as knowledge of power plants.

Since time immemorial these people had known the secrets of *ayahuasca*, a sacred drink made from the vine *Banisteriopsis caapi* and the leafy plant *Psychotria viridis,* used for healing, for contact with the mysterium tremendum, and the unio mystica. In the Quechua language, *ayahuasca* means something like "vine of the soul," by which it is possible to communicate with the spirits of the dead.

All the great pre-Colombian civilizations used sacred plants. The reports of Spanish missionaries recorded the existence of a school of mystery and initiation in the lost city they called Valacamba-la-Vieja, which they described as "an abominable University of Idolatry." Certainly there, ayahuasca was used in particular rituals and initiations. They also wrote about a prophetic tradition handed down within the priesthood of the sun and that the prophecies given by the *Banisteriopsis* drink foretold the end of the Inca civilization.

From this point on, history becomes clouded. Could the Incas have descended from the mountains into the forest spreading the mystery? We can find some clues for the cult of the vine among many indigenous western Amazonian people. At the center of their cosmology are the images of the vine and the leaf, thus indicating their knowledge of the magical drink. The mystery has not only shed light on the origins of ayahuasca but also provides a key to an important inner teaching for our time.

The spiritual knowledge of this secret comes from the *miração,* an inner perception combining insight and ecstasy that can be induced by the ritualized use of these divine plants in a religious context. The miração, contains the model for a new state of being brought forth from an internal reality, revealing an ancient wisdom and foretelling a spiritual consciousness that is indispensible to our very survival on this planet. In this consciousness, our whole being beholds a mystery and shares a secret: Christ is risen among us in a new form! He left the sumptuous cathedrals and now He pulses in the heart of the Amazon forest. The Green Hell of the conquistadores has become a Green Paradise for those willing to enact the conquest of themselves. The forest is the Garden of Eden, wherein may be found both the Tree of Life and the forbidden fruit.

Some theories speculate that at the dawn of time, divinatory plants were indeed the forbidden fruit that influenced us in our passage from biological semiconsciousness to something like our present human consciousness. Thus, spirit entered into matter, and the fall into flesh was consummated with a two-edged sword called free will. We are now at the twilight of an age, and it is not without significance that the evolutionary relationship between mind and consciousness and spirit, brought about by the use of power plants, is confused in the misinformation and prejudice surrounding drugs, one of the most perplexing issues of our times.

For us to arrive at the new era, we need a new path and new knowledge. Many seekers of consciousness have traveled these sacred roads and because of that, new routes were opened. One of these paths is the Santo Daime, a school of self-knowledge, spiritual work, and charity. Santo Daime combines the inheritance of the Christian esoteric tradition with the spiritual legacy and indigenous force of the pre-Colombian people. It is a flower that bloomed in the tropical rain forest in the state of Acre, Brazil. This knowledge took doctrinal form through the work of *Mestre* Irineu Serra. This book explores the life and teachings of one of Serra's main disciples, who not too long ago was still among us.

He was very much a "voice crying in the wilderness," and with the rustic accent of a *caboclo,* a native forest dweller, he was heard in the solitude of the far and forgotten rubber groves, among the *igarapés.* His name was Sebastião Mota de Melo, born October 16, 1920, in the state of Amazonas, in the Juruá Valley; an illiterate rubber tapper, canoe builder, mystic, healer, and prophet of the new era.

In the beginning of the 1980s my meeting with this man changed the course of my life. At that time, without knowing where I was going, I nonetheless felt the irresistible impulse to start my spiritual path. I thought it would perhaps take me to the frozen peaks of the Himalayas and put me face-to-face with some Ramakrishna or Ramana Maharashi. Instead, I found myself before a man with a long, white beard, tanned face, penetrating eyes, a mischievous smile on his lips, and who seemed already to know me. I felt completely disarmed. The scene of this encounter, without a doubt the most important in my whole life, was not Tibet nor was the elder an Indian guru. The meeting with Padrinho Sebastião happened in the great Amazonian forest. It was thus that I had a chance to live with a saintly man and, through his benevolence, dissipate some of the veils of ignorance and illusion that surrounded me.

When the Padrinho spoke, my companions and I would feel such an openness to him that our whole beings were drawn to what he was saying. In a glimpse, he seemed to understand all that was lacking in us. He awakened in us the courage and confidence to live a spiritual life, but always carefully leaving our free will intact.

It was a mistake though, to think that his warm reception showed some special preference or an indulgence toward our weaknesses. When we acknowledged the desire to follow the doctrine, Padrinho always showed a judicious support, outlining the task each one should perform so our intentions would be converted into deeds. But after he had observed in us the repetition of mistakes, excessive self-pity, or a certain laziness about self-transformation, his love sometimes mixed with a righteous and holy indignation. It would last just long enough for him to issue a call to awaken or a reminder to get back to the healing work.

For Padrinho, healing was seen as a clarification of the soul mediated by the Santo Daime. The true path to follow in the moment of crisis, physical illness, or mental obsession becomes apparent through the aid of the Daime. The first step is to awaken our inner self and obtain with it, after many struggles, our spiritual rebirth. The knowledge that can transform us from puppets of our own desires to spiritual beings cannot be transmitted by an ordinary teacher or therapist, but only by a guide or master who recognizes the truth and has obtained the realization of it in his or her being.

This is how Sebastião Mota was. From his presence and words sprang a strong magnetism. Sometimes he would sing a hymn or make a small commentary, and somehow it would correspond to the most intimate thoughts of each one of us. He elevated our consciousness to such a place that everything else we had been thinking or feeling seemed banal. His words awakened an eagerness for the Spirit and the Eternal. He showed us how to maintain our firm faith in God under all circumstances. He taught that as we stop judging and gossiping about our brothers and sisters, we overcome fears and doubts in ourselves as well, and life becomes evermore dignified, harmonious, and sanctified.

It was common for us to walk together into the middle of the jungle and there, all of a sudden, the innocent talk transformed into an intense and unforgettable spiritual teaching for all present. We would be transfixed by the deep meaning of his words, the atmosphere of the luminous forest, and the symphony of birds at dusk.

I remember some unhappy times as well, when Padrinho's illness brought much physical suffering to him. He endured atrocious pain, day and night, without being able to lie down or sleep. In his few moments of relief, he would smile and tell us what he had learned in his agony. For him his illness was part of his work with suffering spirits. In these hours, he would give his body to the pain with the firm conviction that he was practicing charity and helping these spirits.

The old Mota was a great medium. From the time he was eight years old, he had contact with various entities in dreams and visions. He worked with spirits to heal people in the valley of the Juruá, where he lived. When he arrived at Rio Branco, he worked at making contact with entities, as well as at healing and relieving possession from obsessive spirits. He channeled and worked with two entities: Dr. Bezerra de Menezes and Professor Antônio Jorge. Later he participated in Santo Daime healing works with light guides, celestial beings, and all sorts of entities, in known and unknown languages, until his last days, as much as his weakened body would permit.

Padrinho Sebastião was also a prophet. Prophets are those who, because they have arrived at their own self-knowledge and a larger knowledge of being, find themselves perfectly aligned with the Divine will to the extent that they wish nothing else but the fulfillment of Divine laws. They give themselves so fully to the prophetic truth revealed by faith that they may draw a whole people to their destiny. (The prophet's life and work should be coherent with the instruction and visions he receives, otherwise he falls into fortune-telling without any commitment to values, ethics, and spirit.)

Sebastião Mota gathered people around him with the strength of his prophetic revelations and started a widespread movement of which the fairest fruit is the community of Céu do Mapiá, as well as many churches and associations throughout Brazil and in foreign countries. Padrinho Sebastião told us that when he was a child, he dreamed of an immense area of forest burning, only the part where he was stayed green, seemingly indifferent to the fire around it. He said much later that he had been visited by the Spirit of Truth, who asked him to move the people from Rio Branco, deeper in the forest, to the rubber grove of Rio do Ouro. But he became disappointed with the region's problems and he continued searching until arriving at the banks of the Igarapé Mapiá, where the mother community is located today.

A prophet is slightly different from a master, who transmits his knowledge to a disciple to help the disciple realize his own visions. A prophet, however, is the master of a people, committed to accomplish a goal consistent with his community and the Divine order. He is an artisan of Divine will in the material, temporal, and human realities. The master can give himself the space for a serene and controlled personality, while a prophet, because he or she is the guardian of God's words, needs at times to denounce the resistance and rebelliousness of those oblivious or resistant to spiritual realization.

In certain moments, Sebastião Mota would become very agitated. He clamored to awaken us from apathy and to share in what he was seeing. He would reduce to dust any illusion or falseness that we wanted to hold on to in our hearts. It was in these moments that we, his godsons, recognized in him the power of John the Baptist or that being of Divine justice that Christ himself referred to as Elias.

At the end of the 1970s and the beginning of the 1980s, a new phenomenon occurred. Travelers, seekers, and backpackers on the route to Machu-Picchu started to circulate the news of a community in Rio Branco using the mysterious magic drink. It was this news that originally brought me there, and once there I felt at home. Padrinho was waiting for us. Since the 1940s the hymns were foretelling of a new people coming from afar, even from foreign lands, to unite with the ones Mestre Raimundo Irineu Serra had already assembled. Padrinho never forgot Mestre Irineu's words, "Mr. Sebastião, these are not yet our people, they are only the base; our people are still coming from far away."

Thus this rich spiritual phenomenon grew and expanded from Acre in the west Brazilian Amazonian forest into a doctrine that fuses rubber workers, Amazonian caboclos, and people from the edge of the igarapés with professionals, artists, husbands, housewives, and many young people from the more developed areas of the country. Through the Daime and Padrinho Sebastião, they felt a renewed Christianity springing up in their hearts. They heeded Mestre Irineu's appeal and spiritual call and found a new approach to God's words, consistent with the words of the saints, prophets, and other seekers of the way. The Daime offers a new way of understanding the agenda of redemption and the renewal of hope for the spirituality of the third millennium.

It should be fascinating for the metaphysically curious that a powerful spiritual alchemy has emerged from the very heart of the rain forest. Rumors and gossip of all kinds began to surround the tradition. When a great new spiritual epoque is announced to be alive in our time, things like this are bound to happen. We can be charmed and emotional sometimes when reading books, but to live and to make our own history, as Padrinho Sebastião's people do, can be a frightening idea for those who think that God stopped speaking to us long ago and that the sacred does not dwell on earth anymore.

Padrinho Sebastião had yet another role: defender, lover, connoisseur, and protector of the forest where God's people wait for the realization of the promise made two thousand years ago—the return of Christ. While we wait and prepare for this event, we fight at the same time a spiritual and material battle for our daily bread. Mestre Irineu used to say that those who are firm and supple, like green branches, will have a better chance making the transition through the difficult birth of the new era.

To the Santo Daime people, forest preservation and harmony with it are a basic condition, for in the forest sprout the two plants from which our sacrament is made. Moreover, the rain forest is our home, our laboratory of spiritual union and natural self-sustainability. Much is said today about the environment, ecosystems, forest management, and natural resources. There is much tension about mining, pollution, deforestation of native land, narcotics traffic, and so forth. For these problems there are departments, foundations, secretaries, environmental agencies, etc., but very few really know and love the forest; few know how to receive from the forest protection, shelter, and material and spiritual food. We of the forest are hopeful about the possibility of keeping a part of our planet healthy through the coming purifications that are being announced.

The forest is not only the immense regulator of the world's climate, a fantastic natural zoo, a rich repository of important woods and remarkable vegetal species; more than that, it is an area of intimacy with the Divine. The natural world is the habitat of an enormous spiritual energy that remains untouched to this day. Each living pulsation of the forest produces a profound therapeutic effect on the people connected to it. This living connection anticipates the felicity that will be encountered living in the new era, as human consciousness surpasses human destructiveness. Can we actualize a spiritual community that lives in harmony with the forest, with the understanding that the forest is the earthly manifestation of our Celestial Mother? It was no accident that Mestre Irineu received the doctrine of the Daime from the Queen of the Forest.

I never met anyone with more perfect love for the earth than Padrinho Sebastião Mota de Melo. He did not have any problem bringing down a great and noble tree if he saw in it the possibility of making a large canoe that would transport people and merchandise to the community, but he would not like it if anyone hurt even a branch without good reason. Padrinho was like a child when he spoke and walked in nature. He told us extraordinary things about beings seen and unseen, enchanted and ordinary. He loved simple people, the people of the forest, his faithful companions from the first times. But he also loved the new influx of folks from the cities of the south, full of enthusiasm and ideas. He coun-seled the old ones to learn from the education and intellectual knowledge of the new ones. At the same time he advised us, the urban intellectu-als, to abandon our books and pens for a while and take up the hoe and machete.

Padrinho also loved the animals. He was a hunter in his youth, but for a long time he discouraged and sometimes even prohibited hunting, except in great need. He would speak of the *anta's* (tapir) clay pit, springs that were true sanctuaries for all the animals in the forest that go there to drink. He would point to the crisscross of *capybara, paca* (small capybara), and *cotia* (very large guinea pig) trails. For him it was not acceptable for a man to flee the red jaguar by climbing a tree. "The *moçoroca,* the spotted jaguar, I understand fleeing, but the red jaguar is a coward! It only takes a strike at her nose with a piece of wood," he would say calmly.

His uncanny sense of direction was disconcerting sometimes and he loved to behold the rising sun with his eyes wide open. When he said, "Now is the time to plant rice or corn," those who knew him got right down to it. From the behavior of the animals he would deduce many things, including the condition of the astral or spiritual world. If his internal clock started to get off track, he would fix it by the *nambu's* (wild forest fowl) cry, "The nambu cry at six in the morning on the nose," he always asserted. Thus, he would correct his internal timing. "The official time continues to be the *nambu;* I am sorry for those who need a clock-radio."

God blessed me with knowing Padrinho Sebastião in the flesh. He received me as a father receives a son, oriented me on my path, and initi-ated me into the Santo Daime, furthering my spiritual journey. I found myself always attentive to his words. During our moments of intimate conversation, I would make notes and tapes as often as he would permit. Sometimes I would tape a trivial talk in hopes that the old man, as he often did, would turn the talk to the mysterious things—to the sky, the earth, and the spirits. Laughing about my confusion with the tape recorder's buttons, he would say, "Turn it off, friend, we are only mak-ing conversation." After I turned it off, he would start to speak about more profound and interesting subjects. "Padrinho," I would say, "some-day, I am going to write your story."

It is these simple words and teachings so full of profound wisdom and the almost miraculous nature of some of my initial experiences that encouraged me in the publication of this book. It is a tribute of gratitude to the master I much loved and revered. He taught me to be instead of pretending to be, and I am still walking in the way I learned from him.

Padrinho Sebastião—master, medium, saint, prophet, and the spiritual guide of the forest—can bring renewed life and strength to all who seek the transformation of earth into a new spiritual world. From the spirit realm above the forest, where his image hovered and was seen many times, I ask his blessings on this task.

1
...
The Magician of Rio Branco

BEFORE WE ARRIVE at the main body of this narrative, I ask the reader to go back with me many years to the time of my arrival in Rio Branco, the capital of Acre, determined to know the mysterious drink called ayahuasca, or Daime. I was feeling a great need to start on my spiritual path, and like any neophyte who wants to become a disciple of something not yet understood by him, I was split between two opposing feelings: the first was a drive to find an explanation for my emptiness and my conviction that I would only be fulfilled by finding one way and one master; the second was the fear of the very deep transformation this encounter would bring.

Through this tension all spiritual transformation begins. Much stumbling is necessary until our ego, always full of tricks, surrenders to a path of self-exploration, until we understand the road that leads us to the knowledge of God. Further along on our journey we find that this knowledge of God anticipates what only the heart can truly and finally deliver. If we still do not have God in our experience, if we still do not feel sprouting in us the most pure love for this unfathomable and infinite source of creation, we still do not know him. He is love and loved us first.

When I decided to embark on this path, I was full of impressions and judgments about the world and suppositions about the spirit. I felt the same trauma of all who are products of religion without faith, truth without ecstasy, word without proof. In the same way that a child needs the parent's good example to form his or her character, the spirit is an eternal child who discovers itself in each new matter and needs good spiritual food to awaken from the sleep and forgetfulness in which it was immersed when reincarnated. Because the starting point of our spiritual journey depends on patterns acquired in other lifetimes, it is a mistake to think that we are just beginning our path. We are resuming our journey.

Although we are witness to many advances in science and in the knowledge of the mundane world, we have arrived at the point of abolishing truth as a tangible goal in human experience. And in this emptiness is rooted a bigger and more dangerous illusion: that ethics can sustain itself by something other than truth, as if truth could be deduced from a source other than spiritual realization and the proof given by our inner self. Authentic Christianity is a science of self-realization. Through love and charity, we mold our being like the Son of God who was sent to us, discovering his Kingdom on Earth as it is in Heaven. Nothing men did or will do can surpass this eternal truth.

At the beginning of my adventure I wanted to find a fundamental truth, one that like a magnet would attract me to it without my needing to walk with my own legs. At that time my quest did not seem very easy. My path toward a Christian life was still obstructed. Orthodoxy, heresies, the Inquisition, the genocide of pre-Columbian people, all of this darkens and clouds the water of the spring, the clear and pure fountain that is Christ himself. But I had the blessing of seeing this through this new sacrament, the Santo Daime.

I tried meditation as well as other spiritual practices before my final surrender. I pondered the archetype of the inveterate sinner who only repents at death, this passage at which we all will arrive, our last chance to choose between faith and disbelief. This decision may well define what we will or will not find after death, and like the dying sinner, I also waited for a watershed to bring forth my rebirth. But as Padrinho Sebastião used to say, whoever does not attain spiritual rebirth on earth, is an abortion in the spiritual world.

The message preached by Christ is not a doctrine for masochists. From the trilogy—love, forgiveness, and suffering—the last is without a doubt the hardest to swallow. But what He really wanted to show us is that through this inherent human condition we can conquer our own suffering, as well as fear and death.

If in the beginning the Daime's power was revealed to me at once, I believe I could not have taken its force and the intensity of its beauty. Revelation only can come when we are ready for it. Sometimes we surround ourselves with beautiful things that dominate all the landscape, and we wait for celestial messengers to reveal the contents of an old manuscript while angels and cherubim play gold trumpets. We do not realize that the revelation is in life itself, in the nature of God and in the alignment of our external reality without inner experience of the Divine. Thus, we will not know truth until we lose the fear of knowing ourselves.

When I arrived in Rio Branco, all of this was streaming through my head. I was received by the unforgettable Padrinho Mario Rogerio da Rocha. Gnomelike, he was an older man, polite, good natured, of short stature with completely white and thinning hair. His smile showed an enormous self-confidence. His natural nobility, evident to all who met him, was never a chagrin. On the contrary, it charmed us. His small house at the edge of the Acre River was simple and clean. At the end of the backyard there was a small open dwelling made of wood and surrounded by fruit trees. There, *Seu* Mario, as he was tenderly called by his friends, opened his works and healing sessions with various power plants. He explained, "All is within the Daime. All lines of spiritual work that use power plants are, in a certain way, Daime's attributes."

This understanding, however, did not take away his great appreciation for Santa Maria, San Pedro, mushrooms, coca leaves, and so forth. He knew the callings of all these beings, but since he discovered the Daime he would say that there he found everything he was looking for.

During works, while he was seated on his wicker chair, I had the opportunity to see him in many guises, sometimes like a goblin, sometimes like a Babylonian magician, a Chaldean astronomer, a Toltec wizard, a being with an alligator head, or simply as Seu Mario, smiling with his few teeth as if he could observe on my face the landscape of my journey.

Seu Mario was also erudite, and in the simplicity of his language he could reveal, with depth, philosophical systems and spiritual lines. A true scholar of esotericism, he had gathered knowledge from many different schools. He showed great intellectual power, an absence of prejudice, and saw something positive in everything. Everyone who came near him felt great security and peace. I believe that Padrinho Mario's main teaching was to show that the spiritual path, this hard journey of self-knowledge as well as its practical results, cannot be evaluated from a place stagnated by secular life. And that it is necessary to always strive for the perfection of our being, and of being in the world with an elevated mind and an open heart to our brothers and sisters. He would say, "Do not think I am waiting because I am not. I am showing the way. . . . I am here to show Christ in my being. All of us can develop meaningful works to give testimony of the Christ in us. All of us who partake of Daime and assume the doctrine have an obligation to work in the name of our Lord Jesus Christ."

Padrinho Mario and Padrinho Sebastião opened a new understanding of Christianity for me and prompted my reconciliation with Jesus Christ—much talked about, little understood, and much discredited. Seu Mario, with his characteristic way of framing the words, would say, "My son, there isn't anything else to know, OK? Everything is here in clear sight. . . . The Daime within us showing everything. Let's all wake up. Let's all be very awake and see. Each of us giving value to our brothers and sisters. Each of us giving value to our brothers and sisters as well as to ourselves. Because if we do not, we bring down God. If we value ourselves and devalue others, this diminishes the power of God within us. To value all, we need to have a higher mind. You know, we are only now discovering our God, giving life to him, and healing ourselves."

All of this was making a great impression in the depth of my being. It was both simple and complex at the same time. A new horizon was being revealed through his words; a Christ inside ourselves was waiting to awaken, a God whose reality depended on how his sons and daughters assumed his attributes and behaved toward each other. And the bearer of this message was by my side, his voice gentle and halting. When he wanted to give emphasis to an idea he would repeat the whole sentence and smile; as he continued to speak he would observe the effect he had caused in us.

On a beautiful sunny Sunday, he invited me to shop with him at the old market. As we walked, I told him of my desire to continue my journey until Rio do Ouro, where, the previous year, Padrinho Sebastião had already moved with a large number of his people to build the "New Jerusalem," as commanded by the "spirit of truth," to use Padrinho Sebastião's words.

He then explained to me that the situation in Rio do Ouro was still very precarious; pioneers clearing the untamed forest and facing many difficulties, including malaria. We arrived at the market on one of the town's main streets and entered a lane where a dozen small, straight streets converged. It was full of market tents, bazaars, and many other market activities. From there we saw that most of the buildings in that part of town were suspended on poles above the Acre River; down below we could hear the whistle of a river boat maneuvering at the port. There it was before my eyes, a typical Amazonian scene, both impoverished and superb, grave and majestic, where will be written a decisive page in the history of the transition between the old and the new world. Padrinho Mario asked me to wait a bit longer before traveling farther on to Rio do Ouro, where Padrinho Sebastião would take great pleasure in receiving everyone shortly. He would stop our conversation sometimes to greet someone he knew or to show me the stores in which merchandise was better or cheaper.

If not for its obvious tropical and Amazonian landscape, I could have imagined this scene in a Persian market and our polite Padrinho a Sufi teacher who could shorten the disciple's search or send him crossing many miles of desert in search of yet another market and another old man, who might help him or might send him yet somewhere else. While thinking about where Seu Mario could have sent me, he said in his typical manner, "I received this mission. My commitment is with the Santo Daime, with God. When I get up in the morning, when I reach for my toothbrush, I say to myself, in this hour, in this day, right now, I have a mission. Today I am going to attend to the Santo Daime, I am going to value my brothers and sisters; I am going to be with God. Is that not it?"

Padrinho Mario was deeply aware of his mission. For him Santo Daime was the Divine vehicle for the new era that would fulfill the promise of the scriptures, the Word of Christ. Mestre Irineu's and Padrinho Sebastião's hymns, which are songs received directly from the spirit world with a specific teaching or message, and the hymns that followed are the testimony announcing the coming of a great purification. The advent of the era is being revealed in the last great forest of the planet in the form of a sacrament, the Santo Daime, to receive and gather the people who believe in the words of Mestre Raimundo Irineu

Serra and Padrinho Sebastião, and are willing to live out this prophetic revelation.

Padrinho Mario received the mission of calling and receiving the new people, and he saw me as one of the initiators of this process. At a time when I did not yet understand all that was happening, I interviewed Seu Mario for a documentary I was filming. The last thing he said in this interview was, "I am waiting for a people, the people who want . . . to take and further this doctrine."

He believed with certainty that when the people arrived, and we were the first signs, there would be great struggles to overcome the prejudicial confusion between taking drugs and the ritual use of sacred plants as consciousness expanders, observing the doctrine of the Santo Daime. The arrival of Christ consciousness would continue to be a target, only this time the persecution and threats would be by science instead of religion. He often remarked, "Don't we eat and drink what we like? Why should it be necessary to secure the right to drink inside our church and in our homes the things we like? The truth is that the Santo Daime elevates us spiritually, isn't it? It's a sacrament, and you city people working on the political front are the ones fighting for this."

Although I was still looking for my role in the story, for him everything was already clear. Was he not the one who called us anyway? He anticipated the great responsibility we would face when this doctrine began to be known to the world, but it was time to manifest God's mercy. At the end of this cycle and of the millennium, when all doctrines are questioned for their truth, the spiritual medicine that is Santo Daime should become more accessible to everyone in search of it.

I began to see in Seu Mario's words, similarities to the stories of the Hebrew people under captivity in Egypt, the Essenes, the Dead Sea fishermen, and the lame and meek spirits of Galilee. We also are a chosen people, anonymously living the new legend guided by the prophet Padrinho Sebastião. The same millennial history is being continued but with a new hope for those who believe that God no longer speaks to us in these chaotic times. Seu Mario would make this legend resound in our everyday life. He was a humble man but his mind was immersed in greatness each moment of the epic. I was always trying to put together the puzzle: Mestre Irineu, Padrinho Sebastião, the announcement of the great purifications, a messianic gathering in the tropical forest at the dawn of the second millennium, the exotic misinterpretations "of the vine worshipers" . . . things like this occupied my mind.

Much has been written in theology about the human need to bestow Newtonian scientific models on revelation, grace, and faith. But the deepest Christian truth rests in the uninterrupted chain of faith since the time of the Essenes, from Saint Joseph, Saint Isabel, Saint Zachary, John the Baptist, and the apostles, who had the glory of being the precursors and witnesses of the Logos incarnated. And also for those who believed with their hearts in the witness given by God through the self and through the holy ancestors who reached the true Christian revelation better than theologians or doctors of any time.

Back then, I was not always able to accept or understand the form of spiritual training Seu Mario was giving us. But, is it not at that moment when understanding is failing that the need for faith grows in us? My love for these men, Padrinho Sebastião and Seu Mario, gave me more strength to continue on this adventure than did the visions I was getting from the Santo Daime.

I returned home in July 1982 with his message taped on video but without having reached Rio do Ouro. Nevertheless I felt strongly what Seu Mario said at our last meeting about his first time drinking Santo Daime. He had offered, "I drank Santo Daime, do you know? The first time I drank, I found everything I was looking for. I quenched my thirst. I died and was reborn—the man who drank the Daime never returned; the one who came back was a new man."

Imagine my surprise when many of the predictions Seu Mario made came to pass with astonishing velocity. In a short time I was part of an expedition by the Brazilian Justice Department called Cofen. The work of the Cofen was to research the preparation and use of the Santo Daime sacramental drink in Rio do Ouro, and to write a report with recommendations for the authorities. When I returned at the end of November 1982, my first sight was Seu Mario. I went to see him at his headquarters by the fruit trees like a disciple or *afilhado* who had heard the inner meaning of the calling he had made through the documentary and was ready to defend the Daime. After he listened to me carefully, always smiling as was his nature, he explained that the interview was part of the spiritual awakening of the Santo Daime people. He also said that this call was indeed a spiritual inquiry and that I was his messenger, although I was not fully conscious of it yet. He slowly added, "All I do, all I say, is God's will. I say to you and to all of you who arrive at Santo Daime, I called you. Did you know? I called, and I have been responsible for the coming and its challenges. When I started to call I thought I should hide it from God, do you understand? But soon, He spoke to me: 'Call!' Then I called with full strength and felt Padrinho Sebastião spiritually approving of my doing."

I explained to him that I had felt the same as I remembered his words about the first time he drank Santo Daime. His eyes shone like those of a happy child at my remark. He then added, "Well, that day I told you that when I drank the Daime the first time, I quenched my thirst and was reborn. This was what I said, wasn't it? Well, when I discovered these things and quenched my thirst, when I saw all I was looking for and had found, I remembered all of you. I saw that the time was right. The time had arrived for realizing the prophecies, and for that I remembered that many young people would have to come. When I looked around I did not see the people, no youth yet. Then, I asked God to stop time while we prepared our people and waited for the youth to arrive."

He took a deep breath, paused, and concluded, "It was more or less like this; let's see if I remember how I called. I said, whoever needs to drink from the water of life, the water to quench your thirst, come. Whoever searches for the light, come. Whoever looks for truth, come. Whoever looks for justice, I also called. A couple of days later, I saw in a vision people awakening everywhere on earth, all of them coming and bringing light."

"Very well Padrinho Mario," I said, "the many transformations I have experienced in such a short period of time are sufficient to consider the Santo Daime the real water of life."

He added, "Did I tell you yet about the miração I had before you came, of a great number of soldiers of peace awakening all over the earth? I stood there looking at this gathering, so big was it that it seemed without end." The time for the realization of this miração had arrived with the foretelling of a great expansion of the doctrine, an army of light was awakening. Padrinho Sebastião had taken refuge in Rio do Ouro, protecting the original community from the shock of the first wave of newcomers. Padrinho Mario stayed in Rio Branco to receive the new arrivals.

For the first time, government members, Brazilian army officials, university teachers, technicians from the Instituto Nacional de Reforma Agraria (INCRA), psychiatrists, psychologists, and doctors were contacting this humble village, the center of the Daime people, this new spiritual path, which is at once universal and Brazilian. Padrinho Mario, who accompanied the Cofen commission, kept a telepathic connection with Rio do Ouro, receiving instructions to ensure the best outcome for the Daime's quest, as well as the well-being of their guests. He was very comfortable in the host's role. To our surprise, few of us could keep up with him as we walked through the jungle, even though he was already in his seventies.

"My conversations with Padrinho Sebastião are short," he told me. "I receive his orders, the things he would like me to do, and I receive them directly. Do you understand?" He pointed with his finger to the place between his eyebrows to show where the transmissions from Rio do Ouro arrived.

After a couple of days of adventures on the roads and waterways at the edge of the virgin forest, we arrived at the bank of the Indimari River carrying all our equipment on our backs for almost one kilometer. The heavier bags were then loaded into a small canoe that crossed the river and entered a small tributary, bringing our load to its final destination. Before leaving for Rio do Ouro, Padrinho Mario gathered us aside and opened a small works, which are ceremonies in which the Daime sacramental drink is partaken and in which, through prayer and the guidance of the hymns, different areas of the spiritual world are realized as healing, celebration, oracle, consultation, soul journey, etc. Afterward we stayed a couple of minutes absorbed in thoughts, watching the smoke rising slowly to the sky. Meanwhile, the expedition guides were searching for another trail because the regular one had been obstructed by logging. It was late in the day, and we were going to cross the forest at night.

When Seu Mario finished the small works, I felt strong and happy to be a part of it all. It was then that I had the impression of seeing Padrinho Sebastião's face suspended over the forest. It was not an impression, I was really seeing it. I rubbed my eyes but he was still there, as if he accompanied our every move. I clearly saw the giant, three-dimensional image surrounded by concentric waves of energy that soon disappeared to make space for new ones. His presence imposed on all my being a serenity and a silence without precedent. I wondered if this was Seu Mario's normal state of perception when he was receiving his communications from Padrinho Sebastião.

After we crossed the river, the enormous energy field that vibrated from the depth of the forest overtook us. We kept on walking silently through the forest, feeling the vibration of energy arriving in our minds like waves at the beach or like the circles created by throwing a stone in a still lake. Only that, for me, the surface of this lake was the immense blue sky, already tinged by the first purples of the dusk. Framing Padrinho Sebastião's enormous face was his long white beard, which tenderly touched the treetops in the form of fog.

In the silence, one could clearly hear the forest's sounds and harmonies. The animals talked, and their conversations were simple and direct, each realizing its own existence and revering the Creator. Each expressed a different beauty. They did not talk about other animal's lives. The frogs croaked and the stars shone in answer. Fireflies illuminated our way. This happiness would last until I reminded myself of everyday challenges. My mind would then grow restless, the vision would disappear like smoke, only to reappear clearly a bit ahead. There, the face of Padrinho Sebastião was again with us.

After I experienced many hardships on the trail—crossing many grottoes with knee-high water, falling from a high place, and being bitten by nocturnal ants—we finally arrived at a community settlement. The name could not have been more auspicious: Esperança (hope). Full of hope, we crossed a tributary named Trena and made rubber torches because by this time all the batteries we brought had been used up. Singing hymns, our faithful procession entered once more the great forest that echoed with peeps, whistles, and murmurs. We passed through natural portals that looked like doorways into parallel worlds and their secrets. At any point it seemed that we might encounter a clearing full of elves gathered around their campfire. Had that happened, we would have sung their songs and our hymns to the sound of flutes and lutes. It felt like morning but it was still night. I continued seeing Padrinho Sebastião's figure in the sky surrounded by stars, the circles of energy slowly unfolding, drawing webs of silver threads that reflected the moonlight. We had penetrated a powerful domain, but a feeling of tenderness, lightness, and happiness invaded me in spite of my being exhausted by the walk.

When we finally entered the clearing of what should have been the little village in the heart of the forest, I saw neither elves nor a campfire. All was quiet and time seemed to have stopped. I felt like we had walked for days, but it was only after midnight. I washed myself in the Rio do Ouro's waters and slept in the small supply store.

When I woke up, the sun was already on the horizon and Seu Mario was returning from his morning walk. My heart began to pound as I thought, soon I will meet Padrinho Sebastião.

2

...

The Prophet of the Amazon

MY BODY TINGLED as I stood in front of a man who radiated a great aura of light. His face was already a bit wrinkled, more as a result of a life dedicated to intense physical labor than from his real age. The rest of his body was slender and glowing with energy. When I looked into his eyes, I realized that they had already been fixed on mine from the first moment of our meeting. It was a serene gaze, clear and true. It was impossible not to feel an immediate connection with him. After the first impression, intensely tender, I realized that I was in the presence of a being of great light and knowledge. Underscoring my certainty of this was the feeling of security that emanated from his entire being. There was nothing premeditated or false. Everything was true.

In the beginning it was difficult for me to confront his gaze, in spite of its childlike beauty. Such clarity urges us to seek the source of our own gaze: are we caught up in deliberate, fancy pretense, or does the ray shining with love and beauty spring from the bottom of our hearts? "The eyes are the windows of the soul," Padrinho Sebastião used to say.

All of these thoughts passed through my mind before he addressed a single word to me. A sensation of smallness began to overtake me, because in spite of the thirst to know the truth, when a soul is still selfish the presence of such a person is both fascinating and disturbing. I felt like a lover full of expectancy for the meeting with the beloved, and who suddenly, when his or her fantasies are realized, is barely able to utter a sound. Still smiling, Padrinho greeted me, "So, are you Alex?"

He spoke as though he had known my spirit for a long time. It was my physical being he was encountering for the first time. He acted naturally, as if he had been expecting me.

A spiritual mestre is always disconcerting in his actions. That is why his presence is indispensable to anyone who wishes to embark on a spiritual life. At first we marvel at that flesh and bone paradigm. A second later we feel discouraged as we realize the distance that separates us from our model. But if we accept, even hypothetically, the possibility that divine perfection inhabits the material world, soon the inner strength of the mestre, the spiritually realized man or woman, plays a song in the depth of our being calling us to reencounter God. Krishna's magic flute, the psalms accompanied by David's harp, and the sweet voice of Jesus—all manifestations of Divine Logos—provide some of the themes of this poignant, eternal song. Manifestations of Divine Logos, through the grace of God, continue to open more and more hearts to the understanding of the truth. Today those who are misled still refuse to recognize such manifestations as expressions of spiritual truth.

Contrary to scientific and moral half-truths, the validity of which depends on natural phenomena and human concepts, spiritual revelation feeds itself only from true reality, which the awakened spirit perceives. The proof of God is God himself. If we still do not feel him, how can we believe in his existence? To learn to see him, it is necessary to find someone we can trust, who can help us to stimulate our self-confidence and to correct our imperfections.

But all of this was not so clear at the moment of my first meeting with Padrinho. In the middle of the clouds of skepticism, rationality, and doubt, I began to understand that I had a rare and valuable opportunity in front of me, maybe even the goal of my present incarnation.

We feel in a mestre a superior strength that teaches us and prepares us for the encounter with God. This strength elevates rather than humiliates and renders us equal in God's eyes. It invites us to love one another, partaking in an initiatory mystery. The same is revealed by all the great mestres, and by Christ himself, the principal of all avatars who have visited this planet.

Those were also the teachings of Sebastião Mota: to learn to be brother and sister, to form a holy community and to be a truly holy people. The fertile place to realize this spiritual ideal was and is the Amazonian forest where people are once again finding each other. These people are the Essenes of the new era, preparing themselves to receive the Owner of all eras, whose new coming is represented by the second arm of the Caravaca cross, a cross traditionally from northern Spain that symbolically acknowledges the second coming of Christ. All of this emanated from the presence of that man with the long beard and crystal-clear eyes.

Although he was friend to the sun, the moon, and the stars, and told us about his astral journeys through the bottom of the ocean and under the earth, there he was, that old prophet, available to know me and to be known. His presence inspired trust, respect, and friendship, the three small simple paths necessary to reach the main road that is love.

It took only a small spark to ignite my soul. After the ecstasy of the first moment, I became conscious of my underdevelopment, but it evolved to a feeling of much happiness and stimulation. Deciding to ask him for a blessing, I shook his vigorous and calloused hand while I answered his greeting, "Yes, I am Alex. I came from far away to meet you."

It was in this exact moment that my spirit surrendered. It encountered its guide, the spiritual guide of the forest, who knew the secrets and the shortcuts by which the power plants can take us to the most intimate mingling of our consciousness. I felt a great humility being born in me. Until then, I judged myself to be very intelligent. But under the weight of that gaze of someone who truly knew who he was, I asked myself, and I, who am I? Because I did not know the answer to this question, I felt cornered: when I perceived that all these contradictory feelings were products of my own doubts and hesitancy, I became afraid. But as I looked at Padrinho's face staring at me, smiling, my fear dissipated. I smiled back and surrendered.

As if guessing my inner disposition, he gave me courage. He said, "What is important, my son, is that I see you are happy. Soon you will find yourself, know who you are, and discover your mission. We are here for this, to help each other to discover who we are, to become men and women who are truly like Christ. Let's follow His road, isn't that it? It was He who opened the tollgate and left tracks for us to follow. I always say, 'Whoever can follow, follow! Even crawling is worthwhile!'"

"Padrinho, you guessed it. I am very happy to be here, and I hope that this visit helps you and your work. This is also our mission."

"Are you speaking of all these doctors who are arriving? I hope they see many beautiful things and tell us all about them. I myself am illiterate. I only know how to see but not how to count." His eyes shone with the mischievousness of a child. He added in a whisper, "They think they came here to study me, to know me, only that I have already studied myself, and I know who I am. Later, they will realize that they came here for themselves, to study and know themselves." He raised his voice and looked into my eyes. "To find what we are looking for each one of us has to start by knowing what we are looking for. Look at yourself. Nobody invited you, did they?"

"I came because I wanted to."

"You came because you were supposed to come. Nobody invites anybody. Who is destined to come, comes. You did not receive an invitation, did you?"

"You are correct, Padrinho."

"But you came, yes?"

"It seems that way."

"Then be welcome, my son!"

The last words were said with a jovial hug that almost made me lose my balance. As he left for the storage room, he shouted, "Later we are going to get to know each other still better," referring to the Daime works that would take place that evening. I left there light as a feather. I had the impression that Padrinho Sebastião was following me. The images I had from having just been with him seemed to alternate with those that accompanied me during our journey through the forest.

I was so enveloped by good omens that I did not remember any of the other reasons that took me to Rio do Ouro. The encounter with Padrinho was brief but significant. He answered doubts that for a long time I did not know how to formulate to myself. By and by, back to my consciousness would come the fact that I was in the middle of the forest, a member of an interdisciplinary commission that came to study, and maybe even also to decide the future of a drink and a doctrine I had only moments ago accepted when I asked Padrinho for his blessing.

Thinking it through, there were not many reasons to worry. We were there more to know ourselves than anything else. All was entrusted to the power of the drink that, as Mestre Irineu's hymn says, "has incredible power."[1] If each one of the members of this commission discovered his or her self, without a doubt we would better understand ourselves and the nature of the work that we had come here to do.

Padrinho trusted us completely and did not have anything to hide. He foresaw the moment when all would be discovered: at the end of this millennium, which many see as the end of the cycle, when the esoteric sides of all doctrines we have heard about are being revealed, proclaimed, printed, and even vulgarized.

The very thing that for so long has been handed down through a chain of initiates stopped being a privilege of a few to become a treasure available to many. It is divine mercy itself that acts in this way, enabling us through channels of faith and belief to reach one of the many roots of the sacred tree of life and knowledge where each truth-seeker finds rest under its fronded shade and may taste of its forbidden fruit. As it is said in the hymn:

> *I am a shade tree*
> *Like a coconut tree*
> *I give value to you*
> *Value that nobody ever had.*
>
> *But they do not want to thank me*
> *Much less to understand me*
> *If they are someone*
> *It is under my power.*[2]

After I drank Daime with Padrinho Sebastião on that occasion I felt a strong presence that I could not define. Because I could not define this presence, it was the strength of my desire for knowledge that put me on the path, in spite of the painful battles and the suffering that later almost threw me off this predestined route.

After that I spent a long time without seeing again the depths of the miração, even though I always felt its presence hovering around me. Many names came to me, but none gave me a clue as to what was real in this profound experience. Padrinho called miração the state of overflowing superconsciousness guided by the Daime.

Could this be the supreme experience, the ultimate vision, the crown of holiness? I had to believe in what I had seen, and all the names, images, and universal forms were not able to represent what I had so intensely experienced. On the other hand, I also knew that an experience like that is only obtained after many years, or many lifetimes, of initiatory work. How could it be that a neophyte like myself reached it just like that, all of a sudden, without previous preparation?

Maybe it is one of the mysteries of the esoteric revelation that is happening at many spiritual points on the planet. There are no patterns that can contain and keep the succession of events from unfolding from now on. The velocity will be such that only a very dynamic process of spiritual transmutation and elevation of consciousness can accomplish the task of liberation and victory. The whole cosmos vibrates, and a clamor is heard that reaches the doors of the most receptive homes, announcing the return of the Solar-Christ.

By now, I had already convinced myself that I was immersed in a very elevated state of consciousness, reaching a revelation. I judged myself unprepared for it, and deep inside I felt I was undeserving. It was the same shyness and oscillation that overtook me at my first meeting with Padrinho Sebastião.

But what I saw absolved me of all my fears and doubts. Was Seu Mario not saying that whoever takes the Daime and finds what he or she was looking for becomes a new being? All I received and even my hesitation to believe were not misrepresented by Padrinho Sebastião, they were gifts of hope deposited in the heart of the new man being born at that moment. He wanted to know more about what I had seen, which during some moments made me understand all I still needed to become.

It was the first call of the Divine love that was being born in me. The encounter with the Daime brings to our consciousness a kind of cosmic overflow. We perceive the material world, the sun, and the stars becoming a screen of energy through which is unveiled an infinite ocean of peace and good fortune. What divine instrument is thus capable of transporting any miserable mortal to such a summit? It cannot be diabolical, because we feel in our own hearts the desire to rebel against such an insinuation. We remember the sacred content of the Daime experience with its consequences so clearly beneficial and noted as such.

What was happening then? Was all of that the doing of a psychoactive plant, of an alkaloid that induces a kind of mirage called miração? Or is it a true experience of knowledge of our inner being, the goal of all initiation and mysteries since the most remote times? Again my mind would wander, jumping like a monkey on the vines of the forest, through cells, enzymes, amino acids, neurotransmitters, wanting to discover the chemical circuit that takes us to the miração, this genuine weaving of spiritual perceptions and religious experiences. I now understand that my first works with the Daime were of the same nature as those lived by mystics of the past, that I had been graced with a gift, even though I had no pretension to compare myself to any mystic.

I was surprised sometimes by the feeling of a weight in my heart because the whole situation with the research and validation of the Daime was bringing me guilt for communing with God in such a way, for feeling that the divine experience was in some way being artificially induced. I knew many people who felt the same way. But if it was myself who sought and found God in this way, how could I now deny him and not consider him valid?

Suspicion about "hallucinations," visions artificially induced, was the main component of old misconceptions. But a new era is dawning in which prejudice can no longer hold back the truth. Nevertheless, a confrontation is in the air and we were the witnesses being called to testify about this new form of consciousness. This is our first great spiritual battle: to affirm our faith in what we had seen with our eyes and felt with our hearts; to testify to the divine character of an experience that is difficult to frame in any formal and preconceived logic; and to hope that fallible human logic does not once again take God's witnesses and throw them to the lions.

This same question, transported to a plane intrinsically institutional, was moving the government, the modern secular power of our time, to an undisguisable curiosity about the origins and goals of the Santo Daime, a group rooted in the Amazonian forest, achieving communion with God through a drink obtained from a vine and a leaf. To a certain degree the preoccupation was justified because this spiritual phenomenon was as yet unknown to many. And that the religious sacrament is obtained through the mixing of two psychoactive plants stimulates much prejudice. Initiation with Divine plants, a native tradition of the most ancient people of the Americas, should not be confused with the indiscriminate use of drugs and the economic interests that guide this terrible industry, a significant wound of our modern civilization at the end of this millennium.

As Padrinho captured so precisely, the visit of this Confen commission had a special meaning. It was an encounter of national and local governments with a holy people who came from far away, a spiritual community with an ancient legacy, coexisting today in harmony in Brazil. It is not without meaning that many contemporary authors talk about the great spiritual role of our country, also called the land of the Southern Cross, where, as it is said, Christ and his phalanx descended and consecrated the ground of its forest as being the appropriate place for his so long awaited return.

Sometimes I walked through the woods meditating on the mysteries of these plants that cause us to enter into contact with a being so wise and sublime, with power as deep as it is benevolent, to the point that our hearts dare to have the certainty to call it faith and our understanding translates this state as being the presence of Christ inhabiting our interior. I am this! I would whisper to myself and, as I had studied Eastern religions, unconsciously repeat an old Vedic mantra to myself.

Many times, the great negative power present in doubt ambushed my still oscillating mind. Padrinho often warned us, "Be careful with the two thieves at the side of the crucified Christ. They are doubt and fear, the ones who steal our consciousness and take us from our certainty." They were also the ones that disturbed my walks, taking on the role of the Devil's advocates. Doubt and fear whispered in my ears: "Surely you are mad! How can you believe that you are as He is? And what if it was a mirage?"

I was following this being that I felt present in the Daime, even without fully understanding him. One of the hymns that Padrinho Sebastião loved to sing states:

> *I live in the forest*
> *And I have my teachings*
> *I do not call myself Daime*
> *I am a Divine Being.*[3]

By and by, this knowledge was percolating into me. When I drank the Daime for the first time, the great church hall of Colônia 5,000 transmuted in front of my eyes into an ancestral celebration. I felt part of a mystery, the memory of which was being rescued from the mist of the collective human unconsciousness. At the dawn of the great Hindu civilization, our ancestors used the juice of a plant called Soma. It was offered in a ritual form three times in a row, part being offered to the fire and part consumed by priests. Dozens of hymns belonging to the Rig Veda, one of the oldest and most respected religious scriptures, talked about the inebriant power of the sacramental drink dedicated to the god Indra in special rites and occasions. Many researchers associated the cult with *Amanita muscaria siberiana*, a mushroom that has a consciousness expanding active principle, but others point to *Peganum harmala*, a plant that has as one of its components the same active principle of the vine *Banisteriopis caapi*.

Could it be that Daime is the same Soma reappeared at the twilight of the gods, at the moment when Siegfried played the trumpets ending the old Nordic and Arian mythologies and inaugurating a new era of Juramidam, the Divine Being that inhabits the telluric forests of the new world? What does it matter in what form or class of being the Divine Avatars manifest to man and woman? Did Vishnu not come as a turtle, fish, and bird? The Logos, the Divine Verb manifested, adopted in Christ a human form, so why not as a plant?

The various members of the commission spent their days conducting interviews, meetings, tests, and taking photographs. Padrinho, solicitous, attended to everyone. When he met with a more intimate group he would be more open, "I know that further on all of this will not be of much worth. I have a feeling it will not. First one group comes and writes a bunch of papers. Then another group comes and says that the studies done before were insufficient and sends for yet another commission to come to write more papers. In my time there was no need for such documentation. When a man gave his word, that was enough."

"My father also was like you."

"Because he also lived during that time," Padrinho Sebastião said. "But it has been always like this: a sacred world and a confused and illusory 'normal' world. History tells about Christ being persecuted when he came into the world, and it is the same today with the Daime. The Daime shows us our shortcomings, it takes people away from the illusions they dwell among. But no commission is going to discover a secret only by looking at the bottle; they have to drink, partake, to know for themselves."

For some of the members of the commission, there was no "spiritual quest." To see if the use of this drink in its religious context was in any way socially disruptive or pernicious, they resolved to make an evaluation in light of good sense—scientific and moral.

Both the social and the spiritual life in Rio do Ouro testified in our favor. If the rational and emotional blocks of the commission's members impaired their acceptance of the divine nature of their direct or indirect experience with the Daime, they were at least obliged to recognize that the consciousness caused by the drink was far from having negative consequences in behavior patterns or on the productivity of the Daime community. In everything, the results of the visit were favorable. The community was well-organized, productive and orderly, with a level of health, hygiene, education, and nutrition well above the average of any community in the area. That showed that the religious and spiritual practice of the Daime was deeply bonding, socially and psychologically, stimulating coherence and solidarity among its members.

The most important result though, would defy the cold, analytic logic of the scientific man. To arrive at the secret, one has to expand the heart as well as the consciousness. The spiritual phenomena contained in the process of self discovery cannot be deduced from studying the brain in the laboratory. Only sensitive spirits who pursue this quest have a chance to capture it in its totality.

Anyway, a temporary truce was guaranteed. An agreement for the time being was made that allowed for the continued use of sacred plants in a religious context. In the years following this visit, in spite of difficulties, we were able to advance in the recognition of our right to seek the genuine and legitimate religious experience through the ceremonial use of sacred plants.

The laboratories were confirming that DMT, N, N-dimethyltryptamine, the alkaloid in the leaf, had almost the same molecular structure as serotonin, a neurotransmitter. When potentiated by the action of harmine, the alkaloid of the vine, the N, N-dimethyltryptamine (DMT) deeply transforms all our systems of perception and our codes of understanding. What impedes us from seeing the presence of the Divine machinery in the plants, the alkaloid, the consciousness, and ourselves? If these elements facilitate our connection with the divine, why should we fear them as drugs?

To speak of the phytochemistry of the power plant is a descriptive process that does not add any value to the experience. What is important is to feel like our ancestors, who lived in a world "much more sacred than this confused one," to use Padrinho's expression, and did not have doubts that the object of their perception was divine. The Daime has the power to take shortcuts on the road that leads us to a direct perception of God in ourselves, immersing our minds in a state without intellect where the miração imposes itself and silences us.

Still wanting to find a bridge between science and spirituality, we could perhaps say that we penetrated the realm of the archetypes of the human collective unconsciousness, the origins of which may be found in the most distant stars as well as in a helium atom. Confronting the marvelous possibility to rescue this precious memory, a true lost treasure, why then should we give so much importance to labels, judgments, and biases?

When Padrinho Sebastião showed us the depth and range of the spirit, in his simple language, we understood the power present in the truth. He transmitted to us a profound and true conviction, received directly from the celestial beings through their plant vehicle.

He also remembered other visits from the police before this commission. "How they arrived! All the police, tall and big, full of arrogance. What are we supposed to do? Take up arms as well? No. Instead of that, I said, 'My friend, you cannot come in just like that among people with a certain spiritual capacity like us, isn't it true? Here, pay very close attention. One cannot come in and start quarreling and intimidating. Do you want to have spiritual proof? You drink with us and when you leave here you will not want anything else with the illusion, you will want to stay in truth.' Because is God not inside? In your own self? If we do not present what we are, nobody will believe us! The next time they arrived in a more respectable way. One of them even told me, 'Seu Mota, men like you are rare to find and should never be disturbed by these things.'"

Inwardly I rejoiced because I had the conviction that I had found the truth, even knowing that it would cost me a lot to deserve it and, furthermore, to live in accordance with it. I thought, What does it matter how or where I arrived at my self-knowledge and knowledge of God? Is this not the most noble goal that a human existence can have? What could oppose the Superior Power that created and nurtured us with the hope that on the day we find ourselves we will also be able to recognize who we are?

"If a man does not look for perfection in himself," Padrinho would say, "he will never find it anywhere, especially in the one called Christ. The spiritual part was called Christ, Jesus, who walked on this earth, was his physical body. Today we are dealing with the same Christ! Whoever thinks that the initiator and goal of their struggles is someone else is not paying attention. We fight at Christ's side within a tradition that came from the forest." And he would sing:

> *I come from the forest*
> *With my singing of love*
> *I sing with happiness*
> *My Mother told me to.*
>
> *My Mother told me*
> *To bring the holy doctrines*
> *My brothers and sisters, all who came*
> *All bring this teaching.*[4]

Pablo Amaringo
14.04.02

3
...
The Divine Gardener

ALTHOUGH MY STAY in Rio do Ouro was relatively brief, it involved the rapid and intense unfolding of many events. After the dazzle of first encounters, a deepening of the spiritual work with the Daime showed me how difficult it is to remove all the absolute layers of one's personality. My consciousness was a real junkyard, full of useless stuff, a junkyard with aspirations of becoming a sanctuary.

Padrinho's magnetic presence, his words, and the power of his living faith planted a small seed in my heart. This is how the true inner sanctuary began to become more conscious. Although I still lived in the dusty old basement of my inferior self, in a short time the seed sprouted and grew. Now it needed to be well cared for by a Divine gardener. During this time, I frequently heard Padrinho singing this hymn:

> *The Divine Eternal Father*
> *His rose he entrusted to you*
> *But you didn't value it*
> *And because of this it wilted.*

> *The rose that he gave me*
> *Has grown and already bloomed*
> *Because I don't water it with water*
> *I water it with love.*

My Father is very generous
He lets you do whatever you want
But after a long time
You'll receive what you don't want.[1]

The rose that the Father delivered, the most beautiful flower, was his own Son. After Jesus fertilized the earth with his blood, we could through him again have access to the flower of the self, receptacle of the sacred monad. It is righteous to water this flower with spiritual love, because it symbolizes the rebirth: the consciousness that we exist simultaneously on earth and in Heaven. The heart's sacred garden needs to be nurtured with a love that creates deeds, not merely contemplative feelings that indulge the ego's illusions. Love that is full of fantasies and longings is of no use because it produces vague emotions that cloud the lake of harmony. If we do not remain attentive and humble, we may dwell in emotional realms that are far from a state of true devotion.

Every gardener should be devoted to his or her plants, especially when dealing with the sprouting self, the presence of Christ in us. No matter how much care, surrender, and dedication we are able to give, it will never suffice, because this Divine flower, the self, sprouted in our hearts, is at the same time omnipotent, self-created, and universal.

We should learn not to speak of God until we know his intent in full, until we are swept away by love that drives us to the bottom of the mystery, until we love and revere his sublime and little understood intent. As Padrinho used to sing:

My Father did tell me
I could believe
People who have firmness and love
Are difficult to find.

Everyone speaks of God
Because they see others do so
Here within the truth
Behold God where He is.[2]

It is a mistake, therefore, for seekers who have only discovered what they should be to believe that they have reached the final realization. Spiritual rebirth begins with a long gestation. In the Daime, unlike other doctrines in which enlightenment is the culmination of prolonged practices and evolved skills, rebirth can be experienced in the miração quite unexpectedly. Thus, we can become astounded by the gift received and afraid of the responsibility it implies, but we can also become extremely motivated in response to the genuine treasure just encountered.

Many want to practice the love of God within a controlled situation and with a certain composure. They legitimately become absorbed in fighting the emotions, but with that they suppress the devotional feeling created by the intimate encounter with God. They do not allow themselves to be swept away. They identify themselves with consciousness but do not pulsate with Him in the beat of the heart. They do not feel the wonderment of those who have entered the Divine alcove and found the Beloved. There are also those who, by their own temperament, are capable of great rapture and feelings for the many faces of the Divine. They should in their turn be careful not to confuse Divine love with caricatures of the original.

The new being that is gestating is a fragile newborn. The struggle for the worthiness of his or her awakening has just begun. If we have already received the vision that we are truly made in the image and likeness of God, we then need love, charity, and humility to perceive that all our brothers and sisters are so made as well. Like us, they are recognizing themselves.

If we use the divine manna, our experience of the Daime, to feed our vanity, the honey becomes bitterness. Without charity we cannot stand the knowledge of the truth, much less its practice, and we become victims of a dangerous obsession that can, with time, transform into insanity. We need to heal ourselves from the proud pretension that only we are divine, because this is ignorance and can lead to all sorts of mistakes and lies.

If our hearts beat strongly for our wives, husbands, sons, daughters, and friends, how is it that we do not overflow when we discover God as the source of our own divinity? This recognition of divinity in each other as well as ourselves is a manifestation of God's grace, not an achievement of the intellect. To manifest this grace on earth, God, by pure mercy, became flesh and lived among us. Some saw, touched, and listened to words from his own lips; others believed in what was said about him by witnesses.

Blessed be those who did not see and yet believed. Doubly blessed are we, who to this day have a chance to see and believe through the miração of Santo Daime. The quest then is to understand the power of this drink sanctified by Mestre Irineu, which sent us deeply into the garden of our inner selves and to the landscape of the beautiful story of Jesus and Saint John.

I do not know what eminent theologians would think of my considerations, but I think it is time to search for an inner theology—a true science of the spiritual self, alive and pulsating—not an anatomy of dead or fossilized doctrines, but the true root of doctrine, the Divine relic of the heart that produces spiritual deeds. We can receive great benefits by relocating God's science to our inner reality: we can more easily align the inner and outer realities and meet God, who is present on both sides. Those who cannot, through the eyes of faith and the power of the heart, follow the traces of Christian manifestation, in time transform divine knowledge into a tedious autopsy, a dissection of crystallized categories and scholastic interpretations.

During this period in Rio do Ouro, I still maintained a certain incredulity toward many spiritual phenomena. The new thought that flesh-and-bone people could incarnate the attributes of the Divine was a great blow to my paradigm. But Padrinho Sebastião kept saying that these were very special times, and that, like him, everyone should know themselves. "Those who have ears to hear, do it. Those who have eyes to see, do it. Because everything will have to be manifested."

And he would sing an explanation:

> *There is nothing hidden*
> *That won't be revealed*
> *If I so decide.*[3]

He would adopt a solemn expression and then continue, "Thank God I know myself; I know who I am. I am not a fool who goes around giving opinions about what I do not know. We have to trust in the power of the Creative Father and in our capacity to recognize him. Those who thus proceed, believing in the clarity of spiritual revelation, will share this journey together at the end of the twentieth century."

I felt a strong sense of brotherhood with those I met in Rio do Ouro. My impression was that we had known each other before. The prospect of becoming part of this community made me enthusiastic. A great euphoria and love of life overtook me. To balance it, the Daime showed me my painful and emotional personal issues parallel to those ecstatic states. During some moments, I almost felt the seed of the inner self become sterile through lack of patience with and love for my brothers and sisters.

Every once in a while the image of Padrinho Sebastião singing a certain hymn again gave me the direction to be followed. I began, through practice, to understand the seriousness of this path, each situation demanding our attention to learn the lessons we most need.

These special moments when the Daime shows us about our own bodies, souls, or spiritual lives help us to combat our main resistance to the spiritual path. These issues that become *passages* during the Daime originate in our daily lives and are due to the clash of the new consciousness with the mental and emotional residue from old patterns.

First, I had to overcome and give up unconditionally all my compulsive unchecked behavior, noxious to the germing consciousness. True weeds, such behaviors and habits affect deeply the self and can stunt self-development if they are not given up. Through this phase a character deformed by indolent habits and wrong perceptions about nature will miss its opportunity and be induced to evermore distorted and false thoughts. Such self-indulgence conditions us to follow inexorably error after error. A character without boundaries, thirsty for power, glory, or richness, feeble and frail, is a ground in which the Divine self can never germinate.

> *A Love without firmness*
> *Is a fire without warmth*
> *It is a weak thought*
> *It is a body without worth.*[4]

To sprout, the seed of sacred knowledge requires many tears of love and devotion and a strong desire for self-transformation. As in an initiation by fire, we need to burn up all of our character deformities. Through God's eyes, the quality of our sacrifice depends on our discernment, the strength to keep the promise made, the courage to put it into practice, and the depth of our renunciation.

Very few people are offered sudden enlightenment. Because of their determined decision to realize their spirituality, they achieve gestation, enlightenment, and rebirth all at once. For the majority, however, this process requires great struggle and sacrifice.

The most important element is the sincerity with which we seek the truth. Even when we still cannot see it clearly, we have to keep on its path. By correcting ourselves through the light of self-discernment, alignment with the truth becomes easier. When the correction comes from others, we usually resist because we do not like others to recognize our mistakes. This is pride and needs to be combatted. The most difficult task for Christians is not to love God but to love their brothers and sisters.

Saint John the Evangelist said it more or less this way: My sons and daughters, if you do not love your brothers and sisters, whom you see by your side, how can you love God, whom you do not see? When we embark on the spiritual path, we have to learn to accept the positive and the negative testimony given about us because we need both to grow. The positive gives us courage to stay on the path; the negative can help us find a balance between self-confidence and humility, thus stimulating transformation.

There are also false testimonies formulated by less developed individuals with the goal of hurting others. But it is easy to distinguish them from those that assist us on the path toward self-knowledge: positive feedback is given with love and respect in an open and sincere way, while false testimonies are insidious and almost always spoken behind one's back.

Thus, to become conscious and to correct our flaws are the first conditions to be fulfilled on the spiritual path. In a short time this procedure will bear excellent results for the emergence of the Divine Being into the material world. The right discernment, with a real understanding of the goal for each desire and thought, purifies our intent and gives a spiritual meaning to even our smallest enterprises.

The second condition for rebirth is the necessary climate for the development of the flower. Like the ground, the climate needs to be correct because it will influence the growth of the plant. We need to protect it by removing ourselves from environments where other people are spoken of frivolously. This Mestre Irineu called the *correio da má noticia* (the bad news post office), an endless negative chain that goes around the world in all directions, a hurricane of words, false testimonies, and distorted opinions that carries in its belly destruction, misery, insanity, illness, and death. This gossip, which always comes before good news and truth, is the worst form of pollution on the earth. These negative vibrations feed various entities and obsessive spirits that dwell in uninstructed minds and produce doubt and fear.

Mestre Irineu used to say that the correio da má noticia was his worst enemy, and one of the central goals of his existence on earth was to try to end this spiritual plague. As he sang in his hymn:

> *I give permission and I give punishment*
> *Here I do my justice*
> *We need to finish off*
> *With the correio da má noticia.*[5]

Where this foul breath blows through, beautiful flowers lose their shine, the air becomes contaminated and the aura darkens. Deviating from the path of truth is the first of many serious spiritual illnesses and the cause of many more.

Many lives are lost in this way. While the body decomposes after dying, the spirit continues sleeping in the illusion of those who did not awaken within divine consciousness. To join the divine consciousness, it is necessary to have it awakened and manifested on earth in the form of the superior self and its deeds. Padrinho Sebastião was tireless in repeating this very important point. He would repeat, "We have to be born again! Whoever does not acquire the necessary knowledge here on earth is going to suffer a lot to find who they are in the afterlife or anywhere else. Do you think it is easy, my dear, to be able to affirm with conviction that God is and is present in all places?"

To practice charity, the main Christian goal, we are told that we must love our brothers and sisters as we love ourselves. Thus, we have to abstain from feeding the correio da má noticia. Abandoning artificial environments, we naturally get closer to those who speak the truth and can stand by it. By being truthful we perform a great deed, therefore, when we are searching for the truth, everything that is not true should lose its attraction. We lose, by and by, our attraction to the mundane, the main vice of minds excessively focused on the external. And we get rid of obsessive fantasies, the chief ghosts of minds overly interiorized and unilluminated.

If we, as careful gardeners, want to protect our plant from the noxious climate created by bad vibrations, we have to avoid environments heavy in excessive egotism and dense energies. We have to stay away from sexual games of seduction. The true being is totally unlimited but asks for the permanent renouncement of the false shine of what pretends to be yet is not. Those who at the same time cultivate both the pleasure of the senses and knowledge sooner or later will have to make an option for one or the other. The emerging self is of pure knowledge and wisdom. It does not feed on pleasures but truth, in happiness or sorrow, as expressed in a hymn by João Pereira, another of Mestre Irineu's first disciples.

This was a gift
That my Mother gave me
To search for the truth
Until I know.

. . . .

I live in the world
My life is free
Supported by my Father
I do not fear danger.[6]

The alignment of the outer reality with the inner one causes sudden changes. We can no longer follow conventional patterns and take the risk of a big step toward the dark, where faith is the main if not the only guide.

Christ warned us that his name and the truth can provoke strong reactions sometimes, but through contact with the truth we develop patience and tenacity, virtues necessary for spiritual rebirth. Those who keep themseves firm in the truth are not afraid. But how do we know we are living in the truth? Our hearts tell us, and, as we prove our sincerity with deeds, we obtain the recognition and testimony of our brothers and sisters.

As Sebastião Mota explained, "This is a school of Divine knowledge. It is such a serious thing that if everyone really knew, they would not speak badly of this beautiful sacrament that sprouted from the earth itself, as natural as God's own nature. But, since the time of Mestre Irineu, people without this knowledge have spoken dreadful barbarities. They want to force on us the insanity so prevalent in the world today, when our goal is the healing from such derangement. The truth is the only medicine for our time. By receiving the truth in ourselves we show the way of healing to our brothers and sisters."

The Daime also stimulates in us reconciliation and harmony with our own family. We learn about karma, past lives, and the nature of the mission that unites us with other beings. Everyone who begins spiritual work with the Santo Daime feels intensely the need to recognize the role of our predecessors and to love our descendants. We, therefore, must take up the task of karmic cleansing to prepare an environment evermore spiritually attuned and favorable for our perfection and the perfection of our descendants.

Those on the spiritual path with their blood family intact have the opportunity to see the reflection of their own qualities and flaws. When our spiritual consciousness is awakened, the conviviality with our sons and daughters makes possible a great recovery of our own memory and a rich lesson in how to nourish and foster them. To develop our ability to see the truth, a decision is necessary: to diminish the influence of the inferior self on the journey to the true self. Those who totally want to deny the needs of the inferior self, because they are in such a hurry to transform, can become distressed. On the other hand, indulging all the desires and whims of the ego always takes us further from our true self.

These were the issues I was dealing with when I returned to Rio do Ouro after my first contact with Padrinho Sebastião. I was far from the greater certainty that I enjoy today. It was the Daime itself, through the works I started in a small town called Maúa, situated in the mountains outside of Rio de Janiero, that brought to the surface the impasses and the possible solutions. The power in everything was revealed in the Daime where I saw our capacity to influence the material world increasing. This requires a higher ethical and spiritual consciousness, so that we are not tempted to use our newly developed acuity only to satisfy our own egotistic interests.

Before we win the first battles against the tendencies of the inferior self, our personal power can become dangerous. We are like magician's apprentices who yet cannot control our magic. Therefore, there is a need for us to understand the seriousness of the path and the immense responsibility assumed by those taking it. That is why the Daime doctrine brings *apuro* and *balanço* in its own terms. The *apuro* is an exacerbation of the problem. The *balanço* is the purification needed for transformation. This process can happen in the miração, in which each one of us is on an astral journey, in our everyday life, in which we must apply the results of our spiritual lessons, or in both, more or less simultaneously.

The Daime presupposes the search for truth, a consciousness developed enough to hold it, and a community in which to enact the realization of this divine project. But such a reality is a struggle to attain. We need to work on tensions between people and getting rid of conflicts and negative emotions. Hard work and compromises are necessary to achieve a union within truth, peace, harmony, love, charity, and justice that should rule a congregation of beings who have chosen to live a spiritual life.

When the Daime holds sway, all the less-defined features of the personality are revealed. Questions inherent in the process of self-knowledge increase, putting us face to face with all of our doubts. The process can be difficult; brothers and sisters may need to rub their sharp edges together to blunt them. Many give up at this stage. Our own imperfections, or those of our brothers and sisters, give us the excuse to block the true surrender and union. The flower of the self withers without food or care. We cannot distinguish the purity of Divine manifestation when its channels seem so impure. To perceive the truth we have to learn to trust others as we learn to trust ourselves.

Padrinho told me one day, "Without my trust in you and yours in me, how can it be? Without eliminating the doubt and distrust among us, we cannot consecrate the truth, and all will come to naught!" And he sang, "One must trust in oneself / In order to be protected by doctrine."[7] Without fulfilling the injunction to trust one another, it is impossible to achieve the higher mandate of loving each other as the Father in Heaven loves us!

Padrinho Sebastião practiced as well as preached this cornerstone of Christian doctrine. He gathered a people in the forest with this goal:

together to bear the apuros and the balanços to receive the Christian spiritual force that Christ announced two thousand years ago.

I already started to feel in my own flesh the many apuros much spoken of in the hymns. Our first reaction upon entering the spiritual life in search of our rebirth is to notice that everything suddenly becomes terribly complicated and more difficult. This storm is inevitable. We have to decide where to look for protection, in the ego steeped in materialism or in the newly sprouting Divine Being. The difficulties that seem so new and exaggerated are the result of the lifting of the veils of illusion and dishonesty, with which we were accustomed to soothe and mollify our consciousness. The suffering, when accepted, studied, and understood, is the best conditioner of our will, and our affliction should be only ours and never imposed on others. Padrinho would say, "Nothing is better than a mistake to bring our error to consciousness and help us toward spiritual advancement!" There is no real knowledge that does not depend on experience.

While appalled by the intensity of my own internal process, it was with hope that I prepared myself to go to Céu do Mapiá, the new location in the forest where Padrinho Sebastião and his people had moved.

4
...
Zen Canoeing
in the Igarapé Mapiá

IN OUR TIMES there is a lot of talk about the upcoming new era and the need for a new spiritual path. This need is real and urgent, but not everyone who preaches in its favor is in a real condition to do something concrete to attain it. We are waiting for the last veil to fall, for the gnosis to be revealed, for the Holy Grail to be finally discovered. In the meantime, even after all the occult teachings are published, many skeptics still want us to believe that a main direction is missing. Established spiritual traditions should worry less about their administrations and bank accounts. Their dioceses should generate more saints, sages, and spiritual workers who can exercise their talents in this life. For all that men preach, only what is anchored in the truth of their deeds can generate the faith to move mountains and model the world in accordance with Divine perfection.

Humanity needs faith. It is our task to swell the chorus of hope and to soothe the clamor of the tormented, whose cries echo through time until this present materialistic age. Perhaps they were not so different from most of us.

Many people associate spirituality with the reclusive or the simpleminded. They pretend to be modern, ashamed of any devotion. Some are waiting for a spaceship and others for the Logos itself or for the Christ. With a focused mind and a good feeling in our hearts, we can travel many light-years, and our great tool for this journey is consciousness, because its function is to find the presence of Divine imagination in the raw material of thoughts. Spiritual work begins when consciousness recognizes and affirms itself as this tool and opts for a spiritual life and reality.

Any movement toward a spiritual life has to base itself in the ethic of love, charity, and the ideals of solidarity and self-abnegation. True faith means cultivating an altruistic disposition, an energy of union and deed capable of awakening the seekers to come. "We should pray for all our brothers and sisters, the whole of humanity," Padrinho would say.

This is the real spiritual path capable of generating on earth the new era and of bringing to an end insanity, illusion, and lies. Great pathways have already been opened into this new paradigm by men and women of good will. But, be always aware of vanity, for it can cause a detour into insanity. God's victory is found in the realization of useful and good deeds that further the creative life, the Divine intent. Satan's victory is found in insanity and disharmony with Divine laws. This disharmony is present in all the major systems of "civilization" of our days; the ones decaying or already in ruins. The prophets who have alerted people to the insanity of the world have been persecuted, but people who persecute prophets sooner or later suffer the consequences of their actions. War, tribulation, and disunion are the results for those without faith.

The greatest of our sacred battles seems to be the challenging conquest of our own heart, the very heart we need for illumination and guidance. Whoever searches for the self has to search for his or her brothers and sisters as well, discovering the accomplices of God in this earthly realm. It is thus that we form small enclaves and points of light that are opening the way to the new era.

We all are seeds of the Great Mystery, possible prototypes of the new form of material and spiritual organization that is arising from the fragmentation of the old order. The ancient castle has been taken and reduced to ruins. Weeds overgrow the merlons and towers, signaling the end of the cycle. A new foundation is about to be laid. The moving impulse of history is no longer about the struggle of the social classes but about the emergence of new forms of consciousness and a new acceptance of diversity honoring each ethnicity, each community.

This is the new. Without doubt, Padrinho Sebastião lived most of his life planting on earth good seeds able to weather even the difficulties of the "drought" periods. He did not proclaim more than the wisdom found in his hymns. With the simplicity of an illiterate rubber tapper, he offered no ostentation about his knowledge.

Year after year, Padrinho Sebastião gave proof of his further commitment to his spiritual task. Full of faith, his people followed unconditionally the trail their spiritual guide was opening for them: from Colônia 5,000 to Rio do Ouro and from there to Céu do Mapiá.

When I finally reunited with him in June 1983, they had been at the site for about three months. At the location of the contemporary village, there was then only a small camping site. I was immersed in my reflections as the canoe taking me there followed the curves of the sinuous Igarapé Mapiá, a left tributary of the Puros River. I was taken by the same emotion I experienced in Rio do Ouro: Padrinho's presence hovering above the canopy and the energy vibrating in the air. It was like the dream of an argonaut about to discover some site still unknown by the human spirit.

It was difficult to believe that those men and women once again had left their homes and belongings, the fruits of two years of work, to reenter the forest in pursuit of their ancient dream. This time Padrinho was not isolated. His voice had been heard in other places. It had reached the hearts of many people awakening to a spiritual life. Padrinho Sebastião knew from Mestre Irineu that the fulfillment of his mission depended on us as well. He patiently awaited our help and counted on our valor to see him at the "end of the world."

In spite of his growing recognition, he never flattered us or anyone else. He received with equal graciousness the highest worldly authority and the humblest river dweller. To the recently arrived, he apologized for only having rice, beans, and roots. He liked to attend to the poor personally, lodging them and taking all the appropriate measures. He gladly opened as many works as he judged necessary, and his greatest satisfaction was to see healing happening.

The access to Céu do Mapiá was then only by river, we had to navigate attentively to avoid the sharp, floating wood stumps and piles of brush in the zigzag of the igarapé. We often had to jump in to the water to push the canoe through the driest spots. Alternating between meditative states and dynamic focused activity, a real Zen marathon, the journey to Padrinho was itself an initiation. While rounding a bend, all of a sudden we would hear, "Look out—branch!" We had to duck immediately or jump into the river.

The more experienced would command, "All push together! Front! Back! Jump out and push again!" At other times, someone would call out to slow the motor. Immediately, the motor would decelerate, and we would stop by the side of a huge tree fallen across the river. This could mean one or two hours working with the machetes to roll that tree, which was partially underwater, making the work harder. With the obstacle removed, we were back in our Zen mode. Thus, we proceeded from obstacle to obstacle with the boatmen adding to the occasion with tales of snakes and stingrays. Thoughts danced in our minds; we were missing our families and wanting to lie down in a comfortable hammock. We were also full of eagerness to see Padrinho and Madrinha, his wife, and soon would partake of Daime in the middle of the forest.

As I traveled, absorbed in the journey, my thoughts were left behind. At each curve of the river on the three-day trip, suppositions, whims, and masks were being stripped away by nature itself. My concerns seemed empty next to the impressive dignity and harmony of the forest and river. Worldly visitors and natives had to make the same effort and eat the same food.

We slept in simple dwellings at the river's edge, inhabited by humble people of great hospitality. As I sat on the old floor, sharing the provisions and looking at the children's faces, it was hard not to perceive the same dignity of nature present in them, as if the human form was an extension of the forest.

At times I felt as though I was on another planet, but I was not. There in the sky I could see the Southern Cross constellation on the horizon, bejeweled with its attendant stars. Ah, my Father, how I wish to know this mystery! I thought as I swung in my hammock. On the veranda hammocks were piled with fishing nets, shotguns, and buckets for tapping rubber. The night beyond was filled with whistles, screams, mating cries, wheezing, and other sounds of mysterious origin. To this day they have a soothing effect on my thoughts. I could also still feel the hum of the canoe's motor in my dreams. As morning approached, the world changed into gold and purple, and bird songs began to replace the sounds of the night. After coffee and farewell, we returned to our previous places to continue our studies in "Zen canoeing," alternating static and dynamic meditation: jumping, pushing, loading, and unloading the luggage.

After a night's delay in the forest because the motor broke down, we finally arrived at the enormous clearing at the confluence of the Igarapé Mapiá and the Repartição River. There were very few houses, and Padrinho's was easy to identify, being made of planed wood with a thatched palm roof. In the distance, big fields were being burned in preparation for planting corn and rice. There were also many rubber trails, which started practically at the center of the village. In the early days of the settlement, people harvested rubber to pay for groceries. Later, with help from other Daime churches, the focus moved toward general agriculture as well as the production of the Daime itself.

Since I had been in Rio do Ouro six months earlier, I had processed many things internally, and the people of the Mapiá community had made many improvements in their material environment. As I looked into their faces, I could see in their expressions fatigue from the struggles but also happiness at starting over. From the big veranda of his house, which was the community center for the seventy people living there, Padrinho would speak of Rio do Ouro as if it were already in the remote past. The way had been opened for the others who had stayed in Rio do Ouro under the supervision of Padrinho Corrente, awaiting Padrinho's call to move.

By the end of the afternoon the pioneers were beginning to return from the day's work. Some walked slowly from the fields, some left their workshops or sawmills, and others still carried bundles of palm leaves for a new roof. The hunters arrived with their game and fishermen with their fish. The manioc had not yet had time to grow, and Padrinho had permitted hunting for survival.

Activity increased in the big house because in these days before many houses were built, almost everyone slept there. Every day around six o'clock, a couple of women cleaned and swept everywhere, gathering the hammocks, and as if by magic, the main room of the big house was transformed into a small frontier church. Over the table was placed a well-worn, embroidered tablecloth with candles and flowers around the cross in preparation for praying and singing hymns.

We were invited by the message contained in the hymns to examine our consciousness and to understand the mystery that lies beyond prayer itself. Because we sang every day, the messages of the hymns were experienced profoundly by everyone.

Each of our days on this earth should be a prayer filled with work, union, promises, proofs, and consolations. And here in the forest this was actually happening.

After we finished, the women again came and transformed the small church into the house of an enormous family. After eating a light dinner of fish broth, small groups spread out from the clearing to socialize and tired people hung their hammocks for a rest. Seated in a corner, Padrinho would start a circle of conversation.

Fireworks colored the sky earlier on that night of June 23, the apex of winter solstice for the Southern Hemisphere, initiating the celebration of Saint John, patron of the doctrine. The flames from the bonfire reached to the sky, like a beacon of light signaling our presence to all the celestial beings and to the cosmos itself.

As we started our works, the humble church-house was transformed by the changing colors into a spaceship of light and beauty. It looked like Vishnu's chariot pulled by a thousand horses over valleys and cascades that extended for miles. That small village encircled by sensuous igarapés, virgin forest, white herons, and shining stars, seemed to become the spaceship of *Juramidam* taking off from that enchanted place, bound for the unfathomable mystery. Silver and gold lights danced in the sky as if alive, flashing to the singing accompanied by maracas.

Our understanding was navigating through beautiful images, following an irresistible chain so marvelous that it was scary. We were in the miração, the divine language and divine logic opening in our minds and felt by our hearts. Following the miração is like walking on the blade of a knife: if we lose our concentration or courage in the middle of the crossing, we might experience vertigo. We then face images of our fears and doubts and encounter the most difficult of the archetypes of our unconscious. The coexistence of the Daime's teachings with our shortcomings becomes difficult at these moments, thus it is important to maintain a balance between what manifests due to our surrender and our capacity for deeds in affirmation of what has been revealed to us. In the moment of vertigo, we should pray that God not let us fall into the abyss again, and that we never forget the oath made in the hour of danger, when we discovered something fundamental to our being.

At times I felt like an acrobat and thought about a movie I once had seen as a young child in which a man was crossing Niagara Falls on a cable, balancing himself with a rod. States of satisfaction alternated with moments of hardship, and I felt life's mystery palpitating as if it lived independently of me and my senses. I could feel my soul, that immortal spark that entered the ephemeral condition of matter and will one day reunite with the eternal and inexhaustible spring, the feared, much talked about, and much misunderstood God, whom I was trying to understand better so that I could more truly honor His presence on earth.

Everything sparkled in that night of Saint John. The scintillant pulse of the stars illuminated the crown of the centenary trees and invited us to reflect on the meaning of our existence on earth, the living machinery of this biological spaceship. Padrinho danced by my side with his serene rhythm. The big house was the captain's cabin, and there were no doubts that he was the great commander and navigator. Our spiritual spaceship needed a connection to a spiritual current, to elevate the work to the righteous destined sphere, and Padrinho provided it.

The bonfire emitted sparks as the moonlight bathed the yard with a pale light. I felt the unforgettable to be happening. The bitter taste of the Daime seemed to adhere to my cells, and a strange energy was condensed within me. It was the force. The maraca's cadence contained ecstasy and joy within the limits of serenity. Consciousness was awakening in many directions and with many meanings. The best thing to do was to "uphold time," as Padrinho used to say, and to keep, at all cost, the rhythm of the *bailado,* which is the collective dance marked rhythmically by the maracas as the hymns are sung, choreographed to generate an energy field and a spiritual current during the works.

Something in the air hinted of an extraordinary event about to manifest itself in the forest. The works in which we were participating were having repercussions in other worlds. "Stars" talked to us from outside and inside ourselves. The two, the inner and outer dimensions, coalesced intensely.

The force is a powerful energy that precedes the miração. It is as though all the gifts, attributes, and vital functions of our body organs become visible. We become conscious of many processes and phenomena, the end result of which is what we call life, the intelligent principle that gives existence to all that lives. The perception of this undulating pulse, the permanent life within the ephemeral one, made us feel and understand the spirit, the immortal self that is independent of reason or metabolic states. The miração that follows is a pure spiritual perception. It helps to locate and affirm the superior self and so encourages us to discern the labyrinth of reflections and illusions that tries to confuse us.

The true self illuminates everything, using all of the conscious, the unconscious, dreams, and karmic material to articulate its message: the miração. Thus, the synthesis of true knowledge is woven from symbols and images of the collective human unconscious. It is as though God speaks directly to us through a living parable. That is why the character of the true self is at the same time crystalline and profound, bringing a richer understanding of our own life, of our brothers and sisters and of God.

The miração is the "third vision." The understanding that we acquire in it inspires a deep commitment to transformation. Its effect, deeply therapeutic and consciousness-expanding, is due to the abolition of conditioning and illusions that impede authentic spiritual insight. Everything is important in this journey. Our perception increases and the inner voice speaks. The landscape is at once Cartesian and quantum. We may feel like the embodiment of a previous incarnation, or that we are living in a three-dimensional movie, or that we are a living monad of the Creator, an undetermined and leaping electron in the world where the Creator creates and re-creates his eternal and imperishable love.

In the ceremony I saw all the people dancing in the rhythmic pattern as a living example of the oneness in multiplicity. A voice said, "Wake up now! Now you are truly a man, a Divine Being incarnated." As I lost all sense of time and space, I penetrated mirrored galleries that reflected all the forms, names, and images from all my previous incarnations. When I perceived that through my fascination I had become stuck in this or that place, an image from the Ramayana came to me: the devotee Sukha carrying a basin of water on his head and walking many times around the garden of King Janaka's Palace, without spilling a single drop. He did not waver in his attention a moment, in spite of the numerous beauties, enchantments, and sexual distractions that surrounded the palace.

Without precautions, the beauty of the spiritual experience can overwhelm us. In my journey, this sensation was so strong that I thought I was going to fall. I looked to my side, and Padrinho's serenity inspired me. Thus, I began to expand my own limits. Continuing in the works, I looked to find in my heart this Father of love, justice, and forgiveness, begging him to sustain me.

As our bodies metabolized the energy contained in the active elements of the sacred plants, the force was preparing us for the miração in which everything becomes within God. The force touched our hearts, stomachs, and heads, helping our consciousness to see the reality of the body as well as the spirit. All these waves of understanding succeeded each other, presenting themselves as something incontestable. It was as though, in the miração, our human body and brain, which holistic thinkers describe as a prototype of the universe, exercise new aptitudes, ever deeper resources from the field of consciousness. In empirical science, in spite of its misguided embrace of the doctrine of progress, there is truly a progression, an accumulation of knowledge. But in primordial times spiritual insight was more awakened. As the physical body with all its attributes became more deeply incarnated, the clear, delicate perception of the astral, with all its ethical and spiritual dimensions, receded.

Consciousness was submerged in the ocean of unconsciousness. What was left was merely the tip of the iceberg, the parts identifiable with the body and material existence. Under it, in the profound abyss of our unconscious mind, is impressed the spiritual vibration of our very origins, the memory of when a vortex of powerful cosmic energies transformed gas and dust into a whirlwind of worlds and beings.

Life is a fascinating synthesis, full of mysterious attributes encompassing everything. In the human, animal, vegetable, and mineral kingdoms—even on the peaks of icy mountain ranges, in the deep abyss of the oceans, in the solitude of the deserts, at the earth's igneous core, and especially in the immense forest—all things pulsate with the breath of life, the eternal song of the Creator.

An enormous happiness was overtaking the community as the works celebrating Saint John's Day progressed. My appreciation was increasing for the women and men present there, the inheritors of the faith, those who kept alive the knowledge of our ancestors. In spite of the degenerative spiritual cloudiness accompanying the development of the human species, they discovered that in the ritualized use of the sacred plants, a road can be found that helps the spirit to remove the mires of illusion into which it has sunk and to find again the way home.

That day the force, the power, and the light present in the Santo Daime permeated every cell of my body. The Daime sensitized my energy centers, clarifying my self to the point where I could sing with full knowledge Padrinho's hymn, "I am the room and the throne / for my Master to converse."[1] Embedded in the Divine omniscience and seated on the throne of a living temple, we found the way back to the truth of our being. Everywhere, thinking and doing became equally Divine.

When I came to my senses, the bonfire was half-burned and the ceremony was approaching its intermission. A sharp acuity was overtaking my mind. The Daime's force was making everything look alternately green and purple. My body was made of unrecognizable textures. My perceptions were both corporeal and emotional. Sometimes I was pure consciousness, not even remembering that I had a material body. In this clairvoyant state of contact with the invisible, consciousness manifests itself as something preceding the fall of the spirit into flesh and the densification of consciousness in matter.

The hymns kept guiding my understanding and saved me during the hardest moments. When the first part of the works was finished, I felt the power of the Divine Being within me, now soothing, and I supported myself on a low wall in front of the bonfire and promised myself many things.

All was explained by Padrinho plainly. It was his belief that when we invoke the Divine Being present in the ayahuasca, it will come to cleanse and sanctify us in preparation to receive our righteous selves. The drink per se is the vehicle, the sacrament. Its ingestion reorganizes our organic, neurochemical, and energetic foundation, adjusting us to spiritual reality and its multiple meanings. At this point, the Daime helps us to transcend both the positive and negative energies that emerge from the depth of our spirits. After this phase, the miração comes and archetypes, myths, and legends emerge from the collective unconscious. Through this rough material, the universal Holy Spirit becomes accessible through the living images of the miração, the divine language.

The miração is not only the result of the force, as in a cause-and-effect relationship. It depends as well on the choice, merit, and degree of surrender to the Superior Being guiding the miração. Without faith in its divine essence, what comes forth from the collective unconscious will only reach psychological and imaginative levels. In the works, the spiritual conviviality and the inner clairvoyance make us protagonists in an unfinished scene, in which perfection is always our goal. The miração, the divine dream, does not numb us. Instead, our being becomes clear and conscious of its true state of happiness and good fortune. But this dream also can be paralyzed in the middle of our ecstatic flight or produce a series of events revealing deep perceptions about ourselves and others.

Padrinho Sebastião used to say that everything was worked out first in the miração and later transferred and realized. Those who learn to work and receive this light consciousness, synchronize themselves to higher plains of pure cosmic effervescence that penetrate the astral plane of our planet. As we drink from the spring of immortality, we operate through the patterned matrix made by all the constructive beings of the universe. We hear the echo of their pleas for our attention resounding within the depths of our human consciousness.

That night I saw the stars pulsing at my understandings, the bonfire consuming all my doubts, and I thought it would be easy. Only slowly did I become aware that it is not enough to have inner clarity; we need a firm will to achieve the self-transformation required. But even when fog returns after experiencing the miração, a core experience will stay in our hearts to open the new way to access knowledge.

The excessive relativism of all things produced in me at certain moments a languorous and unbalanced state similar to insanity. Only with much determination and humility is it possible for us to discern the illusions that are eager to stop the flux of divine love, muddying its clear waters with desires and falsifications.

For the newcomer the biggest danger is to think that he or she is the only one to whom truth reveals itself in the miração, boasting vainly of a gift that is for all. The sacred fire of the gods and goddesses can be extinguished. All the forms created without it will be innocuous and with a false beauty. If we do not cleanse our lives of all false creations, our righteous self will not be revealed. In the miração only the humble and serene of heart travel with security. The proud, who often boast about their results or wish to be seen as someone they are not, receive only their own derangement as revelation. On the other hand, those who do not have enough confidence in themselves, not having kindled their own light, look to the light of another for strength. I thought about Padrinho's comment on the subject: "It is necessary to learn from moths. Have you seen how they fly to the flame? They hurl themselves into the light with such impetus that they extinguish their own light."

5
...
The Doctor of the Juruá

IT IS DIFFICULT to imagine what the forest looked like millions of years ago. Yet today, where the destructive impulse of humankind has not yet reached it, the forest continues to be what it has always been—the exuberant, sacred garden with which the Creator covered planet earth. And, the earth has been generously giving of her bounty to her offspring.

Since the beginning, for better or for worse, human beings have exercised their free will. The ethical vacillation of the species has produced many extreme results: paradisiacal eras alternating with great cataclysms and wars, echoes of which still resonate in the archaic layers of the human psyche. But nature, always open, invites reconciliation to deeper human understanding and appreciation.

Human beings have been eternally consuming the forest. We have long needed its wood, fruits, game, flowers, medicines, and even its mysteries, sharing and appreciating the magic, the enchanted beings, and the great Divine force that inhabits it. A balance was kept until so-called civilized man arrived in the New World. Since then a waxing imbalance has prevailed, and insatiable human greed has made the realization of the Divine on earth seem less viable.

Love and harmony within cosmic law have been replaced by a methodology of conquest and the myth of progress. With the increasing goal of the accumulation of material goods at whatever price, the human relationship with nature has become increasingly aggressive and self-serving. When native forest dwellers carved a tree into a canoe, making it possible for people to cross previously uncrossable rivers, knowledge arose, but when forests of oaks were butchered and transformed into fleets of warships, seeds of madness took root, and soon a great karmic debt was accumulated by humanity. The forest, this living garland adorning the earth, and woven by God to be enjoyed with love and reverence, was being devastated by the rape of Mother Nature.

Despite the systematic destruction of the planet's woodlands, the Amazon Forest remains one of the last enclaves of the original Garden. So impenetrable were its obstacles and mysteries that vast extensions of land, enclosing kingdoms and civilizations, remained inaccessible. In its multiplicity of life, a tropical forest is a laboratory of interchange and synthesis with spiritual beings and the cosmic energy that constitute the basis for human life; truly the Garden of Eden, where the tree of life and knowledge grows. But when this harmony is broken on earth, the same happens in the cosmos. When we destroy nature, which contains all the elements of human existence, we destroy ourselves.

By Divine Providence, a great portion of primordial nature is still found in Brazil. Somewhere in this vast green immensity, in the valley of the Juruá River, Eurimepe County, state of Amazonas, in a rubber grove named Adelia, on the sixth day of October 1920, Sebastião Mota de Melo was born. In the solitude of a rubber grove, in a humble wooden house with a straw roof, was born this being gifted with great light. God's mysteries always manifest where one least expects.

The rubber groves, today in decline, are great extensions of the forest where the rubber is extracted from the trees native to this area. In the middle, usually on the banks of a navigable river, there is a rustic dwelling for the storage and administration of rubber. From there, following the course of the small igarapés, there are small satellite shelters where the men work.

The dwellings from many years ago are the same as those existing today. We can imagine the igarapé, the pier, the backyard with grazing chickens, the gardens, and some fruit trees. At the edge of the forest, a small hut with a fire pit dug in the earth, over which the rubber is smoked. Access to the house is by way of a rustic stairway made out of logs, a dangerous route for the uninitiated. The floor is elevated high on poles to protect against floods. Inside, there may be only one, sometimes two rooms. In the living room, which is usually like a veranda, hangs an old family portrait, an image of a saintly object of special devotion, or a picture from an old magazine that somehow made it to this isolated place. Old rusted rubber-tapping buckets are stacked in a corner, fishing nets are spread around, and a shotgun hangs from a nail on the wall. In the back of the house, a small extension houses the kitchen with a wood-fired cookstove and a couple of pans and cans. A wooden platform holding a clay pot for water storage projects out over the kitchen window as a place to wash dishes completes the furnishings.

It was in a dwelling like this that this typical Amazonian man was born, whose existence could have passed completely unnoticed if not for the importance of the mission he brought to the world. Sebastião said, "I was born in the forest, and in it I grew up. I did not learn much, but what I learned serves me well. In it I live today and I do not want to leave, no matter what. It is where I found my eternal life, and I cannot forget that for a single moment. Men and women can learn so much when they decide to, but some men and women have been granted a special spiritual gift, a gift and obligation bigger than the others. I do not take away from anyone their worth. I was a rubber tapper; I suffered at the hands of my boss. I do not suffer today because I cannot work harvesting rubber anymore, but still I do not like to see anyone hurt the trees."

Nothing special seemed to be noticed by his contemporaries, but in the spiritual realm there was joy for his incarnation. In a modern tropical version of the three kings, the forest princes, Titango, Agarrube, and Tintuma must have gone to the humble rubber worker's cottage bringing flowers, fruits, and forest tree resins in homage to the new prophet.

I heard him sometimes talking about his childhood in the Juruá, already marked by visions and encounters. He told us, "Since I was eight years old, all sorts of things happened to me! First I started flying around the world and learning everything. My spirit detached itself, and I traveled many places. I thought it was strange, but people around me did not pay attention to it. I heard many things from the spirits, but they thought it was a childish thing."

"Were you afraid, Padrinho?"

"In the beginning I was. I had a lot of fear. But it did not help! I was meant to have this knowledge. Since childhood my inner self was awakened, always helping me. All I needed was to have the patience that I would find the place I truly belonged."

"Did you find it?"

"Yes. If others live in the world without purpose, I at least am living a meaningful life. When I was eight years old I discovered a mystery and pursued it. It began with one dream, and it continued until I realized them all. All my dreams became full of truth and affirmation. Within these mysteries I was never lied to, and for this I thank God."

In a conversation in the bedroom of his house at Céu do Mapiá, the old man sitting on his bed in front of an eager audience related story after story.

"Sometimes I would see visions everywhere. I had them on the water, in the woods, you name it. Once I was walking on a rubber trail. I stopped to bathe, when I saw what seemed to be a monkey. As I took off my clothes and squatted, the monkey became a capybara. This was strange, I thought. Then, it jumped up and became a monkey again but a very ugly one! I was covered with goose bumps."

Whoever has walked alone in the forest is not surprised to hear stories like this. The plant kingdom exercises a powerful effect on our spirits, reinforcing our clairvoyance. We become more sensitive and intuitive. These are the effects of the vibrations and of the beings that inhabit this incredible swarm of life that is the forest. In my travels I have had the opportunity to see many extraordinary things myself, and I marvel at what Padrinho Sebastião must have experienced.

Madrinha Rita, Padrinho's wife, would usually be sewing in the corner of the room during these sessions. Every once in a while she would add a name, a date, or a detail to the story. She related how she met Padrinho Sebastião when she and her sister went to Natal to attend a works. During their astral journey, a voice told him to look attentively at her because she would be the one with whom he would marry and have a family.

Even when the theme was ghosts and spells from the forest, the old Mota did not miss an opportunity to practice his powerful didactics. He would read our reactions and resistances in each facial expression and test our credulity. He would encourage us to believe in our dreams and in the more profound sense of our interior perceptions:

"Have you heard of the *batedor*?" he asked.

"No, Padrinho, what is it?"

"It is a beast that lives in the water."

"A beast?"

"Not just a beast but an enchanted being. The Juruá has it, and here also someone has heard it."

"Why is he called batedor Father?"

"Because he arrives at the igarapé, hangs out, and then starts to make a loud repetitive sound, like drums gradually increasing in volume." He paused a moment for suspense and then continued, "Well, if you do not believe in him, he will come to your backyard and knock at your door, producing an immense noise. As an enchanted being, he can enchant our will even at this moment, if our thoughts are divided between fear and desire to see the batedor. Then he will come even closer to be under our fishing nets, where he likes to swing from side to side. I have only seen him in the igarapé, but there are those who have had him in their houses."

Everyone in the room was affected, some visibly impressed. All of a sudden Padrinho let out delicious laughter. Supporting himself with his arms perpendicular to his body and the palms of his hands on the bed, his small eyes shining brightly, he threw back his head and laughed, full of satisfaction. He considered the necessary time for our reflections and then exclaimed, "Yesterday, the moon laid down on its side; today it is going to rain."

Sometimes a simple phrase about the weather came like a cool shower, awakening us from the trance his presence induced. It was the sign for us to return to the bedroom in the big house at Igarapé Mapiá. I looked out the window in front of me at the river and the jungle stretching beyond as far as the eye could see. Everything was shimmering. I could have stayed like that all my life, seated on the bed, with the certainty of belonging to this new forest world, innocent and profound at the same time.

At other times, the conversational tone became very energetic and disciplinary, demanding of our spirit a more serious search and greater self-investigation. Each word that Padrinho spoke to us had the gift of fitting perfectly inside each person in the group, to the point that each one felt him- or herself to be the target of the patriarch's words. When that was so, it was with relief that we heard him switch to commentary about the weather, or another mundane topic. It was time to end the session.

A year had already passed since the unforgettable celebration of Saint John. Padrinho's big house was now all enclosed and divided into rooms. A small temporary church had been built right in front of his house, and many other new houses dotted the landscape. The fields were widening, and the granary was full of rice and manioc flour.

Sebastião Mota continued to tell us about how he had felt connected with spiritual reality since childhood. Through dreams and visions, he was being prepared for his mission. He had a precocious, strong sense of predestination as a child. The trust he placed in the process of self-knowledge was total.

"As it has always been. I came down to know the earth and the sky. I came down in the hour of my incarnation. And thank God I know the astral, the earth, and the ocean. To speak plainly: I am what the Creator is. It is necessary to have knowledge, otherwise we only talk but do not know. We need to have knowledge, real knowledge; because otherwise people just read a book and think they know something. I thank God that I do not even know how to read! What is the use of knowing how to read and yet not having knowledge of the truth? I cannot take the truth from those who have it and give to those who do not. I was born poor. I am still poor, but I consider myself rich."

When he talked like this about himself, there was not a trace of pride; his words were spoken with the sincerity of a child.

Sebastião Mota was a medium. His mother also had been a medium, but because her gift was not developed correctly, she became possessed by obsessive spirits, which tormented her with increasing frequency. Sometimes a spirit made her stutter. Another would make her work inattentively, letting things fall and break around her. Still another would take her to the middle of the jungle, where she would swoon unconscious until someone found her.

Obsessive spirits penetrate the mind of mediums susceptible to their vibration. When mediums do not develop their gift appropriately, they can easily become entangled in their own thoughts, confounded by the obsessive vibrations. The will of these obsessive spirits produces a struggle, and the tension of it brings exhaustion, insanity, and sometimes death.

When the person develops correctly as a medium, he or she starts to work consciously within this faculty. He or she will concentrate for a few minutes on the obsessive thought without confusing its source. Letting the other manifest through our own body is what we call *atuação*.

Padrinho's mother became progressively worse. Even today the interior of Brazil is still destitute of spiritual as well as psychiatric resources, but at that time help for such an illness was even more limited. She spent long hours confined to her room, chained when the crises increased. Without a doubt, this caused a deep impression on Sebastião. Intuitively, he started to work with the many obsessive spirits with the goal of helping her.

At this point, a man named Mestre Oswaldo came along. He was to play an important role in Sebastião Mota's spiritual development. A medium in Alain Kardec's spiritual tradition, he became Sebastião's first guide and *compadre*. Padrinho thought of him with respect, "The compadre was a good one. He was able to perceive many things that passed unnoticed by others. Sometimes when he walked behind us, only a tap of his finger could make one's whole body shake all over."

Mestre Oswaldo helped Padrinho to work with the obsessive spirits possessing his mother and then slowly transmitted to him the fundamentals of the work of *Banca Espiritá*. Mestre Oswaldo, perceiving Mota's spiritual stature, told him many times, "Compadre, you are destined to have much more knowledge than I. I only can help you in the beginning, but the rest of your destiny you will find in Rio Branco."

At that time Padrinho Sebastião still had no idea that he would move to Rio Branco. With Oswaldo's guidance, he started to work with two spiritual guides, Professor Antônio Jorge and Dr. Bezerra de Menezes. His fame as healer soon spread throughout the region. He began to obtain the respect and recognition of all the poor and destitute along the banks of the Juruá River. More and more people sought his services— poisonous snakebites (Padrinho himself was bitten more than ten times), back problems, broken bones, shotgun wounds, and especially illnesses of the spirit. As he healed more people, more came to him. He recollected, "I also got possessed by many spirits when I used to work. I was a medium. I still work this way today. One never stops being so, right? I worked with Bezerra de Menezes and Antônio Jorge. They were two spiritual beings and they performed many operations with me as medium. Who was the doctor in the Juruá area? I was! There was no one else! Doctor? No one knew of one for many miles around. The people from the rubber groves kept calling me, and with God's help I made many good healings. When I left for Rio Branco, they cried. I do not know if anyone was found to replace me."

The group had already dispersed from Padrinho's bedroom. Only he and I remained, leaning out the window looking at the fields on the other side of the igarapé. He said, "In the Juruá the earth was much richer than it is here. This sandy soil does not sustain a plantation. It is weak soil. In the Juruá there was abundance. Each *pupunha* looked like an enormous mango. And fish? In the season for *piracema* the canoes almost tipped over."

Thus, Mestre Oswaldo's prophecy came to pass. Responding to a call from relatives of his wife, Rita Gregorio, who were living near Rio Branco, Sebastião Mota and his family moved to a place called Colônia 5,000. There a small community formed from among his own relatives and he began a new phase of his spiritual development. Padrinho continued attending to and healing people. Alfredo, his son, remembers, "When Father started, there were just a few people, mostly our relatives. Soon it grew. The works were about healing and realizing the doctrine. I was presiding over the works because Father would be working part of the time as a medium, channeling spirit guides on behalf of the sufferers. Padrinho would concentrate with his two hands on the table and call the spirits. All of a sudden he would start to tremble all over, to the extent that we sometimes had to hold him down. Then the professor would manifest and speak through him. He would greet everyone and delineate all of our errors and wrong actions. He would seriously lecture us, and we all would tuck our tails between our legs. Normally in a healing situation, he would tap his fingers as if he were typing the prescription on a typewriter. After the professor's departure from Padrinho's body, Dr. Bezerra de Manezes would come in, to give prescriptions and to perform the operations.

"The professor was very serious. He noticed that people often commented about each other's private lives and shortcomings, so sometimes he would speak in other languages."

During this period, Padrinho healed many people through these spiritual guides and through his own small *banca espirita*. He exorcized from his wife's relative, Mr. Manezinho, three obsessive spirits that presented themselves as legendary warriors and almost made him commit suicide. Madrinha Rita's brother, Manuel Gregorio, also called Mr. Nel, was also healed. He had begun to suffer pain and unbearable anguish. When Padrinho was called to solve the case, he captured the spirit that was tormenting Mr. Nel. It was a soldier who had been killed with a knife, making Mr. Nel feel the pain in the same place the soldier had received the fatal knife wound. This spirit asked for a mass dedicated to him. When this was done, Mr. Nel was healed.

The professor accompanied Padrinho Sebastião for many years, until the first time he took the Daime in 1965 at the hands of Mestre Irineu. From that moment on, the entity announced that Sebastião should follow the new path opening in front of him and that he would stop manifesting, with the exception of emergency cases, but he would keep protecting Padrinho's works.

This was another landmark on Sebastião Mota's spiritual path. If compadre Oswaldo represented the first part of his initiation, the professor had been the mentor who guided him to full maturity, strengthening him both as a medium and a healer. When the professor perceived that it was time for Sebastião Mota to receive his spiritually destined master, he confirmed Padrinho's new mission, leaving him free to assume the Daime's mission without spiritual commitments.

The professor's influence developed Padrinho's skills, transforming him into an extraordinary medium, and marking him profoundly until the end of his life. Due to his knowledge and his experience in the banca espirita, he knew what Sebastião Mota could be. Beyond the visionary prophet of New Jerusalem and maker of the new Noah's ark, he was the one capable of carrying the doctrine, and even of healing Satan's manifestations. Within the next few years, a sorcerer was to come to the community at Colônia 5,000 for a duel with Padrinho. During the period of this battle, which lasted through the time of Rio do Ouro, was also the time of a flourishing revival incorporating the work as a medium to the doctrine of Santo Daime. Without a doubt, the professor's influences were felt again at the opening of the Star House, destined for healing, cleansing, and teaching.

Padrinho Sebastião told us that one day, while walking near Custodio Freire's property, he passed by the door of Mestre Irineu's center, of which he had already heard. He even walked in to get further information and found that at that time Mestre Irineu was traveling to Maranhão, his homeland. A couple of years went by before the two men were to finally meet. The event that precipitated the fateful meeting was a serious illness Padrinho developed that no one could explain or diagnose. It came all of a sudden, he explained, "I was drinking milk in the kitchen. It came like lightning. Boom! It knocked me over right away. I even said a bad word, as at that time I was still sometimes coarse. The thing stayed there, boiling and itching a whole month. After that, I started to get really sick."

"Did you look for a doctor."

"I went to Rio Branco, I went to a spirit center, sorcerers or doctors did no good, and there were also those who deceived me further. It was a well-done spell. I spent more than a year in this agony. I would work the whole day, but around four o'clock in the afternoon I would experience the greatest suffering of my life. A thing inside me would start coming up to my throat, and then go back down. It lasted from four to eight o'clock in the evening. Every day it was a suffering. Some days I had enormous amounts of horrible secretions. I even tried the help of a Yoruba priestess to extract the spell. But when she saw me, she herself sought my help, as she was about to die. And sure enough, the next day she was dead. It was then that someone told me, 'Go see Mestre Irineu.' I thought a bit and said, 'That's right, I will go to see Mestre Irineu.'"

A case like Padrinho Sebastião's is not uncommon for those destined to knowledge. Previous to the Daime, Padrinho Sebastião's spiritual work already was done in a clean manner, with charity, helping others, diminshing the indiscriminate industry of offerings, for good and bad. Padrinho had healed many people who ended up freeing themselves from the realm of black magic, and some jealous sorcerer probably cast a spell on him.

Even in this case, what gets accomplished is the will of God, which always brings its marvels to the twisted lines of human destiny. Illness, apart from its more profound spiritual cause, is always an occasion for inner study. It teaches us to be humble and battle for our faith, and in the last instance, faith is what can heal us, especially if traditional resources are not sufficient.

It was through the illness produced by a sorcerer's spell that Sebastião Mota, the rubber tapper from the Juruá, met with the spiritual and physical giant Raimundo Irineu Serra, from São Vicente Ferret, Maranhão. In truth, the two founders of the Daime were really reencountering each other. And soon they recognized this themselves.

6

...

Padrinho Sebastião and Mestre Irineu

EARLY IN THE morning I found my way to the kitchen of the big house. Padrinho was already up sipping his coffee, although it was only between three and four in the morning. He would gaze through the window, walk to the veranda, then turn around and go back to the kitchen table. It was his favorite time of the day to give consultations.

Early in the morning, he was always happy, playful, and in good humor. When he was healthy, he would be in the front yard before the break of day with a machete in his belt and a lunch bag in hand, waiting for his friends to arrive to enter the forest, where sometimes he would spend the whole day making canoes.

As people arrived for breakfast, pots of fresh coffee and plates full of boiled manioc root and fried plantains kept coming. When the sun showed half of its golden disc above the canopy, it was time to get busy. Almost everyone in the community passed through that kitchen in the morning, if only to ask the patriarch for his blessings. He would interrupt his conversation for a moment, bless one, then another, answer quickly someone's question, and then return to the central theme of his discussion as he sat at the table surrounded by people.

Padrinho lived harmoniously with all beings. The biggest obstacles to his practice of nonviolence were the mosquitoes that transmitted malaria, and the ones with a ferocious bite. When one landed to bite him, he would tap it as a small warning. But if the insect insisted, the second smack would send it to the ground. I do not know how the Buddha would have behaved in a case like this. There is a legend that when the Buddha went to preach in a city famous for its ferocious mosquitoes, a disciple commented quietly, "The blessed one will not be able to stand being here." Buddha, though, kept himself impassive throughout his meditation in spite of being bitten from head to toe! But this was the only village where he never returned to preach.

Padrinho Sebastião continued the narrative he had started the day before about the first time he took the Daime in Mestre Irineu's church.

"After someone gave me the idea to go to Mestre Irineu, I returned home and the very next day I prepared myself and went. I arrived telling him how sick and hopeless I was. He looked at me and asked if I was a man. I answered him that I did not know. I was not going to say that I was, because I did not know. I know who I am, I told him plainly, but I do not know if I am a man, a real man, because what you offer is not for just anyone. Then he invited me, 'If you are a man, get in line, drink Daime, and afterward come and tell me something.'

"'Very well,' I said, and got in line. I drank the Daime, went to my corner, and sat. After some time things began to happen, and I became fearful. I got up to leave very quietly because everyone was silent. I started to leave on tiptoe and as I passed by the place where people drink the sacrament, the Daime enveloped me in an awful smell. It made me go quickly back to my place. As I arrived at the bench, I heard a voice saying, 'The mestre asked if you are a man, and up to now the only thing you have done is moan.' Then my old body hit the floor and there it stayed. I was outside my body looking at that old junk that was me.

"All of a sudden I saw two men who were the most beautiful beings I had ever seen in my life. They were resplendent, like fire! They began to take out my whole skeleton from within my living flesh without hurting anything. As they worked, they vibrated eveything from side to side, and I, on the other side, was watching all they were doing. Next, they took out my organs. One of them held my guts in his hands. Together they used a hook that opened, separated, and extracted from my guts three nail-sized insects, which were responsible for what I felt walking up and down inside me.

"Then the one who had been seated next to my prostrate body, which was still stretched out on the floor, came very close to me and said, 'Here it is! What was killing you were these three insects, but now you will not die from them any more.' Then they closed my body. Do you see any scars? There are none. Thank God I healed, like a child."

"Were you already well the next day?"

"I was very well."

"Was that the first time you drank Daime?"

"Yes, it was my first time. After that my sons, it unfolded for me. I went on, acquiring knowledge and forging ahead until today when I have the knowledge. But I will not say it in vain."

It was this way that Padrinho Sebastião met with the Santo Daime and Mestre Irineu. From this encounter flowered a spiritual work that has endured to this day, when we are already so close to the end of the second millennium and close to the promises of the messianic era.

Always when I heard Padrinho relate the story of his own healing, it became apparent that his confidence in the Santo Daime and his trust in Mestre Irineu happened instantly, from the first time he took the Daime until the end of his days. When Padrinho went back to his body and got up from the floor and dusted himself off, he was not only healed but had found everything for which he had been searching.

Sebastião Mota was predestined to be a healer since the days of his childhood visions, later as a "doctor" of the Juruá during his first steps doing spiritual work, and still later leading the banca espirita with friends and relatives at Colônia 5,000. Now he had seen the words of his compadre Oswaldo come true, and he knew that he would only find his true spiritual path in Rio Branco.

He decided to side with the mestre who had asked him point-blank: "Are you a man?" Sebastião Mota was one of the men that Mestre Irineu was waiting for. If he still had doubts after that first Daime session, when he presented himself to Mestre Irineu to relate his healing, he received from him many confirmations and much encouragement.

Mestre Irineu recognized and received him as one of his main collaborators. Sebastião, who was already a man with spiritual experience, was clear and available. And now his path was being transformed into a main highway.

I was in a palace
Of sovereignty
When I saw my Mestre arriving
With the Ever Virgin Mary.[1]

These verses are from the first hymn Padrinho Sebastião received, right after being healed, as a testimony to and recognition of the mission Raimundo Irineu Serra had received on earth. In the sequence of his hymns, he narrates with simplicity how he captured the fundamentals of the doctrine that has the Virgin of Conception for its matron.

My Mestre spoke to me
With love in his heart:
"You are to be my son"
And love your brothers.

And to be a brother
One needs to have love
To love the Virgin Mother
And our protector Father.

And to have love
One needs to be a brother
To love the Eternal Father
And the Virgin of Conception.[2]

This is an accurate summary of Christ's doctrine, as given by the above hymn: "And to be a brother and sister one needs to have love . . . and to have love one needs to be brother and sister."[3] Without this proof, the love with which God created us does not reach within us to find its true purpose.

That simple rubber tapper had the distinction of being received in the astral, in the palace of knowledge, where our spiritual works are received and transformed. In this palace he heard a hymn with a message to expand in his *Hinário,* and live them out. In all his hymns, we can see the recognition of his mestre's mission, the request for love and to form a truly united brotherhood and sisterhood.

The velocity of Sebastião Mota's spiritual evolution and the support that Mestre Irineu gave him brought out certain discomforts among the mestre's older disciples. They did not understand or did not want to accept the meaning of the relationship between the two. A well-developed medium, Sebastião felt all of these forces and energies. "In the beginning," he told us, "people were given a full glass, and many fell on the floor or would go to Mestre Irineu to ask for protection. During the ceremony I usually danced in the third row next to Daniel Serra, Mestre Irineu's nephew. Sometimes I would feel a strange energy, but as I was *mirando,* everything would be just fine!"

"It was strong, was it not, Padrinho?" I asked.

"Yes it was! At this point I still stepped on the floor with too much force. Only later the Daime told me, in a miração, to step softly so as not to offend or harm anyone."

"Were there people who did not like you?"

"A couple even mocked the way I worked. I really did work. I gave myself fully to the miração, receiving my hymns and writing them down with Mestre Irineu."

"What would he say?"

"Go ahead, go ahead my son! This is it!"

"And the ones who mocked you. Did you tell him?"

"I never complained directly, but he knew. People said then that there were some people who had been in the Daime for many years but they had never seen anything. Also, that when Mestre Irineu was to make his final passage, many changes would unfold within the board of directors."

"But did you sing the hymns for him?"

"Yes, I sang and sometimes I would tell him in detail the miração that gave origin to the hymn. He would confirm everything. It is necessary to be calm, everyone stepping very softly, not to be proud in our works. Sometimes everything shines and people want to think of themselves more beautiful than others. Be careful not to be proud or you will soon be seated on the bench or prostrate on the floor!"

"But what would Mestre Irineu say?" I asked Padrinho.

"That a people would still come and for me to prepare myself. After he passed away, his spirit came to tell me the rest. He told me not to fear. The Daime is guiding everything, taking Juramidam's people from the city and relocating them in the forest that is Paradise." That day the miração was very strong, and like the first time he took the Daime, Padrinho had an out-of-body experience. As he awakened on the other side, he felt he was very far away. It was then that he remembered *Juramidam*.

I remember somebody
With love in my heart
When I looked up
I beheld Juramidam.[4]

Padrinho always said that these are very important moments for our spiritual apprenticeship. It is necessary not to be afraid of letting go of the spirit, to separate from the body. The more conscious we can become when the separation is occurring, the more we will learn about the reality of creation. It is a kind of rehearsal and a map for the day of our true passage, when the separation will be total. Two times I also lived through this experience. Once in Rio do Ouro, during João Pedro's hymn, another in Mapiá during Antônio Gomes's hymn. The first one was hard. The second time I was more conscious of the flight and received a precious understanding about myself.

"At this hour," Padrinho would say, "we can understand many things. But we must have very strong faith, a real faith in who is present in this sacred drink, in who is being invoked, and in who is Juramidam. We also need to have faith in all the beings of the celestial court, earth, forest, oceans, and a few that live under the earth. And you, what do you think?"

"I do not know, Padrinho. You are saying . . ."

"Yes, I went under the earth, and it was as clear as here up above. Do not be surprised by anything, the superior self is everything and goes everywhere. If I am with him, he gives me license; wherever he wants to go, I go as well."

"But if we get vertigo, should we resist or surrender right away?"

He thought awhile and answered, "Sometimes it is a false alarm, to see if we are looking for a reason to escape. When the force wobbles, the first thing to do is to stand firm and sing the hymn. If you cannot stand up, sit, if you cannot sit, lie down. If you do not have time to choose, just fall." And he mimicked the event.

Everyone laughed. He went back to his seat and continued, "What is important is for us to receive what the Divine Being has to give us in this hour. In my apprenticeship, a couple of times I fell to the ground. You, too, another day, you fell from the bench during the *star-works*."

"It is true!"

"Well, I thank God for my falls because I learned a lot from them. And whoever was looking at me, thinking it was funny, that poor fellow learned nothing."

Another important event from the early days was when he received his twenty-eighth hymn, titled, "I Am." In the middle of the works at Mestre Irineu's place, he started to receive the verses.

> *I am, I am, I am*
> *I can affirm*
> *The Mestre called me*
> *For me to declare myself.*[5]

The power of the hymn, as well as the power of the miração began to overcome Sebastião Mota as he heard a voice saying, "When the lights go out, sing your hymn!" In a couple of minutes the generator stopped and the light went off, interrupting the works. Seu Mota let it out:

> *My Mother is so beautiful*
> *And my Mestre also is.*
> *He is the son of Mary*
> *And I am the son of Elizabeth.*[6]

The first reaction of those present at this works that night was of embarrassment and perplexity. Everything was dark, confused, with some people running from side to side. Padrinho recalled, "I was meant to sing the hymn. It was what the voice told me to do, and I did it."

Some tension was created because Padrinho sang the hymn, but Mestre Irineu continued to stimulate Padrinho Sebastião's journey. If the spiritual path was painful, the material path was no less so. Sebastião's son Alfredo remembers, "We would walk fifteen, maybe twenty kilometers on those roads to take the Daime. The whole family. We would take a single dose and return home. Many hours later, everyone was still having a miração. But later, while still alive, Mestre Irineu authorized Padrinho to open some works at his house and to make the Daime."

In spite of the spiritual teaching that was happening, the relationship between the two men was not biased. Mestre Irineu was not a man to show preference for a person; he treated everyone the same. Nor was Sebastião Mota susceptible to flattery. Nevertheless, their relationship was full of many private conversations.

Mestre Irineu was a man of very few words in social situations. He would not converse at the dining table. He gave thanks for the food and after eating would go to his bedroom for a nap. When he wanted to talk to someone, it was done privately. He would go down from the kitchen to a lower floor where he would sit with the interlocutor on a wooden bench. It is not difficult to imagine that many profound things—many revelations and instructions—were transmitted from mestre to disciple.

Raimundo Irineu Serra struggled all his life for one thing he did not live to see realized—the congregation united as a community. In some parts of his Hinário, his sorrow is very strong. He laments having to give value to those who do not deserve it. He fought to bring unity to his community and to emphasize the importance of love between brothers and sisters. Mestre Irineu was a living example of self-abnegation, work, loyalty, and respect for others. He warned us about the future and the need for us to prepare for the balanço. He would say that we still were in "the good days, but not for long." In his private dialogues with Mr. Mota, he disclosed many revelations of how it will be during the passage "from the old to the new world."

After he marked where he wanted his grave to be, Mestre Irineu finished his destined time on earth. In accordance with the testimony of Dona Percília, a close friend who had known him since childhood: Around eight o'clock on the morning of July 6, 1971, his stepdaughter, Martha, passed by the door to his room and saw him at the window praying, as was his custom. Martha went to the backyard to get a couple of eggs, and when she returned, he called her and said, "Make me some orange tea, for I am in agony." When she brought him the tea, he had already passed away, sitting in his chair. He had enough time to finish his prayers and say good-bye.

His mission was accomplished. Still, as Dona Percília remembers, in the works of the previous week, Mestre Irineu said to her, "Listen, after all these years, only today I received in a vision from my Celestial Mother the presidency of the Santo Daime." It was the crowning of his vision. In spite of not having the satisfaction of seeing a strong and united congregation and of his concerns about the false piety that surrounded him, all he said in his Hinário proved true. The saintly doctrines were replanted. To the surprise of his contemporaries, the teachings of Christ resprouted again around Rio Branco, in a provincial town at the edge of the largest forest in the world. Although the speaking voice of the forest, this black giant, ceased in this world, he left a series of recommendations, named a successor to the presidency of the center, and gave private instructions, particularly to his main afilhados. People say that he personally delivered the biggest secrets to only a few people.

Without questioning the legitimacy of the succession and the worth of many of the mestre's companions, it was undeniable that Sebastião Mota received a great legacy from Raimundo Irineu Serra's spiritual mission. Padrinho Sebastião's legacy was to become the guide for the people, the new people who would come from afar, as had been announced in the 1940s by the Hinário of Maria Marques, one of the *Madrinhas* in the community.

As Padrinho Alfredo tells us, "The mestre said to Father many times that only those holding on to 'supple branches' would survive. He said that the forest was the place of safety for the daimistas, as are called the Daime people. The place where the final summary of the Daime issue would happen was not in Acre, but in the Amazon. And here we are in the middle of the forest to prove it."

The city of Rio Branco received a real shock on that foggy morning of July 6. So many legends and mysteries surrounded this man, perceived by the people to be a mixture of wizard, healer, and saint. At the time of his passing, Mestre Irineu was already a much loved and respected person in the city. He was known throughout the entire state and was sought out by politicians and local authorities. His coffin descended into the earth enveloped by the national banner, invoking many tears and much sorrow. With his passing, a new phase in the history of Santo Daime was opened.

Mestre Irineu had been the great catalyst and pole of aggregation for the daimistas, but during his life there already had been a certain tendency toward fragmentation that increased in the vacuum created by his absence. Many significant things were happening in that moment of the departure of the great man, whose personal magnetism and example had been the inspiration and driving force of this spiritual, administrative, social, and philanthropic organization. He knew that it would not survive after his death in a singular, unified form. It seemed that Mestre Irineu had given precise instructions to all his close collaborators to keep the doctrine as unified as possible without hindering the new and natural development that was gestating.

One of the main leaders was Padrinho Sebastião. For some time, he still tried to work with the board of directors of the Alto Santo Center, the church founded by Mestre Irineu near Rio Branco. But without Mestre Irineu's presence, the resistance to his attempts at collaboration increased.

During this period Padrinho received a series of hymns that attested to the depth of his study. In the first phase, when Mestre Irineu was still alive, Sebastião Mota's emphasis was on the recognition of Mestre Irineu, on the struggle to gain the love of his brothers and sisters, and the affirmation of the doctrine's principles. Now was the moment for him to decide his own destiny, to understand and follow the doctrine in the absence of the mestre, and to follow the path Mestre Irineu himself had entrusted to him.

This was also the time to develop and to affirm his Hinário, which at that time contained about sixty hymns. From that point on, the discipline was more intense. Referring to the recent death of Mestre Irineu, a hymn from this period states:

> *He left the world*
> *But he has the same power*
> *The people don't humble themselves*
> *And all want to be deserving.*[7]

In these simple verses, the hymn confirms the permanent influence of Mestre Irineu; how in the spiritual realm, his presence continues among us. In that phase of transition, Padrinho Sebastião indirectly prompted all who, even under the shade of the mestre's spiritual legacy, continued deluding themselves.

> *It is in the sun and in the moon*
> *That we must firm ourselves*
> *Many who want to be great*
> *Will be surprised afterward.*[8]

This hymn, received at the same time as the one discussed above, shows that the knowledge and the confidence in the celestial beings who preside over our existence are much more important than the quarrels and misunderstandings about status. While others lost themselves in the mundane, Sebastião Mota worked to follow the spiritual reality deeper, without measuring the sacrifices made to achieve his intent.

Once he attained all the knowledge of the Daime, he would speak of it without holding back. He also charged against dishonesty.

> *What the Mestre orders*
> *Must be done*
> *Correct yourselves*
> *Your falseness.*[9]

In another hymn he emphasizes his abhorrence of falsehood.

> *Falseness never served anyone.*
> *It was the only thing He found*
> *Even when He died*
> *Everything here was altered.*[10]

Imbued with the intent and purpose of clearing falsehoods, he invited his brothers and sisters to search for the proof with Mestre Irineu himself, who continued living in the sacrament that united all his sons, daughters, and disciples in this hymn:

> *It is necessary to take Daime*
> *To come to know*

Whether My Master is truthful
Or if you, my brothers, are truthful.[11]

And finally he consciously affirms the mission entrusted to him:

I come to gather
The flock that belongs to me
To be a son of God
You don't need to be bad.[12]

As Padrinho would explain, "I was told not to fear anything and to start to gather a people. Gathering the sons and daughters of Juramidam. Who is not, will drink Daime, leave their name, and go away." And he sang this hymn to remind us of the gathering entrusted to him:

Each one looks after himself
I also look after myself
I'm taking care of this path
I'm making my garden.[13]

Within a relatively short amount of time, Padrinho channeled many hymns with these same themes. In them Padrinho makes clear his role as a disciplinarian. He warns against falsehood, weakness, and ignorance, especially from those who like to talk about God. They hear from someone else but have neither the conviction nor the knowledge necessary to "hear within the truth" of the Daime and see where God is.

To complement this "good spiritual warfare," to use Saint Paul's words, Sebastião Mota continued to work toward unity. After all, it was in that place that he took the Daime from the hands of Mestre Irineu and was healed. But now all his attempts to bring the group closer would meet great resistance from a few of the most influential members of the board of directors. The greater the opposition Padrinho Sebastião suffered from those who wanted to deny his leadership, the more firm he was in becoming his own Divine Being. His hymns and lectures became richer and more profound, and he was joined by more followers and collaborators. In his final attempt to work with Leôncio Gomes, who Mestre Irineu had named as his sucessor to the presidency of Alto Santo, Sebastião proposed to raise the national flag in the center, as a symbol of unity and to salute this hymn he had received. He sang:

> *I lift up my flag*
> *Because my Father ordered me thus*
> *All who look at it*
> *Have the same worth.*[14]

In the board of directors meeting the proposal was not accepted under the excuse of some formality. Gomes suggested that Padrinho raise the banner elsewhere.

Padrinho accepted the board's decision with serenity, but from that moment on, without any formal recognition of separation, it became clear for both parties that their paths would part. Some veterans remained loyal to the original center and the old administration of Alto Santo, dedicated to the doctrine and devoted to Mestre Irineu. Others found their own way. But many followed Padrinho Sebastião and came to Colônia 5,000. All were nonetheless valuable companions and soldiers of the first order.

It is surely true that a lot of emotional conflict accompanies this type of process of fragmentation, a lot of misunderstanding and correio da má notícia as well. But as the years went by, everything became clear. The excess was balanced and the truth arose, slowly establishing itself. God is certainly more demanding with his own people. As in the hymn of Antônio Gomes, one of Mestre Irineu's first disciples:

> *All that already happened*
> *It was because God wanted*
> *If we do not live more united*
> *We cannot be happy.*[15]

Not a man to retaliate or slander others, Padrinho Sebastião never showed rancor to people. As he once told me, "My name runs the world like a soccer ball on the players feet. It is like Christ; wherever he went there would be all those people talking. Sometimes someone comes here after being with someone else and unloads on me—on me, when I do not speak about anyone else's life! I also have to hear the lies they put in the newspaper about the Daime and me. God shall give light to those who have it not."

Padrinho Sebastião was conscious of the truth of his mission. While some preserved the traditions and adored the memory and relics of Mestre Irineu, Padrinho Sebastião had been given a different mission: to open new paths, gather the people, build a community, and prepare for the purification.

Concluding the process of withdrawal from Alto Santo, a new banner, representing his Hinário, was posted on the grounds of Colônia 5,000. After the disciplinary phase, Padrinho's hymns became more poetic, almost lyrical. His teachings became broader and assimilated many esoteric sources, all of which stemmed from his direct spiritual apprenticeship.

Little by little, Sebastião Mota's spirituality detached itself from the material level and reached progressively higher levels where his spirit fused with the cosmos and with creation.

> *In the sun, in the moon*
> *On the earth and in the sea*
> *I sought this truth*
> *And I know where it is.*[16]

Dating from this time are his famous lectures, delivered during the works of his Hinário. From the head of the table and in the Daime's force, he would warn the people against illusion. In his simultaneously simple and suggestive language, he would develop great themes of spirituality. Through this time he was able to complete the main instructions initiated, defined, and passed on to him by Mestre Irineu as his hymns continue relating. He sang:

> *My Mestre left*
> *His body is in the night dew.*
> *It's in my heart*
> *And doesn't leave my mind.*[17]

In spite of Mestre Irineu's physical absence, there was no loss of the uninterrupted flux of orientation that kept coming directly from the miração and pouring into the hymns.

In this period, persecutions from the local government office against the Daime in the city of Rio Branco began. There were threats, including orders by some of the local police to close the centers. In Alto Santo the Daime was hidden, buried, and even poured out. But the old Mota did not stop his works. His banner continued flying. It was then that he received this hymn:

I went on a journey
To see how things are
I found everything obstructed
I almost couldn't go through.

As I was arriving and talking
I was ordered to correct myself
To be sure about
What's going on here.

The Mestre isn't satisfied
With this union
He's seeing everyone being wicked
Deluded with illusion.

Talking with my Mestre
He said to me
I want to see who is with me
On this very occasion.

The story that's happening
Is null to me
It's like the journey
Of the men who went to the moon.[18]

Remaining loyal to these instructions, he kept his works with the Daime open in spite of prohibitions and threats, and from this same astral dialogue came the order to construct a temple at Colônia 5,000.

7
...
I Raise This Banner

THE HISTORY OF the fellowship of Santo Daime is essentially no different from that of other esoteric societies that ramified during the course of their evolution. It is a mistake to think that what happened resulted only from the clash of personalities or differences over the doctrine's semantics. A more profound meaning lives beneath the mutable forms with which eternal truths clothe themselves. The imagination and the elements of the unconscious that link the human psyche with religious systems and devotional cults need reconnection with the Divine.

Certain rites and systems of knowledge are more appropriate for certain peoples, cultures, and times. It is the evolution of spiritual needs that diversifies beliefs and systems, but authentic lineages know that their essence is the same. Deep truths nourish us.

Behind the apparent confusion that sometimes places brothers, sisters, and friends in opposition works a powerful logic, sometimes difficult to understand. All of this is part of a self-regulating mechanism. Whoever only partially surrenders to the spiritual life frequently believes that those who give themselves completely are foolish. In the beginning it is still possible to reconcile the spiritual search with a mundane sensibility, but as the journey progresses, the surrender has to be total and unconditional.

As we develop on the spiritual path, we go through experiences that naturally stimulate our surrender to God. The true surrender is a spontaneous giving, an act of love, and is never due to fear. After we encounter doubts and fears, we may lose the need to understand what is happening.

What is happening is what God is giving us. As less energy is spent rebelling against our destiny, we will attain optimal conditions for transforming it. This unconditional surrender guides us to a new channel of intuition and a sensibility for the truth. Without this, the experience is purely intellectual and only reveals God to the mind but does not receive Him in the heart.

We do not lack good reasons, real or imaginary, to be disappointed with the spiritual path; nevertheless this hampers us in our confrontation with obstacles on the path of self-knowledge. Many followers are shocked by spiritual hardships but not by the hardships created by their own egotism in the material world. Egotism is the main culprit for some fragile spirits who, full of moral judgments, abandon the fighting arena.

A certain dose of common sense is necessary, especially for seekers who surround themselves with all sorts of spiritual options. In the beginning, good sense serves as protection until the neophyte finds the right path and guide. Until then, the more "free thinking" is valued, the easier it will be to fall victim to predators disguised as lambs. There are psychotic spiritual lineages as well; but even they should be evaluated carefully and without prejudice, considering the level of spirituality to which they correspond.

Without doubt, spiritual knowledge makes us confront the challenge of moral improvement. Working spiritually one discovers oneself evermore, thus accumulating strength, because the fountain of all power resides in self-knowledge. But the usual mistake of the aspirant is in believing that the use of this power is his or her privilege. All prerogatives that violate equality are born of pride and vanity.

Sometimes I saw myself questioning the undisciplined minds and emotions present in the spiritual community, maybe more so than I would in the mundane world. The question should ask why "spiritual discourses" always stumble upon contradictions—for example, between the ultimate and the practice of everyday life.

The Santo Daime doctrine had taken a big step that would make it outstanding among all religions, and that was what attracted me to it. A people were being gathered and taught about the fulfillment of a prophecy announced long ago. However, considering Mestre Irineu's life and our own recent history, I saw that in spite of the progress the Daime had achieved, the search for proof of the truth had been until then in a context of a brotherhood and sisterhood not completely united, at least not at the level described in the hymns. Neither was the community united in a spiritual understanding of its own mission and the role of individual followers.

The doctrine was evolving or was being "reformed," with a reconsideration of the elements of community, planetary expansion of the doctrine, messianic emphasis, and the acceptance of other plants as sacred. Many of these elements could not be absorbed by the institution in place at the time of the founder's death. So Padrinho was obliged to be the instigator of certain new developments.

With dynamic movements such as the Daime, traditions are always in a process of becoming. With excessive attachment to form, it is difficult to be open to new spiritual demands and new psychic patterns emerging from the historical interaction between mind and spirit. The evolution represented by Padrinho Sebastião within the Daime tradition was without a doubt what propelled the sudden expansion of the doctrine during the last decade, as well as the development of a more socially diverse Daime community.

We had started to develop Daime works in the south, and we were feeling in our flesh how difficult it was to overcome the dominance of the ego and the everyday struggle to build a community. Tribulations and the confrontation of personalities are normal in this phase, until the leadership can transform these experiences into a rich apprenticeship that, once realized, helps to form a solid bond and true unity among the fellowship.

While we are still learning, certain disharmonies make us face the struggle to overcome our habit of judging others, to work to better our confidence in others and in ourselves.

The Superior Power stirs up the emanations of our egos. The Daime doctrine has two goals, one static and the other dynamic. It asks of its practitioners a knowledge and at the same time the strength to realize it materially and spiritually. To gather a people in the forest with the goal of a sacred encounter at the end of the millennium is a considerable social task, logistically and materially.

The encounter with ourselves and others is the encounter of each of us with God. Interactions with others teach us about ourselves and are lessons provided by God in accordance with each karmic situation. While friction among brothers and sisters may prevail, it is because they have not yet conquered full knowledge. Like another of Padrinho's hymns says,

> *The truth cannot be denied*
> *The truth cannot be hidden*
> *For the truth is God*
> *And God is the true Man.*[1]

To arrive at the knowledge that "I am" is everything and is God in all beings, it is necessary to experience this feeling in an illuminated way, as an enlightenment that, all of a sudden, transforms our vision of this world and detaches us from our preferences for labels and forms. This process allows us to enter an understanding of the fundamental unity of all life, from the pulsations of a quasar to the simple act of breathing. Through the miração, the Daime opens the spiritual lucidity of superconsciousness, but to maintain oneself in this state permanently is a task demanding an entire lifetime.

During the first two years of my initiation, I passed through many processes full of strain and pain. But slowly I mended, seeing that these passages were part of the therapeutic as well as the didactic action of the mysterious Divine Being who acts through the sacred drink.

Personal power struggles belong to a kind of test for sorcerers. Trust generates love and confidence in the teachings and ends up being a rich spiritual apprenticeship. Thus, Padrinho's first commandment, expressed in his hymn, is fulfilled, "To have love one needs to be a brother" and "to be a brother one needs to have love."[2]

All knowledge that does not come from this principle and does not generate love between beings is an empty and useless knowledge. Sebastião Mota's own verses express this idea.

> *Many want to be knowledgeable*
> *And it's God who gives knowledge*
> *If you don't have knowledge*
> *You can't firm yourself.*

. . . .

Knowledge is very good
Better still is to correct oneself
To tell with certainty
About this Divine power.[3]

My periodic meetings with Padrinho Mario in Rio Branco, and with Padrinho Sebastião in the forest, were the balm that healed all my doubts and apprehensions. When I approached the vibratory field of these men, many pains and anxieties would evaporate, and everything would be clothed in meaning and depth. They would help me to believe that each unsuspected stone in the path had its reason to exist.

Padrinho explained many things about his own life that corresponded to my needs without my ever having to ask him one question. Sometimes while navigating a canoe on the igarapé, I would compose mentally all the lamentations and questions I was going to ask Padrinho. But it was almost never necessary. His words, his smile, his simple presence restored my confidence and toned my hope.

If anyone confessed fear and doubt, he would not hold back.

"Padrinho, why is it so hard to be brothers and sisters?"

"Everyone wants to be wise, but we do not want to humble ourselves to others. 'To say that you are with God / is very easy to say / But to obey His commandment / that's what I want to see.'[4] Who says this through me in this hymn is the spirit of truth itself, speaking with all its purity. It is not me, a poor old man. Whoever thinks that all of this is craziness, does not understand what life is! Life lives in all and in everything, and it knows how to work. Life is one. Even the cockroach, ugly as it is, life is in it. God gifted it with the pleasure of running. Do we not also run about in our cars? People think they are important for various petty reasons."

"Some find more advantages in having rather than being," I added.

"Tell me, what does it matter if you do not have self-knowledge? Do you think money is meaningful in Heaven? For an eternal life? No, it is not. How much does it cost to understand something so simple? Is it not so simple that it becomes complicated? But enough is enough. Slowly the understanding comes; we begin to leave bad habits and avoid bad thoughts."

He continued: "People come to the doctrine, sacrificing much to get to Céu do Mapiá, but they arrive still full of pride, not paying any attention. Therefore, they will bang their heads for a while. They do not understand that they have been called to a very fine test, as we are also waiting for the final audience. Everything is marked and we should be alert. To be with God is not to be with the world, nor even to have one face for God and another for the world. No! It is to be equal. Balance yourself, positive and negative, so that your light shines even more! We should not have complaints about anyone, materially or spiritually, and all aggression that comes against us we avoid peacefully."

"Everyone being a friend," I said.

"Yes, we have to go ahead with the faith we have in the superior self that is God in us and everywhere, in our Mestre Juramidam and in Christ Jesus. Our dear Mother is up above watching us night and day, checking to see if we are on our path.

"But about the doctrine, my son, I did not find any like the Daime before! And I tell you I went to many of them, but I saw a lot of illusion. It is better for one to believe in oneself than in a paper or clay image."

After receiving the spiritual sign from Mestre Irineu to build the church and to organize a people, Padrinho insisted, every time with more emphasis, that the organization should take the form of a community. In his mind, the community was the solution for the stresses of our time. This distress was the sign of a new goal that Padrinho received years later: to enter even farther into the jungle with his people.

The community experiment initiated at Colônia 5,000 was thus the first step in Sebastião Mota's process, bringing him later to establish a community of God's people in the middle of the forest, the landscape chosen by Mestre Irineu for the transition from the old to the new era.

Padrinho continued his recollection. He was sitting on the steps, surrounded by his afilhados. The full moon shone on the backyard, and everything shimmered.

"So it was, my son, many things came to pass through the early struggles in Colônia 5,000. There were even persecutions. Many times the federal police were there, they arrived suspicious, and left as friends. We needed the difficulties to forge a people."

"Did Mestre Irineu think like this as well?"

"In the time of Mestre Irineu, he was already trying to create this mentality. We gathered the colonists and we worked as a team."

"But it was not a community, was it?" I asked.

"This was what was still lacking in the doctrine. It was lacking the people. Mestre Irineu told me that this aspect was yet to come. There were people starting to gather, but the community was a very young and innocent child, but when these people become conscious and discover that 'God is our knowledge,' when each person understands this, he or she becomes sure of it and changes his or her mind, becoming a stronger person from inner certainty. A strong mind gives strength to the will as well, does it not?

"Now, what is still missing is our desire to identify with God's will. We must have equality among us to reach God, because God is always where there is unity. This is what I want: that you will be like me, having the spiritual knowledge that I have. I am not interested in how rich anyone is! What interests me is to have enough rice and beans to share with my friends when they come."

"Padrinho, sometimes I hear people saying not to stir things up because we are already close to the final *balanço*. Others are making plans for their grandsons and granddaughters who will come . . . what will happen, Father?"

"It is possible that God wants us still to be. If so, very well. But we will be all different, another life form, another love, and other thoughts. Truth, justice, and abundance do not hurt anyone. And plenty of prosperity. This is also our right. No one feeling the need for this or that. This is the way that it is supposed to be, a people who do not see differences in the value of each other because everyone is equal! Equal to me, to you, and to all. Everyone being one with no desire for anything. This is what the man asks for, a clean and pure people. Intelligent! You see for example a professor who knows this and that. When the spirit of the truth comes to him as in this hymn and asks:

> *What are you going to do?*
> *Listen to what I have to tell you*
> *If you do not have light*
> *Try to understand.*

After understanding
Is when you will be enlightened
There is neither sun nor moon
My brilliance is Divine.

If you don't have light
I don't know where you are
Seek my Jesus
For He came to save us.

No one should want to be great
One needs to be humble
Make oneself tiny
To enter the celestial.[5]

"And that was what I did," continued Padrinho, "instead of getting big, I humbled myself. I took many pushes from others quietly in my corner. But thank God, I am here today, proving what was said by the Divine Being. I am not lying."

It was thus that the identification between the church and the Colônia 5,000 community represented the first big step in favor of the later development of Rio do Ouro and Céu do Mapiá. The people organized themselves in teams and opened many fields for cultivation. Livestock was gathered. A sugarcane factory, a church, a market, and many houses were built.

It is common, when taking a retrospective glance, to recall the past as always lighter than the present. This envelopes us in a certain nostalgia. All the "here and now" confronts us with pressures, urgencies, challenges, and decisions, while yesterday has already happened, and it is easier to understand its pure and simple essence. It is a memory devoid of what we do not want to remember.

For the people of the Daime, the period from 1973 until about 1978 was a very fertile time. Everyone remembers and misses this period. The works in which Padrinho gave his best lectures, the hard-headed, long-haired people and foreigners arriving, the Feitio (the making of a sacred sacramental drink), and the developing of teamwork.

These moments when the spirit steers time with its favorable winds are relatively short. Periods of calm sometimes foretell of another rainy day. If we would only consider the material, spiritual, and emotional planes, our happiness would depend more or less on the formula announced by Padrinho: "To have our rice and beans and the pleasure of sharing them with our friends." Besides that, health and a good family karma can help. But money and even beans end, health suffers changes, relationships can disintegrate, and all that happiness attached to external objects is ephemeral and illusory.

On the plane of spirituality, everything we do adds up. All the apprenticeships, positive and negative, external or internal, are necessary. All that happens is a lesson for us to study, the Divine script of this game of life, the starting point for all transformation. Thus it is through these bumps and shocks, the more or less harmonious dance of energies that constitutes the everyday life of a community, that the great lessons of spirituality are learned, especially when the community is united around the same spiritual goal.

Padrinho's Hinário bloomed in this period of great fertility and harmony. In the hymns we can find the guiding thread of Sebastião Mota's spiritual path. The hymns contain basic information, enabling us to understand the doctrine. They embody the essence, the spiritual synthesis of the miração, and are messages directed to all brothers and sisters. Regardless of their origin, the hymns are considered the property of the community, cared for by all.

During the Daime's force and miração, our understanding is elevated, and everything that happens in the works is transformed. Like a flaming battering ram knocking down all the walls of illusion, true knowledge penetrates our hearts. It is in this state that the music of the spheres resounds within our beings and the celestial messengers bring to our consciousness their words, praises, and warnings. Our souls become exposed to each other's sight, allowing a clear view of what is happening in the interior of each person.

Padrinho Mario once told me, "My son, I had a miração in which I went all the way to the astral to the house where the hymns are stored. There are many drawers, each one with a little light. They are very beautiful, the beings who take care of it all. All the hymns of the doctrine are there, the ones to come as well, OK?" To the practitioners of the doctrine, receiving a hymn is a special moment in our work; if we have the facility, an intense dialogue with the Divine force becomes established, as with Moses in front of the burning bush. As clean and pure a person is, the crystal of her mirror will reflect the higher vibrations and messages. Padrinho Sebastião always said, "I know what I saw and experienced to find each word of my hymns. But I did not say anything in vain, because I live with intent and do not care for what others say. What I said is my truth. I went through the birth pangs to give light to all those hymns."

Besides its direct relationship with the astral world, the hymn can be considered a testimony as well as an affirmation that correlates perfectly with the personal history of whoever receives it. They help us to understand better the real context in which God's people engage in battle for the affirmation of spiritual values. In this period, Sebastião Mota's hymn often brought up the Saint John the Baptist story, which he felt to be as his own.

> *I live in this world*
> *Remembering what happened*
> *Saint John was decapitated*
> *And my Jesus was crucified.*[6]

Still from this period, we can follow his doctrine in this hymn where he asked the brothers and sisters who are still immersed in illusion and forgetfulness to awaken.

> *The time runs and the hours are passing by*
> *Everyone sleeps, they don't want to wake up*
> *It is good that it happens this way*
> *So we can listen and know how to respect.*[7]

To the ones who judge others and gossip he warned in this hymn:

> *I ask my brother*
> *For each to look after himself*
> *Don't worry about the lives of others*
> *For the Mestre doesn't teach that way.*[8]

In the spiritual practice of the Daime doctrine, the hymns are a direct form for Divine expression. But the efficiency of the spiritual message depends also on the person who receives it and on the deeds he or she gives as proof of the hymn's teachings. People who do not behave like a brother or a sister have no power to persuade others. In extreme cases, if someone is deliberately lying, pretending, or inventing messages, they will suffer because the Divine Being is present in the Daime's force and will come and ask the liar's account of conduct in trying to falsify the Divine teachings.

We also find him sending messages from his own experience to the community, as in this hymn:

> *Each one looks after himself*
> *I also look after myself*
> *I am taking care of this path*
> *I am making my garden.*[9]

All was happening at once, Colônia 5,000, like Padrinho's Hinário, was growing. His older sons, Alfredo and Valdete, dedicated themselves to cultivation of the fields and more practical organizational tasks, while Sebastião Mota focused on building the church. As in the Essene communities of antiquity, everyone handed their belongings to a central administration that was in charge of planning the spending, production, and provisions for all families. At six o'clock in the afternoon, everyone would gather in the church to pray, where hymns would be sung, speaking of work, loyalty, and unity among all.

Until the 1970s, the existence of the community and of the doctrine was a religious and cultural phenomenon of regional proportions only. But soon youths, backpackers, and seekers of every kind came from many different parts of the country and from foreign lands. Some of them stayed in the community, others left and came back later bringing more people.

The news started to spread around the world of this simple and amicable people who use ayahuasca in their rituals, living in a community guided by a rubber tapper with a long beard and great knowledge. The message of the Daime and the beauty of the miração were moving beyond the confined limits of the forest. Padrinho Sebastião's community was the point of reference for the first waves of a new kind of peregrination, which became

common in the next decade. Those who were paying attention saw signs
of the transition that had been predicted since the time of Mestre Irineu.
Padrinho announced:

I came to remind
This I have to say
God is for everyone
This cannot be hidden.[10]

The cycle of two thousand years since Christ's last coming is completing itself, and another era is drawing close: The time when the Divine
truth cannot be hidden, even to protect it from the attacks and scandals
of the world. While many daimistas were jealous of the sudden attention
given to Sebastião Mota, he, humble as he was, interpreted these tensions
as the confirmation of the mission Mestre Irineu had given to him. Was
it not Mestre Irineu himself who told him that his destiny was to be the
guide of a great people, a different people who would come when the right
time was approaching?

In February 1985 I was at Céu do Mapiá one more time with my
Padrinho. I arrived full of doubts relating to the doctrine and my own
role, but all dissipated completely at the first contact with his magnetic
and loving presence. At the edge of the big outside cooking fire at the
Daime's second Feitio in Mapiá, I was being initiated into the mysteries
of the ritualized making of this sacred drink. Padrinho Sebastião along
with Padrinho Mario and a big crew, had just arrived and were sitting
in the *Casa da Bateção,* which is a house full of stumps where sections
of the vine are beaten into a pulp before being cooked together with the
chacrona, called the *queen's leaves.*

The power of the stars was so great during this time that I had the
sensation I was going to be sucked up by them. At that moment, the earth
answered me, increasing my perception of the effect that gravity has on the
body. The silence was absolute. Focused, we heard only the soft whistling
of the boiling pan and, occasionally, sounds from the forest.

At that instant the miração descended. I saw a being like an angel
among us playing an instrument that sounded like a mixture of rattles
and sirens. A low humming was coming from within me. I felt pulled to

an area of the sky where sudden changes of pressure would have threatened to tear me to pieces had I been there physically. I was mounted on an immense undulating cosmic serpent, like a cowboy in a rodeo.

The sensation I had in my body during the miração was like being inside an airplane encountering turbulence at great altitude. In my mind, many scenes, symbols, and indigenous myths related to the Daime were streaming. I believe the waving movement of the snake represents the primordial energy, the movement of the spirit penetrating and giving life to the material world, inaugurating a new era.

From the smallest electrons to giant galaxies through the mysteries that quantum physics endeavors to understand, everything was explained to me in this moment, in the waving rhythm of the cosmic serpent. Marvelous symphonies and painful clamor coexisted in my brain.

All of a sudden, by the force of gravity, I fell into my world, the earth. With my eyes still closed, I saw the long journey of human beings that in some way crown Divine creation. From a simple aggregation of cosmic dust, he or she became an organism able to receive cosmic intelligence and great evolutionary power. A being capable of asking about its own origins may remember the love that generated us. Thus we find the way back to the celestial dwelling where Christ himself has secured our destined Father for those who do not deny him. I saw all of this in a vertiginous form, like a movie in fast motion—wars, victories, sublime moments, and harsh punishments—the long journey of the human being on earth.

I stayed for a while estranged to myself and to all around me. Slowly, the sensation of being inside a vacuum disappeared. Only the soft waving of the feathered serpent was left and the verses of a hymn dancing in my head.

This our empire
Is of our Father
Way before time
And of the beyond.

It is necessary to praise
To be able to follow
The truth of life
That now here it is.

I am here on this earth
It is to fulfill
The will of God
So I can live.

I am remembering
What is real
Majesty in life
Only in the spiritual.[11]

Slowly I opened my eyes, carrying with me a sensation of having crossed all eternity. After I opened them, the scene I saw in the Casa da Bateção was the same as before: the pans humming, my friends holding pieces of wood and hovering over the pans, Padrinho Sebastião and Padrinho Mario seated with all the others. As if everything had obeyed an invisible command, everyone was opening their eyes at the same time, giving the impression that we all had had the same journey.

The day after this experience, we were in the old church next to Padrinho's big house, singing his Hinário. I was still under the spell of my vision, and I listened to the hymns with a new receptivity. The singing of the girls and young women seemed like a chorus of angels.

My father is with me
All can believe
He gave me this glory
Only he can take it.[12]

8
• • •
The Duel with the Sorcerer

PADRINHO REPRESENTED THE birth of the Christian self in each of us as a flower that we must water with love. But even a rose has its thorns, and it is also with the spiritual life. Our progress is not linear, because self-knowledge depends on our failures as well as our successes. Even when we identify the error as evil and the other option as good, this does not really clarify the nature of either. Nor does it explain why God, the primordial cause of all forms and creatures, permits negative options so clearly against His own supreme will. We believe that God's will is good and what goes wrong is due to mistakes in our discernment. Our free will is a double-edged sword.

The tension between God's perfection and human weakness cannot be ignored in the spiritual science of self-knowledge. It can be mistaken to a certain point as a requirement for virtuous moral conduct, but this study goes far beyond that. Truth and "perfect conduct" are often preached by men, but God is less interested in attempts than in results. Everyone has to live out what their karma holds for them. Thus we contain both good and evil—right and wrong, all possibilities—inside ourselves. These may be discerned in a clear and real perception of what we are, so that all we are capable of can be manifest within us.

This self-reflection is essential for spiritual growth. Otherwise, we may pretend to be what we are not, thus wasting our present incarnation. We must take responsibility for our lives and not blaspheme against God as if He were guilty of causing our misfortune. Padrinho Sebastião often commented, "All is contained in God, the eternal present. He has nothing against anyone. . . . God does not bother anyone! People keep on complaining, 'Ah! My God! He is sending me this punishment!' This is a form of raising false testimony against He who has only light to give! If someone falls ill, it is likely due to his or her misdoings and insanities, but some people go around saying to others in a loud voice that God sent it! God is clean and stays away from worthless things. Do you not see how the sun dries all the garbage? The sun always stays clean and clear. Through sunlight, God illuminates us all equally, continuously renewing our opportunity to understand His will.

Saint John the Evangelist advised us not to worry about the origin of evil, because God, who is the Good and the Supreme Charity, comes before evil and loved us before evil existed. A deeper meaning exists in his consent for the existence of this apparently negative force. Within the purpose of Divine creation, evil ultimately comes to serve the good. On a cosmic level, the negative force can be comprehended as part of the destructive and dispersive element that must exist. It is present in many representations of the Holy Trinity, and its field of action falls within Divine will. It is part of His manifestation since the dawn of time.

In this way human beings with powerful intelligences came into being by which the Creator began to conduct his cosmic symphony. The excessive importance that some of those beings began to attach to the fruits of material creation, originally of Divine conception, little by little, through greed, generated evil. As the fallen angels, who were rebellious and jealous of God's power, these beings began to exercise more influence over the evolution of the material world.

But human beings also represent an important level in the evolution of the spiritual and material processes that the Supreme Being set in motion. Man and woman were put into this Paradise, the ancient myths tell us, with their spiritual evolution dependent on the exercise of their free will. Thus Divine Protector and evil tempter, within the microcosm of human consciousness, reproduce the universe itself with its elements in opposition and the possibility of synthesis on a final level, depending on genuine spiritual knowledge. Padrinho Sebastião often exclaimed, "Balance yourself, positive and negative, so you shall be light!"

In our material, moral, and spiritual lives, we should learn to identify these constructive and destructive forces present in each one of us, as well as in the universe. This study is part of the process of self-knowledge, the basis of all spiritual realization. For the mind to liberate itself from all illusory states of consciousness, it needs to seek deeply in the duality that is, in and of itself, another level of illusion.

There are energies, vibrations, thought patterns, entities, and disincarnated consciousness that operate on a level of destruction, disunity, egotism, and cruelty to others. They can be incarnate or disincarnate, and they work inside our minds in the form of desires and emotions. Their influence is worse when we are open to their vibrations.

What should we do with this cosmic polarization, especially when we are conscious of it not being about us or our actions? The answer must be sought in the realm of spiritual charity. In part we must see ourselves as mediums whose mission is to help and to clarify the spirits themselves, which is done through the medium's own illumination. The medium becomes host and mediator for obsessive and suffering spirits, whose healing depends on charity and compassion.

The main attribute of the Supreme Avatar is that through the grace of His total and unconditional compassion for humans, we also can perform the deeds and the wonders necessary to heal the sick and the obsessed. It took me a long time to discover that compassion is one of the main virtues needed in the modern world. It is one of the rarest as well. Observing the Padrinho's life and seeing his compassion, I understood that, through compassion, a truly wise person learns how to differentiate between the true and false pains of human experience. He or she is thus able to discern the degree of neutrality, identification, or participation appropriate to each.

If charity feels to us like an outward act of consolation, compassion is internal, psychological, something we give privately. We need to be able to feel and understand the pain of the other in our own being. This is done through a kind of mediumship. First, we open ourselves to the pain or illusion of our fellow creatures, being careful not to confuse it with our own. We then make a good effort to discern all the elements of it in ourselves, for them, and for the them in us.

Based on our own understanding and experience, we penetrate the mental, emotional, and astral chaos that is always looking to communicate with incarnated beings. There are those who, without the proper instruction, but moved by love, endeavor to help others. Such work is indeed a dangerous mission, and one should always look for good guidance. But if we are pure in our intentions, we approach ecstasy without being threatened by the monsters who inhabit the depths of our unconscious, and who thus lose their power over us.

But if in our bosom we carry a heart of stone, full of guilt, fear, self-doubt, and insensitivity to others, the weight of our conscience will make us drown in the sea of our own insanity. The medium should be careful when trying to salvage a spiritual shipwreck. Those who, so to speak, are materially or selfishly drawn to self preservation will cling with such a desperate grip that they may drown in their own experience.

Padrinho would advise, "That's why I say I do not know how to deal with all the spirits, but I am always learning a bit more. I am working to make them all our friends so they can have true knowledge of God, accepting and understanding the power of God above all things, including ourselves. Those who accept are on our side and on God's side, and those who do not accept encounter eternal death. They may never again enter the incarnated world. They are losing their chance and will disappear from the earth and from the astral. In the astral realm there are many hospitals for beings who are existentially sick. They are like mental institutions here on earth. It is hard to go there because they are for beings who are very sick and hard to educate. Once, I passed by a place like that. The 'screamers' began to call me, and I went to attend to them. But when I put my foot there, the clamor, the horror, and the teeth-grinding were such that I had to fly out of there. I told Mestre Irineu and he advised, 'The spiritual knowledge I have gained leads me to respect all the spirits, but of the ones I know, I give the most importance to Juramidam, the one this world calls Christ, the Redeemer, who truly can lift the darkness.' My desire was to arrive at the place where God is and thus to come to the knowledge of who we are. With a lot of suffering and sacrifice I arrived at that place. Now what else am I going after? It is necessary to learn how to master everything with calmness and tenderness, to learn how to treat our brothers and our sisters. Whoever wants to come with me, come—but as a man not a vagabond. Because a man should not enmesh himself with smallness nor listen to gossip. I am going forward, and the Voice of the Desert is guiding me."

All these considerations—good and evil, spirits of light and darkness, and the way to confront them with charity—help us understand the events that unfolded when a sorcerer known as Ceara arrived at Colônia 5,000.

The church at Céu do Mapiá

Ritual in the church of Céu do Mapiá

Creche with children at Céu do Mapiá

The old church of Visconde de Mauá

The main center and arrival area at Céu do Mapiá

House building in Céu do Mapiá

Padrinho Sebastião and his family at Céu do Mapiá, 1984

Padrinho Sebastião at Céu do Mapiá, 1985

Padrinho Sebastião making a canoe

Padrinho Sebastião, Alex, and Madrinha at Céu do Mapiá, 1985

Padrinho Mário and Alex, Visconde de Maud, 1985

Padrinho Alfredo holding a jagube vine

The vine (jagube)

Padrinho Corrente washing and cleaning the leaves, Visconde

Beating the vine before cooking the Daime tea (Batistô)

Alex and Padrinho Alfredo cooking Daime tea, Céu do Mapiá, 1985

He proclaimed himself king of the *macumbeiros* (sorcerers). Ceara worked with the entity referred to as Tranca-Rua.

The theme of becoming a medium and the struggle with suffering spirits occupied a central place in Padrinho's life. After his healing with the Daime, his main guide, Antônio Jorge, announced his withdrawal so that Padrinho Sebastião would learn from his own experience. Padrinho then received the orders from the astral to erect his temple and begin the organization of a people and a community. During this period, Padrinho had many warnings and visions of an approaching confrontation with a spiritual lineage not well known to him.

In Padrinho's first vision he was walking on a road when he saw a horseman dressed in black following him. As he walked, the horseman gained on him until they finally met at the end of the road. From this warning, Padrinho understood that something serious was about to occur.

After that he saw an entity smoking a pipe, a tricksterlike being from the forest. This being leaned on him with great force and told him he was going to run him right out of the doctrine. After this second vision, Padrinho Sebastião became somewhat skittish and worried as he waited, day by day, for the fulfillment of this threat.

A few weeks later, Padrinho had yet another vision in which he was held down by a very large man who was speaking of "a great test" Padrinho would have to pass to obtain the degree of knowledge destined to him. He knew something was approaching.

While these lugubrious pronouncements were in the air, many things were ripening in the community. Padrinho asked more and more for perfection in the works, for everyone to awaken and learn with the great master that is time, which "does not deceive nor have compassion for the flesh."

It was then that Ceara arrived. He was a medium of high capacity, but he had dedicated himself to the practice of evil. Padrinho received him graciously, already knowing he was the opponent whose coming the visions had announced. A black moth, Ceara saw the light in the white-bearded old man, he felt attracted to the light but also wanted to destroy it. Was it not jealousy of the light that made Lucifer rebel against God, the source of all light, for the right to govern humans?

The sorcerer arrived with lots of talk, offering his abilities and promising "to help eradicate falsehood from among us," as he put it. Ceara would repeat, "Padrinho, I do not drink the Daime, because it is forbidden to me. My spirit guide does not let me, but I am going to straighten things out for you." Then he would say to others, referring to Padrinho, "Now, I want to see what forces really are with the bearded one. I am going to expose all the hidden powers in the community!"

From the first day of Ceara's arrival at Colônia 5,000, he began opening all sorts of spiritual healing sessions with a variety of excuses. Finally he opened a small permanent place for his practices. He would not even be finished with the one ceremony, which sometimes took days, and he would start another one with the excuse that "there was something wrong in this or that household."

As soon as the sorcerer arrived, the old Mota received instructions from the astral realm to let him work in the community for five months. During this time Padrinho should be aware of but not stop Ceara's work. Padrinho should "bear the impact" because this was part of a mission of charity—to convert the satanic entity that was incarnated in the sorcerer. The old man's hope was that the sorcerer and the entity guiding him would become influenced in some way by the force of the Daime.

This happened after a while, during a works at which we were singing Saint John's Hinário. Ceara asked for Daime for his entities for the first time. But not for himself yet. He said, "Padrinho, everyone whom I bring here, give them Daime because they are all untamed, and need the doctrine." But at the same time he announced, "The Tranca-Rua will not surrender so easily."

And so Ceara channeled one of his entities, drank the Daime, and we continued the works. After a certain hymn, Padrinho sensed a confrontation coming and asked everyone to stay calm because after the entity that the sorcerer channeled drank Daime, it would denounce many of the troubles within the community, causing a great commotion.

The efficiency of a sorcerer's power depends on how much energy he can draw from negative situations. Even when unmasking something genuinely wrong, his intent will always be to instigate strife, setting one person against another and maintaining all the negative energy available. He does this through sorcery, blood offerings, and other symbolic operations of black magic.

The negative power that feeds on our little imperfections can make the weaker-minded corrupt, leading them slowly into a conscious pact with malevolent spirits. And yet there was a positive side of this process because many things were coming to the surface.

The pot of distress was boiling. Padrinho Mario said later, "The entities that worked against us were our judges. We could not but recognize their role. They were the ones coming to change us. They were the ones asking for our testimony and demanding, 'Are you not a living saint? What are you afraid of then?' If everything in our consciousness is clear, and our hearts make no accusations, no sorcerer has power over us."

In the week after Ceara drank the Daime during the channeling of one of his entities, his behavior began to change dramatically. In some moments Ceara would stop pretending to be a helper, the one who presented himself as a simple instrument to discipline the people, and would put on a sad face, showing his need for help. This was already a sign that, even against his will, the Daime was healing him. But in these moments the sorcerer would try to resist.

"You are going to win Padrinho! You are going to win! There are only two great ones, God and Tranca! But God is bigger, is He not? He will win. But I am still in the battle."

Caught in this crossfire, Padrinho would ask everyone to study this spiritual manifestation in discourse. To those who rightly understood, the battle being played out was really big. Slowly though, Ceara started surrendering all his entities to the Daime. Only he, the self, the Tranca, his main entity, were not.

The risk was great on some occasions. As Ceara himself later confessed to Alfredo, Padrinho's son: "Alfredo, many times I had the desire to crash the car with your father and all your family. . . ."

But he was surrendering evermore, and his behavior announced an approaching resolution. The time given, five months, was almost over. During a works when Padrinho drank Daime, he had a vision in which he traveled to the astral, to a house where, in the living room, a big tarpaulin covered something. He picked up the tarp at once. Underneath it were all Ceara's doings represented in the astral: "only trinkets and pretensions," in accordance with his own words. It was then that Padrinho understood that the time for the final decision was coming. But he was still waiting for the final scene.

Less than a week later, the sorcerer arrived at Padrinho's house, saying: "Padrinho, you win! I am not going to work here anymore. Here everything is as it is supposed to be. What I had to do, I have already done."

But the price of the battle had been high. The sorcerer had done great damage and offended many good people. The duel and the contact with a dark line were so hard that Padrinho later recognized the effort he had made not to doubt the instructions he received. His son Alfredo said:

"There were hard moments in which Father confessed to me to have struggled spiritually with Ceara's strong entities. I remember him saying: 'Alfredo, there were moments when even I wanted to doubt that I was still within the light. But sometimes this is the way it is. All those dark entities that came through Ceara, they came to ask for our understanding and healing. Only that this kind of work is very heavy and I almost got hurt.'"

Alfredo continued: "Ceara kept giving Daime to his entities saying to Padrinho, 'Sir, give Daime to those whom I am going to channel, they are all bad and untamed. But I still will not drink, because the day I drink the Daime . . . ah! my God, I will lose the battle!'

"So one day, I was in town and Ceara appeared at Padrinho Wilson's house. I greeted him saying, 'Here comes the *macumbeiro*!' We called him *macumbeiro* to his face, and he took great pleasure in that. He said, 'Alfredo, how are you man? Do you know? Today is my day.'

"'Today is your day for what?' I asked. 'Today I am going to drink Daime.' Then I said, 'Is it true Ceara?' He confirmed it. Padrinho Wilson asked me, 'Shall we give to him?' and I said, 'Yes, do it!' Then Padrinho Wilson opened a works, Ceara drank Daime and sat in a chair. In twenty minutes he said he was experiencing miração. 'I am *mirando,* Alfredo, I am seeing.' With ten minutes of miração he said, 'It is enough! I do not want it anymore! It is already decided, I am going.' Old Wilson still wanted to keep him, 'Man, you are still mirando—stay!' But he got up, saying, 'No, what I had to see I already saw.' He left and within three days he was dead."

"How did it happen?" I asked.

"In three days he slowly surrendered himself. That is how I interpret it. First he tried to trouble all of us. Then he saw that he could not. So he began to lose his strength from all the bad doings and sorcery he had done, do you understand? He began to surrender, passing the doctrine to all his entities. When only the Tranca-Rua was left he drank the Daime and so did Tranca-Rua. Ceara journeyed and Tranca accompanied him. It could have been that he would have softened, begged for forgiveness, and become a decent man. This was what my father was hoping for the end of the story. But his death was destiny. He had been possessed by the entity and had done many evil things." Ceara was taken by his own wrongdoings, and now Padrinho, the only one able to help him, was going to continue the healing of Tranca-Rua.

"If Ceara had continued in the doctrine, he could have resisted the entity, so paradoxically, maybe the entity did get rid of Ceara?" I asked.

"Right! After this, the entity shifted to the old man, and almost killed him. But this was later, in Rio do Ouro," Alfredo added.

"How was it that Padrinho started to feel the presence of the entity for the final duel?"

"It was gradual. The health of the old man got visibly worse when Ceara died and he felt the presence of the Satan who had come to surrender. I was at Colônia 5,000 organizing the people who were staying there while Father opened Rio do Ouro. He was working hard and was the first to enter the forest. Before dawn, he was already in the dark forest where no one had stepped, and he would start to clear. If we were not careful, he would be out there with a machete, contracting all kinds of malarias and other bad things. But going back in time a bit, before going to Rio do Ouro, he still saw one last celebration of Saint John at the Colônia 5,000.

"He stayed for a long time on the floor of the house. We helped him into a chair, and then when he recomposed himself, he went back to drink more Daime in the church."

"That was when he felt the being?" I asked.

"According to him, on that day it locked onto him, that spirit being called Tranca-Rua, the demon who came to be healed in Sebastião Mota's church."

"It is hard to have perspective when things are happening. When Jesus expelled demons and dueled with Satan it also generated a certain scandal among the doctors of the law, Pharisees, and other cultured people, did it not?" I added.

"Yes, but whoever is spiritually aware knows the importance and the meaning of these facts. If during this period our fellowship rested on firmer foundations, it would have been easier for the old man. The being could have been indoctrinated by all of us, instead of just my father. His capacity and knowledge as a medium made him alone bear the weight of this process."

"Do you mean he already left for Rio do Ouro knowing that he carried the being with him?"

"Yes, father went back to Rio do Ouro feeling the consequences of being possessed by that being himself. He worked with bodily disorder, spiritual confusion, agony, desire to die, and thousands of other things, none of them pleasant," Alfredo continued.

"Father spent the next celebration of Saint John in Rio Branco. He arrived very sick, as if he were going to die. I was fighting in the Colônia 5,000 against a group that was turning everything upside down. Several deluded youths, one thinking he was Christ and the others believing themselves his disciples, wanted me to change the order of the works. Well, during the works, Father manifested something so strong that he said in a loud voice, almost screaming, that he was with God and whoever doubted should get ready for the test. It was then that it happened: a spiritual interaction between him and an outsider from a southern community. In another incarnation, the outsider had been a king and he had come to reconcile himself with the old man that day. Father started to speak in a foreign language and the southern man answered in that same language. After that, the man fell on the floor and rolled in the backyard until the end of the works."

"Did Padrinho go back to Rio do Ouro after that?"

"Yes. It was then that he entered into a true spiritual alignment. The satanic being was able to express himself with full liberty in Padrinho. Father was always suffering. There were times when he spent days vomiting blood. Then Tranca-Rua would manifest and say, 'This is not his! It is mine! I was the one with the stomach full of blood. Black chicken's blood from all my misdeeds. It is not his! Do you want to see? Tomorrow he will stop bleeding. But everyone has to stay calm, otherwise he will not be able to stand to cleanse me.' Then he would threaten, 'And if he does not do so, there is no one who can. Say goodbye to me and to him.'"

"Did the blood really stop?" I asked.

"Yes. And when any disharmony among the people occurred, the symptoms would return. The old man, poor fellow, was nailed to his own cross, so he would understand what Christ had experienced, and as for Tranca, sometimes he valued the doctrine more than we did. He would say, 'This medicine of yours is of great value, but I can only help myself if you all do well your part. If you act thus, I am cured, healed in each and every one, this is what I say!' There were times when he would manifest while the old man was in agony with us gathered at his bedside and say, 'You are all very nervous, and you will end up killing us both!' In response we sang the doctrine's hymns as Tranca would scream through the old man, 'Slowly, slowly! For God's love! Otherwise I will make away with him!' It was like this that he bargained. And we had to sing very calmly and slowly so he could stand it."

"Didn't Tranca-Rua come to ask one day to be part of the doctrine?"

"This was the decisive moment for his conversion. We had an open works in Father's room because he was in bed. Then all of a sudden Father sat up and his ashen face gave place to a beautiful countenance, really shining, as if he were completely well. Ogum Beira-Mar, an entity of Yoruba origin, manifested in him, saying that he was there as a messenger and that Tranca-Rua was asking for Padrinho to be taken to the living room. There Tranca-Rua, through Padrindo's body, was transformed into a cripple. When we sang a couple of hymns he cried and begged forgiveness for his transgressions."

"It was the judgment of his crimes, by man's law and by God's law, was it not?"

"Right. He would say that these medicines were uncrippling him to a point that soon nobody would recognize him. He had hopes not to be a spiritual cripple anymore. He explained that the reason for his lameness was the jealousy and envy he had of God. He said that he was fed by all of us, the ones who 'drive off evil' during the day to follow their own desires under the cloak of darkness. This can bring only illness and death. Then he, Tranca-Rua or Satan or whatever name is given to him, asked for an opportunity."

"What kind of an opportunity?" I asked.

"To be a brother. He said to Padrinho, 'If you accept me as your brother I will watch over this house and the proof will be the old man's healing.' That was the sign he promised: When the old man healed from Satan's influences, so would the people."

"So what did you say?"

"I said, 'Tranca-Rua, this is the way! If you are seeing things better than we are, if you are giving value to our spiritual medicine and the doctrine, then we accept you as a brother.'"

"And he?"

"He said, 'From now on, Tranca is in favor of God and this doctrine. You can count on me. When a worthless thought goes by your mind remember me. You can call and I will be here to help. But I must say, with me on your side, it is better to be disciplined.' Then he made a request. If the doctrine is so clear as to be understandable even by him, a major mess-maker, it is our obligation now to understand Satan's work in each one of us and at the same time to love and practice charity with all beings. We should also correct them through our efforts to correct ourselves. Is it not right to love God and our fellow men as we love ourselves? Only through this can we attract good things. And when the bad spirits come and find the doctrine being practiced, then they convert themselves. God sends Satan to challenge us! Even Tranca-Rua himself was saying that his power was to be exercised the way God wanted."

"This story has a great meaning," I offered. "God is interested in gathering all His children again." I remembered a hymn I received and sang it.

This works
It is what is happening
God is casting the nets
For His children to return.[1]

"This is it," confirmed Alfredo, "further on, Divine justification will ask, 'Who are you? Are you Mr. Lucifer, who rebelled so long ago?' Even knowing that these fallen angels are sons who have power and that God is not going to discard a son only because he erred, he will have to roll around until once again he sees the light. Is that not so?"

When the conversation turned to those events that marked the transition phase between Colônia 5,000 and Rio do Ouro, a strong energy was felt. Padrinho Alfredo, now one of the leaders of the movement, was finishing his memories with the last words pronounced by the being named Tranca-Rua on the day of his conversion.

"Tranca-Rua said, 'Make a house to give light to all spirits that will come. Work honestly for their healing, otherwise everyone will lose. Make a house even if it is the size of a matchbox.'"

"From this was born the Star House!" I exclaimed.

"Yes, the first one was in the forest at Rio do Ouro, the one you know. Afterward we built one here in Mapiá."

I left there that night full of thoughts. The theme of the confrontation between God and Satan was indeed very delicate and as old as human history, but even today analysis and understanding of this battle can bring forth precious keys to self-knowledge and inner illumination. On many occasions when this theme was mentioned I had felt a certain indulgent mocking from some people. Really, it is much easier to suppose we only are going to deal with the higher spiritual plane in our spiritual path. But we should remember to help those who abjectly fall. This is called charity. This is why Christ fought against his tempter: to have the power to expel him from us and others. Jesus lived with prostitutes, ate at fishermen's tables, and was crucified between two thieves. As in the image of the sun that dries all things used by Padrinho Sebastião, Christ did not become impure from his actions. On the contrary, many had the chance to be healed and sanctified by the presence of this Son of Love during his brief passage on earth, some two thousand years ago. Now I was bearing witness to something very similar.

Pablo C Amaringo
14.04.02

9

...

I Light My Candlesticks

AS I PENETRATED deeper into the history and doctrine of the Santo Daime, into its more intimate processes, I also transformed inside myself, overcoming much resistance and self-indulgence. Spiritual surrender is unconditional. When we are surrounded by myths and legends of bygone saints and old books, it might be easier to be a believer. But when we live with a saint of flesh and bone, who greets us daily and eats rice and beans with us, we have a tendency to feed our doubts by noticing his shortcomings. Padrinho believed that it was worthwhile to overcome this habit. He advised, "Instead of worshiping a piece of paper, each of us should choose a man or a woman to look up to and respect as the living presence of Christ or the Virgin."

Not that I was shocked at all the stories about sorcerers and black magic, but contact with the dark side of a spiritual path is always traumatic for the neophyte, adding to our fears of Satan and of the personal demon contained in our most egotistic inclinations and motivations. Padrinho Alfredo reassured us, "A friendship has to be developed, an understanding between God and Satan. God has never done anything useless, and there is nothing outside God. This is the truth, otherwise nothing would exist. God is everything and made everything so He can show and prove his creation at the right time." Men and women have to undertake a conscious internal struggle, but to use Padrinho Mario's expression, it is a struggle for love, wherein we only attain victory over the enemy after he is no longer perceived as the enemy, but rather as connected to the pure will of God.

Padrinho synthesized all the knowledge that the spiritual seeker of inner reality needs to understand: self-knowledge is a path to the correct discernment of reality. He offered, "We must understand what is happening with each other and learn how to trust or we will never be free. We have to transform an enemy into a friend. Without our doubts of people, material or spiritual, all of these disturbances will end. As long as we do not understand, we need neither fear nor courage. But if our own universe, when it manifested itself, began the duality, so it is with humans, who manifest the universe on a small scale. The unification of opposites is necessary for all spiritual realization."

Padrinho, with his perspicacity, perceived all that was happening inside me. I was hesitant to assume the role of medium. When I said good-bye in March 1985, we had a brief dialogue. We reviewed for a few moments our earlier conversations, and as always, he joked a bit about my tapes and annotations. Then he said,

"So the task is, my son, to unite the negative and positive: therein the mystery lies. The spirit and body must unite! If your gaze fastens only on the negative, it will give no light. If only on the positive, that will not work either. You have to unite both. Bring together all the demons and all the gods—this is the work. Discipline yourself and walk the middle path. The inner self fashions its own dwelling and sits on the throne of its own temple, well seated, seeing everything!"

While my mind recapitulated the facts, words, and recent lessons, I answered, "Padrinho Mario liked to sing the hymn, 'I am the living room / I am the throne / Where my master converses.' In the end I was certain of being with God. I looked to all sides, and only hope was left to me. Beyond all reason, I could still depend on hope." Then, I fell silent, wondering how long hope could sustain my faith.

Padrinho must have noticed something in my expression, and he teased me, "So, young fellow? Are you thinking a lot, or are you doubting me?"

The question was asked with a playful and tender tone, but it went right down to the depths of my being. I stuttered in reply, "What Padrinho? It is nothing like that." But as it always happened in such moments, I felt naked in front of this man, whose deep perception revealed the most subtle aspects of my inner process. His few words had an immediate therapeutic effect, so that I ended up smiling when the time came to step back into the canoe. I waved good-bye to that old man with long beard and shining eyes, who stood there on the wooden veranda, watching my departure. Almost shouting over the sound of the canoe's motor. I added, "I don't doubt you at all, but maybe I still doubt myself."

I was carried by the canoe and the roar of the outboard, zigzagging through the curves of the igarapé. On each trip, the processes of saying good-bye and returning to civilization were intense. I was absorbed in reflections, trying to put together ideas and feelings, taking in the new teachings, and at the same time imagining what would be waiting for me in the mountains.

My state of restless questioning gave way to a great clarity. Everything was being revealed. Even my doubts had clarifying significance. When the canoe crossed the channel of the farm that is located at the mouth of the Mapiá River and we entered the voluminous Purus River, it was almost evening. Flying fish were leaping over the canoe. The clouds were hiding the sunset, producing beautiful reflections of blue and pink. I started to receive a message, and as I was writing, the wind sprinkled water on my face and tugged at the pages of my notebook. My pen flew across the paper and my mind accompanied it, agonizing over the sequence of ideas with fear of losing them. For two hours I wrote, filling almost half of my notebook. The keel cut the surface of the water, and that was how I felt my mind being penetrated by that intense energy. When the message was concluded I started to read what I had written and many things became clear. I had received key information about my mission in the future. The message spoke about a "divine game," about good, evil, and charity, touching on all the questions that had become my main focus in recent years.

When this trancelike state left me, I became aware of the silver moon shining in the sky among the shimmering stars. All of us in the boat were absorbed in thoughts, dominated by the grandeur of the night.

When I arrived home, many new things had happened and the community we had dreamed of was beginning to become a reality. At that point I was further confronted with the issue of becoming a medium and working with the spirits.

Soon it came time to go back to the forest.

In August 1985, we organized the church's first big Feitio, at Colônia

5,000, Feitio being the ceremony by which the sacred sacrament Daime is made. After that many of us went up to Mapiá, but this time, the happiness of arriving was lessened by the news that Padrinho was having another heart crisis. They had become cyclical since the physical and spiritual exhaustion in Rio do Ouro.

His heart became merry at our presence, with the happiness he had in receiving the newer sons and daughters in whom the hope of the future lay. Sometimes the emotions were too strong, and he would succumb to their intensity. In addition, it was an especially difficult moment in the village of Céu do Mapiá. The government was not paying the community for the two years of work they had done in Rio do Ouro. The rubber production had practically stopped and the bills for basic supplies for the community were increasing.

Many healing works for Padrinho were done in this period, and slowly the old man's health improved. In one of these works, done in Padrinho's own room, I sensed very strongly the spiritual presence of the many sufferers who came to be cleansed in the light of his presence, which further stressed his tired body.

Since my last trip, all the questions I had about becoming a medium were, in a natural way, being answered through practice. We now needed to practice the same charity that Sebastião Mota had demonstrated throughout his whole life so that we could attempt to heal him. But how? Very few had a notion of how to work in a form that could genuinely help him. He himself, after the works, explained how he understood this help.

"You pay attention because I am trying hard to manage this mission the Master and the Virgin Mother gave me, to give light to all these spirits. Let us learn to value and to love with authentic charity all that exists. What I want from you is that you be very conscious of this struggle. Now is the time to unite and to have the certainty that Satan is not our enemy, do you understand? We need to work always with the good, for the sake of good, so as not to feed Satan. And if temptation comes, we remain still and watchful. How is it people say?"

"Passive?" I offered hesitantly.

"Yes. We should remain passive and know with certainty that, with the Daime and with our conscious intentions, we will not become confused between ourselves and those we are healing. If the patient is ready, he gets better. And if he still has things to work out, in visiting our inner temple, where the Daime is constantly cleaning and adorning, taking what is pure and reinforcing it. The person wants more of this healing. If people are intractable and do not want to be healed, then that difficult path they will have to walk alone."

"But we cannot become confused, is it not true, Padrinho? We have to be calm so that the influence of a negative spiritual force that wants us to make mistakes does not overpower us, causing us to risk abandoning a place of balance to take advantage of situations for pleasure or whatever else!"

"It is true. We have to be firm in the Daime. With the Santo Daime there is no room to cling to ugliness and mistakes. And we have to learn to let go at the right time as well, otherwise the spirit can stay, like an uninvited guest, and in a weak medium, become an obsession."

Alfredo, who was sitting in the corner, completed the thought, "All of this differentiates the true prophets and sages from all sorts of false Christs and vampires, so that they can be corrected at the same time as they have an opportunity. In time, the dividing line will become clearer. The ones with the Divine do not procrastinate."

"And it does not mean that in the face of temptation we should give in to them," I added.

"No. We are required to have knowledge and doctrine. The temptation is very strong to give light to beings that sometimes only desire to realize one wish through us. But it is imperative that we keep our clarity."

"How can we understand the call?" I asked.

Padrinho Alfredo clarified, "It depends on each one's mission. Sometimes it is not a choice. Thousands of things appear to test us, and it is with great effort that we understand. Otherwise we flunk the test."

"So, my son," spoke Padrinho Sebastião, "God lives in harmony and nobody can finish Him. Therefore, we should live in harmony and nobody will finish us. Evil, yes, has to be finished! Upon finishing evil, there will be no more difficulties of any kind, all our wills aligned in one direction, is it not true, Alfredo?"

"So it is. I feel myself to be a helper of my father in this struggle.

His illness has to be well understood by the people, for it has a spiritual cause and each one of us plays a role in it. Each one of us should untangle ourselves and assume our places, so that we can save these beings that are with us, and consequently save ourselves as well! Suddenly the Devil may come; he is always saying things here among us, and it is this that we are afraid of, is it not? But we always have these fears within ourselves."

"Confronting these internal fears, it becomes easier to trust others," I agreed.

"Being firm and united is all that is left for us. All is nothing, and nothing is all. I know it to be right for us to discover one another and discover that victory is found in knowledge and nothing else. All the rest is deception! And further on we will see that; even if we do not want to, we will realize this."

Showing signs of being tired, and wanting to finish our conversation, Padrinho began to sing a hymn.

> *My brothers and my sisters*
> *Please start unraveling yourselves*
> *I am small and keep my word*
> *I'm showing my truth.*[1]

I started to leave, while Padrinho, still weak, rested his head on a pile of pillows placed over the arm of the chair. It was in this way that he rested during the more acute phases of his illness. Swollen because of the edema, he could not lie down without intense coughing and a sensation of suffocation.

The grace of God is given to his children in such a natural way that sometimes it goes unnoticed. Sometimes we have a heavy heart and the reason seems unclear; suddenly, we see the sunshine, nature's harmony; something mysterious gives us comfort and new hope for our being, renewing our union with God and with life, inspiring a great force of transformation, and we leave our previous lethargy behind.

Then one beautiful day Mr. Mota was giving blessings in the middle of the backyard. His small tired face was smiling, and he seemed better. When the health of the patriarch improved, the village's mood changed. We experienced a great relief and a sudden change of humor.

Every day became pleasurable again; the forest seemed perfumed again and showered forth its beauties.

Life returned to its former rhythms. Lines of people again came to ask for Padrinho's blessings after the six o'clock prayer. He would walk from the kitchen to the living room and from there to the veranda, where he would converse until it was time to go back to his room for a nap. One night when we checked in on him, he was already awake, sitting in his immense reinforced bed, continuing spiritual conversations. The chair where he had survived his greatest agony had been taken away from the room and replaced by an abundance of flowers.

"So my son," he would begin. "I was half here, half there, but now I am better. It is the weight of many things we receive, especially I, who am a prepared medium, an old mule who takes on all kinds of loads of others! But I have a great hope, as I was saying, that with your help and everybody else's, we will prevail, by God's will."

"But since Rio do Ouro, your heart has suffered some, has it not Padrinho?"

"That is how it is. There were many serious battles I had to live through then so I would be able to teach and help you all avoid some suffering today. But some of you will have to experience it yourselves as well."

"Yesterday you spoke about doubt and fear and said that we cannot have enemies, did you not?"

"Yes, and thanks I give to my Supreme Virgin that I trust people. I do not have doubt and do not need to say anything about anyone. If I gossip about someone, the invisible lower spirits by my side are listening. And I hear the spirit, saying to another spirit friend, 'Let's go tell on this person.' These beings are serious, if they do not find truth in what you say, they will come to demand the truth from you. There can be bad ones that say, 'Let's go disturb him.' And they come and come on strong."

"So it is necessary to be very careful with them, isn't it?"

"Yes, we need to be very careful in the spiritual life because they are listening to everything. One day, although I was very alert, these lower spirits arrived, and they taught me some hard lessons. As time passed I realized my protector was always with me, and I had no more fear." Then he sang:

I am here
I hear the voice in the desert
Everybody be alert
We do not know where we're going.

In paradise
One must watch one's step
Walking very clean
In the presence of my Father.[2]

"Here we need to have a lot of respect," he continued. "Many of us think we have no power, but we do, by knowing ourselves. Until this happens, you live in an old world, tied to material things, chained to many idiotic things that do not even belong to us. He who has only one wing does not fly! Another day I saw a dove over there; someone had trimmed one of its wings. It would take flight and fall. So it is with a person who lives without knowledge. Imprisoned by the old body, tied to trinkets, imprisoned in nothingness, zero! Sometimes we struggle to attain spiritual knowledge. We try to deny the negative. When seeing, only seeing the Devil in others, never in oneself. Look inside you, don't you know where it is? That is why I say, let's be equal in everything! Spiritual and material. Respect everything, so we become equal. You see a lizard: what an ugly creature, one thinks. I am going to kill it. No, it should be allowed to go on its journey and I on mine. Be it a snake, frog, whatever ugly creature. Do not disturb anyone!

To love and have loved
One must know
God in your mind
God is your knowledge.[3]

"If nature creates everything," continued Padrinho, adding to the theme of the hymn, "should I fear anything? No. I am friend to everything, so nobody can do me harm. Rather than feeling afraid, we should talk accurately about the nature of spiritual reality. How it is, how it is not, how it can be changed. Today the Tranca-Rua we knew is no more. He can be for others, but for me who won the fight, there is no more.

Thus you must understand that if you want to follow the spiritual path, you must not gossip against anyone."

The flow of Padrinho Sebastião's words, the grace with which he was leading us with the power of his vigorous images was opening our understanding in a surprising way. With his extreme simplicity, he explained intricate themes of spirituality. In some moments I was aware of the similarities between his talks and passages that came from Genesis interpreted by Meister Eckehart or Saint John of the Cross. But Padrinho did not quote passages from books but always from his own life, which was an open book to us. His power of persuasion was this uninterrupted creative discourse that sprang from his own knowledge.

When Padrinho felt his energy returning, he would become loquacious. He had satisfaction in transmitting what he knew and had a special way to teach each person.

"Very well, this is Satan's story. Satan is like this. He does not have a human consciousness and is in opposition to everything, fighting this and that. The world is very small in the face of the Divine Presence—it's like looking through binoculars from the other end. Have you done that? Everything is very small, is it not? And it has to be very small really, because we become inflated in illusion and pride, thus taking a risk when passing through the eye of the needle. Even those who discover some things and arrive at some knowledge, if they became proud, they will die in the same way. Pride, envy, and jealousy are our biggest enemies. I am speaking because I lived through all of that, so I could converse with and teach you today."

"We learn only by experience, but we should not need to learn the same lesson twice—unless we want to stay at the lower levels, right?"

"Do not act like dogs that, after regurgitating, go back to eat the same garbage. Look, I am going to tell you something: everything is possible for us, and nothing is sin!"

In these moments, the theology of Padrinho Sebastião became daring. I wanted to ask him to speak more slowly so we could read between his lines. The phrase "all is possible for us and nothing is sin" stayed in my head for many days. Immediately, the figure of Dimitri Karamazov came to me, who cynically summarized his idea of religion in the statement, "Because God does not exist, then everything is permitted." This extreme notion made me restless during a period when I was compulsively dedicated to philosophical reflections. Many years later, I realized that I was seeing in Padrinho's face the perfect incarnation of Staretz Zossima, the good monk from Dostoevsky's book, inverting the dangerous affirmation of a statement as daring as because God exists, for us everything is possible and nothing is sin. Far from preaching the same amoralism with a spiritual glaze, Padrinho wanted to say that there were no advantages for those who, in the name of any morality or goodness, avoid confronting the experiences that bring knowledge. In a simpler form, the old Mota cleared my doubt with a parable.

"The story of sin is that no one from that time understood the language of the common folk. Even today it may be hard to understand what foreigners are saying, but in those times it was even harder. Are they not discovering things to this day? Was it not a little while ago they discovered a new Gospel?"

"Are you talking about the Dead Sea Scrolls?" I asked. "There was a group living by the Dead Sea called the Essenes. They were similar to us, and the time they lived in also was similar. They were waiting for the Messiah and the end of time," I added.

"We came from far away, the spirit of the Daime came from far away. I am not a professor, but I know how to make a canoe. Many doctors cannot. I do. I enter the forest, I find a piece of wood, tap to see if it has been emptied by ants, make a bottom, and there I go to the other side of the igarapé. But the doctor, if he does not know how to swim, he has to stay on this side of the river. It is said that Buddha once visited a wise man who lived at the edge of a river. As he arrived, the man came and began to tell him all the knowledge he had accumulated meditating at the river's edge. Buddha asked, 'And what is there on the other side, on the other edge?' The wise man answered, 'This I do not know, I never went there.' Then Buddha said, 'You do not know much! You have lived so many years at the river's edge and never went to the other side to see what there is.' So it is, my friend. We think we know a lot, but God is the one who gives knowledge! When everyone realizes that materially speaking we are nothing, that all depends on the spirit, then one is really going to give value to oneself, no? Because dwelling only on the material level is mostly ignorance. Matter by itself has no value."

I would hear those words, take my notes, and check them against my own experience. The intention of Padrinho Sebastião's teachings was becoming clear in my heart, and through it, the clarity and simplicity of the doctrines of the Santo Daime, Juramidam, and Mestre Irineu.

Everything was coming together. The questions about good and evil opened the understanding that, on our own, we can gain access to the spirit and be shown the right use of mediumship. From there, we need only to study the nature of the superior self, how to awaken it among the other "illusory selves" that try to present themselves as if they were our true self. Whenever we are at home within ourselves and honor the superior self within us, it means that God's presence is shining on earth.

Satan's envy for God's place also made him envy men, God's living expression. Satan wanted to take over and dominate each one of us. Thus it happened on a cosmic level, since the time the Creator manifested himself. And so it continues to happen during the brief lifetime of each creature. Opposites in search of synthesis struggle in the universe and in ourselves.

After reaching the nature of our authentic inner being, we may remember in succession our previous incarnations. Padrinho Sebastião called them "memories of the past." Our main focus of inquiry into those memories should fall at the time when the Savior of humanity was incarnated among us and in other significant passages where this testimony was requested. Even when we do not have a retrospective vision of our past lives, we should learn to discern in present situations which behavioral patterns and mental conditionings should be avoided, because they are the fruits of bad karma previously acquired.

With more people finding themselves, finding the thread, we can wait for the fulfillment of the promise of the return of the messianic times, the return of Christ for his harvest. The true Kingdom is spiritual and internal but must also be proven in the material world. There is always the supposition that a generation, maybe even our own, will witness everything with their own eyes.

Remembering the past is a dive into the fog of spiritual memory, what the Theosophists call the "Akashic Records." Their function is to help us to reconstruct our journey, to attain the clarification and forgiveness that may still be missing for us to be ready for the appointment, what others call purification or the cleansing of Earth's crust.

Therefore, from the memories of the past, we go to the memories of the future, if we are still unclear of what we should be doing when the Messiah manifests. We have already heard in our heart the echo of this spiritual knowledge, which is eternal and can take us to the realization of our own Divine Being. We know what is to come because we have the spiritual memory of what has happened in other times: lost cities, the flood, the Essenes, the Incas. Each end, in reality, is a new beginning.

The time we now live in is the end of a great cycle, and the demands on us are, in many cases, greater than those of earlier times. Thus, the announcement of the reaping and harvesting and the separation between the chaff and the wheat. The "chaff" is going to be thrown into the fire of extinction, which results in death. Where love and knowledge prevail will be the "wheat," which will be saved in the silos of eternal life.

So let us now pass beyond the initial phases of spiritual experience, the gradual process of the breakdown of the ego, karma, personality, and the obstacles to character, until we arrive at the point of unification of the negative and positive and the transmutation of the inferior to the superior. Freeing and opening our medium channel, working on our perception and level of consciousness until we are able to separate the pure self from the others—then we are freed from the bonds of this materialistic time, so as to become more conscious of our incarnations. The "memories of the past" are, as it says in one of Padrinho's hymns, an attempt to justify or to repair our position in front of Christ, John the Baptist, and other characters of the great story.

We should focus our efforts to discern the future. The present is the prejudgment that prepares us for the final one. After the union of positive and negative, we can see our own light shine. This is the allegorical meaning expressed in Padrinho's hymn.

I live here in this world
I do not owe anything to anyone
I live in the land of God
Where he also dwells.

I live in the sun and in the moon
I light my candlesticks

I have a supreme life
As my Father does.

I live in the sun and in the moon
I light my candlesticks
Receive this as a present
Because it satisfies you.

If it satisfies you
Receive in the heart
This gift of love
Of my Lord Saint John.[4]

This is a synthesis of the spiritual doctrine of Sebastião Mota, which he never tired of repeating to us, with the rich and good-humored language of a forest native. It is a teaching of great esoteric significance to be developed as a true social science inside an enormous crucible: the community. But it is through spiritual rebirth that the foundation of the Kingdom is realized in each heart. Padrinho Sebastião insisted that we should always be conscious of who we are on earth, as in Heaven.

All of this is a long journey, maybe a trajectory for a whole lifetime of searching. The sacrament, Daime, is both a shortcut and a medicine. It shortens and clarifies things. It helps us find our spiritual identity. I remember the words of Padrinho Alfredo that without this realization "it is not worthwhile to have fear or courage on the subject."

As a medicine, the Daime acts in the form of light that illuminates our false consciousness, heals moral wounds, and rebuilds a serenity out of angst and obsessive recollections.

Spiritual rebirth is another cornerstone of Sebastião Mota's thought. He explained with the image of an unborn chick that has to have perseverance and strength to peck the eggshell and to put its head out. If what is alive does not break the shell of illusion, it does not participate in an authentic existence.

The invocation of Daime inside our being provokes a cleansing of ourselves, our inner temples. Then we are expelling the inner vagabonds accustomed to loitering there due to our weaknesses. Once such energies are expelled, the Daime strengthens our consciousness to deliver the rightful owner to the throne. Because God, as it says in one of the most important of Padrinho's hymns about this theme, gave a house for us to choose "those whom you find worthy."[5]

The most extraordinary thing of all is that this drink Mestre Irineu affirmed to have "an incredible power" not only generates an expansion of consciousness but amplifies our feelings, develops our devotion, and creates a sensation of a deeper and more integrated knowledge that harmonizes with all the levels of our being.

On the other side, the miração and the state of ecstasy give us a great power to evoke our previous incarnation and a new light that takes our soul back through the labyrinth of its old journey through the material world. When it does not give us a direct vision, it facilitates our understanding of patterns that we acquired in our previous incarnations. We become stronger in discerning how to act in our everyday life, avoiding the repetition of errors. The compulsion to repeat mistakes produces great spiritual stagnation and opens the door to many types of obsessions, neurotic patterns, and even psychotic distortions.

In the ritual, in the initiation, and during the many spiritual works that are opened in this sacred journey of the Daime, we learn to move with care the pieces on the board of the Divine game of life. Gradually, both our own being and our way of being in the world become attuned to the supreme harmonies that rule our spiritual evolution and its connection to the material world. The doctrine asks us to look inward and to realize outwardly through an approach that uses repentance and avoids guilt. The recognition of mistakes develops the capacity to forgive ourselves and others.

The paths and the options that the miração propose are deep visions that cannot be described in words. But miração is not static like meditation; it contains also a certain dynamic element. It is an ecstasy that holds us regardless of our will and one that we also are asked to direct. Because of all of this we consider the spiritual work developed by the Daime a sacred journey. It can free us from a lot of karma, but for that to happen, a great effort is necessary. The struggle for spiritual rebirth can be as painful as childbirth, but each newborn is a new light that shines and helps others to find themselves.

This is the mission the Divine Beings have presented in the sacred plants and are bringing forth at the end of the millennium. A light is coming from the forest, and we are stewarding its emergence, illuminating the way for those who are taking this shortcut. We do not want to offend, scandalize, or judge those who mistake a spiritual path, perhaps the oldest one of them all, with a hallucination or a psychotic state. But shortcuts do manifest themselves when time is short.

Much is said today about the end of time, but even of those who speak about it, few really believe in what they are saying. For us, the spiritual master present in the Daime, whom we invoke by the name Juramidam, speaks to us through the miração, which is His language, teaching us progressively to face this awaited meeting.

All who seek the same goal will one day see fulfilled their hopes of being freed from bondage to the physical plane alone. We will become intimately conscious of what is happening in the higher cosmic planes, beyond our familiar physical dimensions of existence.

This path, in the heart and mind of each one, is the inner landscape of the New Jerusalem that Padrinho Sebastião fought for his whole life and the quickening of the same quest of his disciples and afilhados. The forest is the external setting for the consecration of a people. The call for this gathering is not made with trumpets and fanfare. The clear sound may only be heard in the depths of our consciousness, and it takes a lot of attention to hear God's voice. As it is said in this hymn:

I am very small
But can be seen
I am the infinite
For those who perceive.[6]

Pablo C Amaringo
14.04.02

10

· · ·

Feitio

God's Will, Human Action

THE YEAR 1986 was a year of much apuro and balanço for the Daime people. A decree from the Division of Controlled Substances of the Brazilian Health Department included harmine and dimethyltryptamine (DMT) in the list of prohibited substances. The main alkaloids present in *Banisteriopsis caapi* and *Psychotria viridis* thus became "dangerous" substances. Dangerous to whom? Maybe to certain official concepts of civilization, especially to those concerning health, culture, and nature developed inside laboratories and pretending to understand from test tubes the phenomenological complexity of sacred plants used in a ritualized context.

The suspect substances had their alkaloids posted with rewards offered, much in the same way that famous outlaws have their photographs advertised on "wanted" posters. With this kind of focus and approach, the problem becomes more political and legal than social and ethnographic. Luckily, even after this sudden inclusion of the components of the Santo Daime sacramental drink on the list, good sense prevailed in the Federal Council on Narcotics. The department in charge of legislation in these areas and the police looked the other way.

The prohibition, even if not enforced, again raised the stigma for the Daime people of being a "drug cult" and brought back concerns we had not had since the time when the two other commissions visited Rio do Ouro in 1982 and Mapiá in 1984. The final reports of both commissions emphasized the seriousness of the ongoing spiritual work in the community, its fitness and productivity. As a result, the commissions made positive recommendations regarding Santo Daime to the military authorities, the government of Acre, and academic institutions, with the hope that the issue of recognition would be finally resolved.

But in 1986 the government's approach to ayahuasca churches changed with the creation by the Confen of a study group, presided over by Dr. Domingos Bernardo, with the goal of doing field and interdisciplinary research at the many communities and centers that used the sacred drink.

The bureaucratic ruling that included harmine and dimethyltryptamine among the substances considered illegal needed a scientific and phytochemical foundation, as there is for cocaine, heroin, and other illegal substances. The prohibition had been based on vague bibliographic references and pressure from a certain antidrug lobby, with its prejudice, paranoia, and confusion.

Furthermore, this sudden inclusion of the ingredients of the vine and the leaf in the category of the forbidden or controlled substances was unprecedented and explicitly biased. Even if they were, by themselves, considered dangerous substances to the physical and mental health of those who used them, not one study had been made until then about the resulting concoction of the vine of *Banisteriopsis caapi* and the leaf of *Psychotria viridis*.

Precisely at that moment, the most recent chemical research around the world was uncovering much significant data. One of the most curious characteristics of DMT is that it is not active orally due to the action of the enzyme known as monoamine oxidase (MAO), which is present in human tissues. The group known as beta-carbolines (harmine and harmaline, which are present in the vine) temporarily inhibits this enzyme, making DMT orally active. But this activity becomes regulated by each human organism. The strong emetic effect of the drink prevents extreme intoxication or any harm from long-term usage. Everyone in the Daime community knows the impossibility of drinking it in quantities larger than the regular ritual dose.

The studies remove much confusion, even for opponents hiding behind chemical and neurochemical arguments. Every serious study in this area unanimously agrees that this drink has incredible power. It cannot be analyzed without cultural and anthropological considerations because both mind and culture are important factors in the transformation of the drink's biochemical effects into ecstatic and transcendent revelation. There are beneficial effects on personal and social levels. The old term *hallucinogenic plants* is giving way to more appropriate ones such as *power plants* or *sacred plant teachers*. These terms recognize that these plants open a doorway and mediate the energy of Divine Beings. This age-old tradition probably developed in many parts of the world, but in the Amazon has enjoyed an unbroken tradition.

Archaeological research in Ecuador revealed that these plants were already being used in religious ceremonies at least three thousand years before Christ. Many clay artifacts have been found in an ancient archaeological site, including decorated small cups for the ceremonial ingestion of a drink. This allows us to suppose that a version of ayahuasca, a sacred drink of some kind, was received in a ceremonial form by the gods, goddesses, and guardians of people in remote times as the myths attest.

All of this is enshrouded in deep mystery. How could the ancient shamans have discovered, among many thousands of species of plants, nearly a hundred that are psychoactive. Could spiritual revelation be a factor? Science had to follow in the tracks left by the accounts of adventurers and explorers, who preceded the ethnographers and botanists, to research the chemical composition of these plants and their powerful effects on the human psyche. In the case of ayahuasca, this question becomes even more disconcerting, because it is a drink made of two different plants. Their combination potentializes and harmonizes the active principles contained in each, delivering to the celebrant an ecstatic experience *sui generis*.

In spite of the absence of historical records, there are legends of ayahuasca use by the Inca Empire. If the Incas did not receive this Divine gift in their pharmacological pantheon directly from their own predecessors, it was certainly through the course of the empire's evolution, expansion, and assimilation of other peoples that it came to them. The first time the term *ayahuasca* was recorded in Western history was by two Jesuits in the eighteenth century, who described it as the *Devil's Drink*. They mentioned its use in certain rituals of South American indigenous people and believed that it caused them to lose their minds.

Today we live in a world of vivid contrasts. Religion and science present different faces of the same reality, and they alternate between periods of peace and conflict. Earlier religious dogmas overshadowed scientific knowledge, lighting the Inquisition's fires to prosecute heresies. Now we encounter a new myth: the scientific paradigm wearing an almost papal infallibility and judging arbitrarily the rediscovery of an ancient spiritual and religious consciousness through the ritual use of sacred plants. But reclaiming the science of our own ancestors may well be a solution for the crisis on planet earth at the end of the millennium.

Civilization has led us to the point where the political power machine and the electronic media transform millions of human beings into automatons, consumers manipulated by their own desires and habits, preyed on by advertising and media agencies. People live out their lives with a few basic concepts and some abstract assurances. Ideas of citizenship are stereotyped, and there are few examples of noble and idealistic behavior to follow. Padrinho Sebastião, in his simplicity, would not have had difficulty analyzing this scenario: Satan is loose in the world! When the inferior nature is not integrated within each of us, the end result on a planetary level is chaos, visible evil, and hopelessness. Plagues, wars, and epidemics seem to drive us to further pollution, social insanity, and ultimately the death of the planet.

The myth of science lives with all of this in a dubious manner. Some well-intentioned political activists join the fray because they are able to identify some aspect of the evil at large, but very few have what it takes to diagnose evil found inside oneself. To do this demands direct experience and self-knowledge. Padrinho Sebastião said that "the wise man is one who can control his own great beast."

If science does not spiritualize itself, the result will be a materialistic, all-powerful scientific council hovering over the spiritual consciousness of the new world. True spirituality will have to overcome stifling dogmatism in a new disguise.

A new spiritual vision needs to be created. If what we call science, and its progeny, the information age, are spiritually bankrupt and unable to help in this latest turn of human events, we will have small chance of reaching a positive end. It is necessary to put brakes on those branches of knowledge and technology that rape and dissect nature with the intent of extracting from natural laws new bellicose and lucrative applications. If this new spiritual option is not brought forward, many problems await us in the material world, hyperspace, or the ethereal planes, where Divine justice has jurisdiction as well.

The systematic denial of opening intuitively to the new spiritual knowledge that rises to meet us is a kind of scientific arrogance that quickly shows the limitations of our current paradigm. It is like a servant who works with devotion and is able to ascend the ladder until he is the top administrator but never owns the business. He who worries only about external things is unable to own the genuine spiritual realization, which is always simultaneously both internal and external.

Sebastião Mota always insisted on the necessity of being oneself, never pretending to be what one is not. A knowledge that merely imitates a lack of spiritual truth. It is a mimetic knowledge that never arrives at the inward understanding of the truth, nor the meaning of the gifts God bestows on all his creation.

Nature, mind, and cosmos were, until today, unknown oceans through which the new argonauts of the spirit travel in search of the golden fleece. All that humankind has up to now understood, conceptualized, and created has come from three spiritual sources, "springs," as stated in João Pereira's hymn.

> *From the three noble springs*
> *I have a lot to tell*
> *A King and a Queen*
> *And an Imperial Prince.*[1]

Nature is the first and most exploited of these "noble springs" and the one that has suffered most the effects of human conquest. The disrespect of cosmic laws, upon which life on many levels depends, set in motion irreversible processes and destroyed precious life-forms that will never again be known by humankind. Some put their faith in great spaceships that will evacuate the planet at the decisive moment, but for others the solution is to be found in a process of transformation of consciousness. Individuals grounded in their own spiritual experience must begin to prepare for what is coming.

An institutional solution on a planetary scale does not seem possible anymore. What is left is a deep dive down to the roots of being to repossess the ancient forms of community and solidarity in the hope that the seeds of the new spiritual and ecological life can germinate and bear fruits on this earth. Thus it would begin, this new world so much talked about, the birth of which will depend on a great purification, and a gradual modification of the relationship between the physical, astral, and etheric bodies. Confronting such a serious issue as the formation of a new spiritual consciousness, we hark back to ancestral sciences: power plants that can help us both unveil the past and prepare for the future, providing a priceless service to humanity in this frightful period of transition.

In the past decade, many scientists and researchers, following in the steps of the great English naturalist Richard Spruce, have given due reverence to the most complex and fascinating ecosystem in the world, the Amazon. Their intent has been to study the potentialities of the sacred plants in general, ayahuasca, yage, or Daime in particular. These plants, which the hymn calls "the teacher of all teachers," have so much to teach us.[2]

I remembered Rio do Ouro on the occasion of the first visit from the commission that came to study the Daime phenomenon. The commission had agreed to a series of visits to Santo Daime churches and communities located in the south of the country and in the Amazon. I was to accompany the commission.

In Rio Branco, they participated in the works at the União do Vegetal, Alto Santo, and Colônia 5,000. After that, we flew to Boca do Acre, and there we rented canoes to take us to Céu do Mapiá. Again destiny had united so many people of different backgrounds—legislators, psychologists, psychiatrists, anthropologists, and federal narcotics officers—all going to make contact with the sacred drink, the doctrine, and the Daime people.

The day before our trip, in my bed at Hotel Rosa do Acre, I was remembering the words of the old Mota when he received the pioneer commission in 1982, "You did not come here to know me, because I already know myself. You came here to know yourselves." The heat in the hotel was intense, the fan made a noise like a helicopter, and it was difficult to decide which was worse, the noise or the heat. I walked to the front porch at the end of the hotel to look at the tropical view—the merging of the Acre and the Purus Rivers, which many days downstream merge with the Amazon. With each trip this landscape was becoming more familiar: the riverbanks, the city lights, and the houses on poles. I was surrounded by the most beautiful and exuberant forest in the world: the Garden of Eden, the sacred laboratory where its ancient inhabitants learned the secret of the plants that speak to our consciousness.

Direct contact with the community and the Daime would influence the decision of the council more than the results of their methodical studies. Before initiating this field research, the Confen temporarily revoked the government proposition to pass a regulation on the psychoactive substances in the vine and the leaf, and leaving the final decision to be made after the conclusion and recommendations of the work group.

Early in the morning, our three canoes left Boca do Acre. Before noon we arrived at the mouth of the Igarapé Mapiá, where after a small stop we continued upstream, taking advantage of high water to arrive at the village still in daylight. The commission's visit would coincide also with the realization of a great Daime Feitio, including delegations from other states.

At the end of the afternoon we arrived at the village pier, near Padrinho's big house. The new bridge was already up right in the place where the Igarapé Mapiá meets the Repartição. Much to our dismay, as soon as we put our feet on the ground, we discovered that Padrinho was suffering from one of his strongest crises yet. The old man, in addition to his cardiac insufficiency, continued to be a sensitive medium, and sometimes his body would succumb to the weight of emotions and tensions inevitable during the Feitios.

During the first day, I led the members of the Confen on a tour of the village. We were a long time in the Casa do Feitio, where the Daime is prepared, and they asked many questions about its preparation. At their request, we resolved to speed up the construction of the place so they could see the beginning of the Feitio. That night I went to Padrinho's room to see if he was in a condition to receive me.

He greeted me as warmly as ever, but I was shocked by his condition. His eyes, which usually shone with life, were somewhat clouded, and in spite of the effort to smile, his expression was showing the stress of many difficult nights of vigil. I asked for his blessings and wished him improvement. He asked about my family and about the brothers and sisters he knew from the community at Mauá. The effort seemed to tire him, and I did not want to prolong the conversation.

He coughed some, got up with difficulty, and held on to a wooden bar secured above his head to assist his breathing. His life was reduced to the stoic forbearance of his suffering. When the suffocating feeling increased, he would hold on to that wooden bar, breathing deeply and dilating his lungs. When he felt better, he would sit in a wide armchair full of pillows. It was like this that he slept, sitting with his head supported by the pillows, while we stood guard so that his small rest was not disturbed. Through these hours, everyone would approach the room on tiptoe to ask about the patriarch's health.

Despite this tense mood, the day of the Santo Daime Feitio was arriving. It is perhaps the most important and festive ritual of the community, and practically everyone is mobilized to make the sacramental drink that is consumed on the occasions of calendric festivities, *concentração,* and healing works. For the Feitio, a great unity is necessary among the members of the community. It is tradition to say that when the enormous pot is put on the fire, all the questions and all the problems are being cooked, transmuted, and resolved inside it.

The commission's members, especially the federal police, were very curious to learn about the details of the production and distribution of Daime to all outposts. We explained that the work was practically uninterrupted for the men in charge of the search and collection of the material. Many days are spent walking through the forest to locate the "kingdom": natural gardens, in which grow great amounts of the vine and the leaf used in the preparation of the drink. Sometimes the search is based on concrete information from someone who knows the species employed; or the indication is given by nature herself, by the type of vegetation and soil, or by the intuition of those who go to the forest. Under the effect of the Daime and in harmony with the forest, it often happens that these men are "directed" to the vine and the leaf. In some cases, luck and chance also intervene, as when I took part in one expedition in 1983. The old truck broke down in the middle of the road that goes to Xapuri. When we pulled over, there on the other side of the road we saw the braiding of many branches of many *jagube* plants, *Banisteriopsis caapi,* reaching up into the jungle canopy.

In the old days, the searching and collecting was done simultaneously. A large group would go to the forest with some reference, only returning when they had obtained the number of bags desired. Progressively everything became more complex. First, the areas with large amounts of jagube and *rainha, Psychotria viridis,* were becoming more scarce due to systematic collection and deforestation for the big farms. In addition, the growth of the Daime community with added centers called for a progressive increase in production. To meet this demand, the system of cooking the Santo Daime passed through many modifications, with the goal of taking the most advantage of the evermore scarce material. It was discovered that the same piece of vine could be cooked many times and still produce a Daime with the same strength and light as that prepared by the first cooking.

In 1986 the Eternal Daime Project, as named by Padrinho Alfredo, began so that we would not lack our sacrament through difficult times. The search parties started going out beforehand, and the production, storage, and consumption of the Daime was planned and vigorously controlled. Each center would announce its needs for the fulfillment of the official calendar of works and gather the amount of money necessary to pay for the expenses, being responsible for bookkeeping and recording the activities of storage and consumption of each liter that was entrusted to them.

The contributions obtained by each church are periodically sent, in accordance with the project's necessities, to subsidize the acquisition of equipment (canoes, motors, gear for the forest, pots, etc.) as well as the fuel, food, and maintenance of the group. A percentage of the cost of the Feitios is applied toward the replanting of jagube and rainha, as a precaution against the times when the sacred plants will be even more scarce.

In August 1986, we were ready to begin the festivities. The carpenters were putting the finishing touches on the house. The group members of the Confen were asking questions and taking photographs. We went to the pier to receive the canoes with the material. The jagube came cut in bundles of 120-centimeter pieces and the leaves in large bags. The men were tired, having carried bundles and bags as heavy as fifty kilos from the point where it was collected to the canoes, sometimes more than an hour's hard walk through the forest. This is without saying anything about the difficulty of recognizing the right kind of vine and leaf, because there are many similar species, which only an experienced person can discern with certitude.

The Feitio is a ceremony rich with spiritual symbolism. It is the biggest test and the most eloquent testimony of cultural strength and the purity of the ritual of the Santo Daime doctrine. It is a ritual in which is relived the origins of the indigenous people who to this day inhabit occidental Amazonia. The Feitio is the production of our sacrament.

It was very important for the Feitio to be happening in the presence of all researchers in order to make a strong case for the legitimacy and legality of the ritual drink, which some members of the health department suspected to be a potent and dangerous hallucinogen.

A celebration and an initiatory rite for the production of the sacrament, the Feitio demands of all the participants great physical, mental, and spiritual fitness. The Feitio corresponds completely to the category of an initiation ritual, in which knowledge is passed on in a progressive form and in accordance with the capacity of each participant for surrender and assimilation. In it the search for the perfection of the process leads to the realization of spiritual perfection. The dexterity, intelligence, memory, and technical precision collectively required for a successful Feitio are also the same skills essential in each individual.

There are many stages in the process: localization, harvest, transportation, washing, examination, scraping, pounding, cooking, and the final apuração of the Santo Daime. Each one of these phases demands familiarity with certain techniques that help to perfect the beauty and efficiency of the works, and each is related to the development of certain gifts, qualities, and attributes that need to be learned from those who are more experienced, so that the Daime produced will bring much strength and light, completing itself in the miração, the personal transformation that began with the Feitio.

Each stage of the process completes itself in sequence, and the end goal is harmony and the perfection of the works. The Feitio is spiritual alchemy through excellence. In it, we are the makers of the sacramental vehicle for the beings of nature and the cosmic powers to manifest as the expression of Divine Love that they are.

While we are making this material vehicle, we are re-creating ourselves as well, through the many initiatory stages, from the material to the spiritual and back again. For those who work with Daime, the inner work necessarily accompanies the outer. Everyone has to come to terms with and develop a high standard of efficiency, responsibility, solidarity, abnegation, and loyalty during the work. Everyone feels strongly about not harboring resentments and bad thoughts about other brothers and sisters while the pans are over the fire, because these vibrations penetrate into the drink, and the disharmony can be felt in the miração.

In the big room where the Daime is cooked, total silence is demanded as well as concentration and a high level of consciousness in each movement and gesture. When the vibrations are high, the work unfolds in a harmonious dance. The inner and outer worlds are superimposed without duality. We are obliged to function with precision in the body, while receiving the revelation with the spirit. He who keeps himself within this flow sees with clairvoyance, communicating through thoughts and understanding from intuition.

The only thing one hears is the boiling and the vapors escaping from the pans. It was in a time like that in a Feitio that Mestre Irineu must have sung his hymn.

> *I call the vine*
> *I call the leaf*
> *I call water*
> *To unite and come to show me.*[3]

The result of this union is something more than the drink. Something more than the effects of certain alkaloids on our nervous system. The power that acts over our consciousness is also the same power through which we can realize this Being that is expressed through our own perfection.

The more we give of ourselves in this surrender to the Divine, in trying to overcome our barriers and limitations, the greater is the grace we receive in the miração. The Divine Force, expressed on the physical level through the effect of the alkaloids on our brain chemistry, produces an energy that facilitates our consciousness to reach the spiritual reality, the highest and most subtle levels of perception. Over the fire the molecules of the sacred drink are released. In the same way in the heart's fire we are asked to grow in love and skill in search of the greatest perfection possible in everything. This is the essence of the initiation rite of the Feitio.

Being initiated is not like receiving a diploma that you hang on your wall. It only happens when a real goal is achieved in the physical and the spiritual simultaneously—on earth as it is in Heaven. Because of that, a new form of consciousness and spiritual knowledge sprouts from the greatest depth of our existence and stays indefinitely in our being. It is a light that sprouts from the source of the superior self that will guide us until the end of the search.

The members of the commission observed the work with a lot of attention, but they certainly could not perceive the real significance of many things they were seeing: the secret, the spiritual treasure that Christ said was open to all who are peaceful and humble in their hearts. Those with these traits will always see, regardless of their form or name. If our visitors believed they woud find something similar to cocaine production, even the little that they could understand was sufficient to destroy this suspicion. What is made in the Feitio is the pure and genuine alchemy of a sacrament.

There are many symbolic phases in a Feitio. It starts in desolated silent places of the forest, when the vines are cut with reverence under the attentive gaze of all the elemental, enchanted, and invisible beings who are their guardians. Transported over great distances, the plants arrive at their destination in bundles, which are cut again in equal pieces measuring a hand and a half. Some tribes justify this procedure by saying that the miração gets evenly distributed to all.

The leaves of *Psychotria viridis* are spread out in an airy shaded place. Then they are examined one by one by the women to remove any impurities such as small animals, cocoons, and so forth, in a process called *catação*. They are then carefully washed and taken in big drums to the place where they will be mixed in the pans with the macerated jagube.

The pieces of the vine also receive careful cleaning by the men in a process called *raspação*. With a pocketknife or a wooden spatula, every part of the vine is cleaned, especially its folds. If the vine is too thick, it is unbraided so that its center also gets cleaned. It is necessary to be careful not to hurt the bark, which contains the highest concentration of the active principle. Some of the tribes that drink ayahuasca use only the bark, not the whole vine. In these phases, the catação of the leaves and raspação of the vine, dexterity and patience are necessary. While the hands work quickly, the mind has to keep a thought pattern of high quality. The point of the knife called self-discernment should run through our minds as well, liberating us from impure thoughts, so that we can approach the cauldron of Divine Alchemy.

Before daybreak, the cleaned vine is taken to the Casa de Bateção. There twelve men partake of the Daime and sit in front of tree stumps. With a wooden mallet weighing around two kilos, they begin pounding the vine on top of the stumps in a process called *bateção*. This work can take hours depending on the amount of material to be cooked that day. This phase demands, especially for the neophytes, the breaking through of one's own limits. The physical effort demanded is great, even for someone used to the process. The bateção has to be accomplished with the same rhythm, the tempo of which is given by the lead singer. The mallets are raised and lowered in unison while the hymns are sung. Through our own physical effort and the need to empty the mind to do the work, we feel the great responsibility to remain calm.

The internal discipline demanded by the bateção is for one who has already examined his impurities and scrutinized the vices of his mind. Now it is the time of firmness, perseverance, renouncement, and sacrifice to consecrate the transformation and pass through the most difficult part of the journey. We put on top of the stump to be macerated all our negative side upon which we have meditated and analyzed during the raspação. The mallet goes down, the sweat drips, and our respiration becomes difficult.

In one hymn that tells of King Jagube being massaged, the *batedores* are the blacksmiths of the Divine foundry. The stumps are the anvil where the hot metal is shaped. The vine starts to lose its fibers, and these fibers are also the fibers of our being.

At sunrise, the sacred plant is macerated, reduced to small pieces of fiber and dust. The matter is sacrificed to facilitate a transmutation. The ego is broken not in a metaphor as in other initiations but by the mallet. Under the weight of the mallet's impact, our "vine being" is macerated on top of the stump until the rhythm diminishes our doubts, fears, sins, and guilt. All the dust on the floor of the Casa da Bateção is the ashes of the Phoenix, and in the cooking we are reborn purified. We then also understand that when we are enjoying the beauty of the miração, that brothers and sisters are making an enormous physical effort for that to happen.

The pans are filled, alternating layers of vine and leaf. Vine, leaf, water, and fire are the physical agents in this sacred vehicle, the Daime. To it we give our best energy and vibrations. We work hard. The fruit of our effort impregnates the liquid in the same way that we are impregnated by the vibrations of the spiritual Being that inhabits the vine and the leaves of the forest.

The Divine alchemy is realized during the cooking of the Santo Daime. The material from the day before will be cooked now, while the catação of the leaves and raspação of the jagube begin to be readied again for more bateção the following night. The workers drink herbal tea, eat roots, and rest, while those in charge of firewood come to split the wood needed for the day.

In the furnace room stay only those responsible for the cooking and apuração of the Daime. This phase demands total attention and concentration. With big wooden forks called *gambitos* in hand, they watch the boiling, giving instructions to the fire-tender and performing many maneuvers, making sure that the boiling vine does not spill, burn, or pass the point of readiness.

The pans are cooked down and the liquid replenished in a synchronized choreography. The gestures are precise and the words few. The attention is total so there will be no confusion or mistakes. The cooking continues, and the material is recombined and recooked, resulting in a process of many degrees in which the Daime yield is maximized.

Night falls and the stars twinkle. They are the same stars that twinkled for the Mayans and Aztecs above their pyramids. They were present at the Feitios held by the Inca and at the time when the forest covered almost the whole American continent.

The Casa do Feitio is transformed by the miração into a golden temple. Time is suspended, and the past is remembered. For a moment, I saw a furnace inside a crystal pyramid, and the next moment the scene changed to ancient Atlantis. This is the same drink used millions of years ago, the source of all knowledge of forest people, and there is a secret inside it. We hear in the silence the echoes of an ancient past and remember who we are, following the instructions and signs we find it inside our own selves.

The flames tremble in the furnace. Those responsible for the making of the sacred liquid examine the level of the liquid in the pans with a wooden fork. One of the pans needs to be *suspirada* (aired). With the fork he brings up the fibers from the bottom of the pan, using his knee as a lever. Sometimes he will lift the fibers in the copper-colored boiling liquid until he can see the liquid boiling just above the fibers. Stopping longer at the last pan, he presses gently with his fork and smells the vapors. Everyone is concentrated around the vapors in a mysterious and magical mood.

After a period that varies between a second and an eternity, in accordance with the miração, the person in charge knocks three times with his fork at the edge of the pan, calling the sun, moon, and stars. Two men approach silently, one on each side of the furnace. They pass a cord through each of the pan's handles, cross them with a long piece of wood, and lift. While the flames from the fire rise up, everyone sings, "All this mystery / In the pan exists."

The pans are taken to be drained. Now silence and concentration are broken only by the noise of the pan being turned while someone else on the other side holds the pulp with a wooden tool. At this point it is impossible to think of this liquid as a drug, and not a Divine sacrament.

All of this happened that night in the presence of the Confen members who were sent to give an opinion about the ritual use of the Daime. While the Feitio was in progress and the furnace being tended under the direction of Padrinho Mario, we were listening to the hymn.

All this mystery
In the pan exists
This is a secret
That only my Father gives.

This is the science
Bigger than this there is none
This is the power
And who wishes may come forth.

The Master told me to say
That everyone must listen
Some power bigger than the fire
I doubt it exists.

The Daime which brought
It is for all to contemplate
For he is leaf, vine, and water
Plus the fire that is there.

All the wonders
That boil in the vine
It is thanks to the fire
There from the second floor.

Inside the furnace
There is an underground kingdom
I asked permission and went in
Even inside our Divine Mother.

To her I give thanks for
All this remembrance
Her car will pass again
And I want to be in the front.[4]

11

...

The Spiritual Rebirth

THE MEMBERS OF the Confen commission departed very impressed with everything they had witnessed, felt, and learned. Once more, with God's blessings, the authorities who visited us left as friends, both parties benefiting mutually from an intense time together. Padrinho Sebastião was feeling a bit better, and we decided to use the excuse of the last crisis to take him to Rio de Janeiro for medical exams. But when the canoes carried the guests away, many events were still to happen in that Feitio. Without a doubt the main event and the strongest of them all was the passage of Padrinho Mario Rogerio da Rocha.

Padrinho Sebastião was so advanced spiritually that, in spite of his great simplicity, we dared inflict our grossest doubts and hesitations on him. Padrinho Mario was my confidant, and the person with whom I shared the most on a personal basis. At his "headquarters" in Rio Branco, he listened to our silliness, mediated our conflicts and ego clashes, helped couples to reconcile, and gave us valuable advice.

His spiritual philosophy was founded on giving of oneself as an example. He did not like to lecture or defend the principles of the doctrine. He would say that "nobody indoctrinates anybody." Only when the truth is mirrored in a person's actions can it be understood and emulated. As in the story of the Abbot Poemao who lived in an isolated community in the desert and was asked by a younger priest: "Some brothers are living with me, do you want me to govern them?" The old man answered, "Not in any way. You give them the example first, and, if they desire thus to live, they will put the lessons in practice by themselves." But the brother responded, "Abbot, they are the ones wanting me to govern them." The old man still answered, "No. Become an example, not a legislator."

It was in this way that Padrinho Mario conducted his life. Our attention was always awakened by the way he acted when confronted by each spiritual question that was presented to him. My sadness was so deep when old Mario left his body on that sunny morning of August 4, 1986, in the middle of the Feitio, while the pans over the fire were cooking with all that intensity. His liver had borne, since young adulthood, many malaria attacks as well as hepatitis, and in the last years the crisis had worsened. Nevertheless, his death process was so sudden that it almost went unnoticed. The day before he got sick, he came to the Casa da Batação and passed the day with us while preparing the Daime. At night, at the end of the work day, we sat on a stump under a jagube plant and he told me a secret, reconfirming a talk we had had long ago when he received me as a son. As he bade me good night, he said, "It was only today that I truly saw that God's creation is really perfect and marvelous. I have no doubt, thank God; everything is happening just as it is supposed to."

At the time I did not see any further meaning in what he said. It was after what happened that I understood his words and demeanor to pertain to the intense moment of farewell. That day he told me about his mission and my mission, that they were complementary. If a mission is genuinely spiritual, he said, it automatically complements the others. There is only one mission.

Two days later, I woke full of presentiments. I arose with a strong urge to go to the house where Padrinho Mario was lodged. On the way, my uneasiness increased when I crossed paths with someone who was already going to the village to call the doctor.

I arrived in time to see him take his last breath. We even put a couple of drops of Daime on his lips but his consciousness had already detached from his body. The women began to sing the hymns of the Mass.

It is difficult to evaluate the intent of men of great knowledge concerning their passage, the last "power dance." I do believe that they offer themselves to be harvested, and that this voluntary act is far from the inverted narcissism of suicide. On the contrary, it is the height of the teaching of radical charity, a conscious agreement with destiny when it presents itself in an incontestable form. Besides this secret, Padrinho Mario took also with him a lot of the spiritual weight that had been producing illness.

Many days after the Feitio was finished, almost at the time for our departure, we met at the Star House for the final meeting and Padrinho Alfredo's evaluation of the results of our works.

"In spite of it all, I am happy with the results of the Feitio, and I hope you are, too. We shall be evermore attentive so that the next Daime will have double the force. Until then, let's give strength to our thoughts, body, and spirit. This key to knowledge is inside all of us, and it is also contained in this liquid that we made and in all that nature created. The greater our surrender, the greater the knowledge in the sacrament and in us. If we do not know how to surrender—and thus how to penetrate— we see everything and know nothing. Because the Feitio for us finalizes everything; Feitio means God's will and human action."

"The men from the commission left satisfied," I added.

"Truth is true to itself as is the Divine Being. There are truths deeper than the ones the commission perceived, but there were moments when they were perceiving many things about us also. The miração does not deny anything to anyone, and if we present something, we have to do so correctly for the Daime to be seen as it is in the astral, and thus to be respected without problems. My father and I are at peace. Man's law also has its place, and if they make it possible to allow the Daime to be put in these terms, it is because God wants it in those terms."

"But at the same time, the lawmakers need to understand at least some of what they have already seen without confusing it with drug use and hallucinogens," I said.

"Yes. We have to be prepared and believe in ourselves and in what we are saying, helping the spirits to heal. The police and the law may want to take the Daime, examining, detaining, even prohibiting. But this is a limited prohibition. Everyone has to know that they are holding the Divine in their own existence, with their own example. The law sees, respects, and feels the power of our people when we are one. Thus it is in us, in our hearts, in accordance with the law, everything correct, with no mistakes. Keep on following our consciousness and the truth, because this is the main law and once it is accomplished everything else comes."

It was getting close to the time to leave. I asked everyone to go to the field next to the Star House for a last farewell to Padrinho Mario. Padrinho Alfredo spoke, "When the commission left, Padrinho Mario thought about traveling with them to Rio Branco, but in the last minute, he came to my room and said that he was not going, saying he would stay to go on the last train." We who were going to travel surrounded the grave in silence and great emotion. Padrinho Alfredo continued, "Under this sun that shines on us all, we are here to say our good-byes to Seu Mario Rogerio, present in spirit, on the seventh day of his passage. We ask of his spirit, now dwelling in the Divine, harvested here among us in the middle of the Feitio at Céu do Mapiá, to keep helping us spiritually in the same way that he always helped us while he was alive. This is because we who lived with Seu Mario know how much he helped us and the weight he bore in his own home receiving all sorts of people. Spiritually he continued to have contact with this circle of which he had been part and continued to give us spiritual guidance. In talking about Seu Mario, I am talking about the Feitio, because he was an essential part of it, was he not?

"Because our Feitio was marked by the passage of Seu Mario Rogerio da Rocha," he continued, "the memory of this beloved being is in our hearts and in the Daime that we will drink when we get to our homes. We pray for a lot of tranquillity and happiness so that we can move forward in our Project Eternity, our Eternal Santo Daime. Thank you, Alex. Thanks to everyone here present. I ask the people to be ever stronger in everything they undertake, and soon we will be together again, in the south, with Padrinho as well."

Then it was my turn. After the final thank you, I limited myself to asking for a minute of silence and for us to sing Padrinho Sebastião's hymn that was Seu Mario's favorite. Full of emotion, we all sang:

> *My brothers and my sisters*
> *Please start unraveling yourselves*
> *I am small and I keep my word.*
> *I'm showing my truth.*[1]

It was confirmed that Padrinho Mario had taken with him some of the negativity causing Padrinho Sebastião's illness. Slowly, the old Mota was recovering from the serious phase of the crisis and, after a lot of insistence on our part, he agreed to travel to Rio Branco to see a doctor. He spent a couple of weeks in the hospital and then traveled to the south for better medical assistance. Along the way Padrinho visited many churches and communities that, although separated by almost five thousand kilometers, were close to his heart. We walked by the ocean, in the mountains, through new and unknown landscapes, but we knew that nothing could replace for him his beloved forest.

In February 1987, after he had recovered, we accompanied him back to Mapiá. A group of almost fifty people traveled with him by riverboat from Rio Branco to Boca do Acre. The old man was lodged on the top deck. The commander had to insist energetically that not everyone go up on the second floor, because of the risk of overturning the boat, but people kept creeping up to stay by his side. His favorite theme then was life in the city. He loved meeting so many new afilhados, but his opinion about the multitudes that lived "on top of big buildings" was not as cheerful. He complained, "My God, everybody squeezed in drawers one on top of the other . . . they only know how to go places by car, even to the corner store. They do not know how to walk anymore . . . they buy everything in a so-called supermarket and cultivate absolutely nothing. How can it work? I do not know any legume that will grow in asphalt. The sand of Copacabana Beach is not like the sand on the Puru River, where everything grows. When the hard time comes, many will cry, 'Help me God!'"

Everybody was laughing at Padrinho's stories as the old boat was making the curve toward the beach at Boca do Acre. The setting sun would show up once to the right, then to the left, in front or behind the boat, due to the great curves the river made. Again, I immersed myself in reflections and meditations. This last Feitio and the passage of Padrinho Mario closed a circle for the Daime people. The expansion of the doctrine, the fight for legalization of our sacrament, our material organization, all of this was a new challenge for us.

Organizing this spiritual and material group seemed more complex every day. It was necessary to overcome many attachments, the most difficult ones being related to the conveniences and illusions of the "modern world." Sometimes I felt Padrinho challenging me, testing my surrender and detachment, demanding of me a decisive action in our move to the forest. Other times he was the one to ponder, to ask for patience, and to hold our excitement. He would say we had still a lot to do in the south. Everything was happening quickly, and we needed to focus to prevent being dominated by faults or by misplaced excessive courage.

When we were with him in this forest, which was his element, he made an effort to satisfy our smallest desires, but he did not like when someone would not take the next spiritual step, trying to escape in the name of comfort and attachments. In these hours he would say, "Ah! My son, if you do not get used to making everything simpler from now on, you will suffer a lot. If you stay, it will catch up with you, and, if you run, it will certainly eat you. Better not to run away—at least you do not tire yourself and can face the beast with more of a chance. In the Scriptures, Jonah was eaten by a whale because he was running from the instructions God had given him, was it not so? He was lucky because the big fish had indigestion and spat him out."

During this two-day trip, I was evaluating all the transformational processes that were boiling inside my being. I dreamed frequently of the Feitio, pans boiling and almost overflowing. The idea of spiritual rebirth, the theme Padrinho Sebastião repeated each time with more emphasis, tormented me. The torment was not unlike the tempest that surprised Jonah, throwing him into the water as a sacrifice to save his crew. So was my own personal boat oscillating in torment, to follow or not God's will. I had to differentiate, through correct inner discernment, all obsessions and illusions that get mixed in with desires and fantasies. In some moments, I felt with extreme clarity the rudder of my ship given to the control of the superior self. In others, egotistical motivations and vanity were too evident, and I confronted these intruders that attempted to take command. As the boat taking us up the river swung and swayed trying to hold its course, I perceived how completely all experience was metaphor.

Some of these intruders were easily recognizable, and their unscrupulous intentions were so clear that it did not take much effort to avoid them. Others though, entered into the inner sanctum, tiptoeing with dignity and a solemn posture. They tried to disguise themselves as the superior self, and it was difficult to recognize their true intention, so great were the mental subtleties and the feelings of false consolation they like to inspire. Diacone, a bishop in the fifth century, affirmed that true compassion manifests when someone has an ardent recollection through God's love, taking that experience even deeper into His indescribable love. False compassion produces in the sufferer a light sleep, a dullness of body and soul and a veiled recollection of God. Thus the result is a state of indecision and disoriented happiness that comes from the liar within, a marked contrast to the clarity and indescribable happiness of true compassion.

Everything is subtler in the inner world. The biggest danger is to be induced by our self-pity into a trance of complacency. We feel our difficulties and suffering are unique and under this pretext want to exclude ourselves from a greater surrender and transformation. The latter will grow as awareness of its necessity comes to our consciousness.

It was clear to me that the deserved process of rebirth, at least in the beginning, was marked by inconsistency. The spirit, when it receives a body and carnal consciousness to help face life, is conditioned by the karma already acquired and by the connections made during the present existence. This individualized spirit, conditioned by existence and physical consciousness, is what we can call the individual soul.

On the astral plane, where dematerialized conscious thoughts, emotions and diverse vibrations exist, there are many spirits in the form of souls still conditioned with the identity that they had while in the body. Underdeveloped spirits, they further regress in the density of their attachments and inflict them on those with whom they come in contact. During their stay on earth or on other planets, besides not realizing their definitive spiritual rebirth, they further themselves even more from Christ with the accumulation of new karmas, each time more regressive.

These "souls" remain individualized spirits, conditioned and attached to the illusory scenes of the earth, including scenes of human pleasure and suffering. They do not pass the ordeal of the purification because of the quality of their incarnated spiritual consciousness, and this impedes their return as Christian flames to the Celestial Father. They do not awaken to overcome karmic obstacles, each new one more difficult than the last, which were produced by ignorance, especially of spiritual things. These souls do not have a chance to liberate themselves unless they are encountered by a truly holy person who can reverse the process. They are therefore taking the risk of becoming a "spiritual abortion," as defined by

Padrinho Sebastião—beings that have lost all their light, forgetting all the knowledge they once had, until they descend into complete darkness, without the capacity to illuminate even the vermin of the earth.

Many of them have been in this situation for a long time, without another chance to reincarnate. They do not have a physical body of their own and want to take over others who, although incarnated, are in a situation similar to their own. They get confused by the worst illusions and false representations of themselves, the rags of their spiritual being. These are the so-called entities, adored or feared, invoked to attend to the desires of those who are incarnated on the same level of regression as their own.

In certain ways, these entities can be considered spiritual androids, parasites, or thought patterns that are attracted by the lamentations of our hidden "selves" and by the false consciousness of the human ego. Some entities are attracted by more illuminated inner temples, where the voice of the inner self has already been heard, even if in a weak and inconsistent form. Like moths attracted to light, they ricochet in the chambers of the sanctuary and cause damage.

Still others are spirit beings conscious of their disciplinary role and by God's mercy are permitted to maintain themselves somehow attached to someone's inner self. They may even sit on the throne in the inner temple of men and women with the intention of testing their discernment and free will and perhaps provoking the pains of rebirth. These "negative" spirit beings, if we can call them that, enter into contact with the "positive" forces that are mobilized by the true self to help fight the fear, doubts, and seduction into sin, the favorite tricks of these demons. And this ends up making possible the healing inside the person, the dialogue between the positive and negative forces thus coming into the light. These are also the spirit beings or entities that "having not prepared the ground, the spirit remains wandering," as Mestre Irineu's hymn says.[2] All of them are attracted by the quality of our vibrations and by our own inherent weaknesses that open our flanks to them.

When the superior self wants to emerge, it is in some way mixed up with these aggregations of regressive spirits that cluster around and feed on one's shadow. This explains the swing of the pendulum between the true inner self and its semblance. Only through consciousness of our conduct and perseverance in our aspirations can we guarantee the presence of our inner Christian flame. The one inside us wants very much the meeting of Him and us. Until the day this meeting happens, the seeker should fight all the battles without getting tired or losing enthusiasm, even when immediate practical results seem to be lacking.

To close our flanks to these negative influences, as explained by the Abbot Barsanuti, another monk from the desert, we encounter three basic obstacles: the egotistical will, self-justification, and the desire to please. Those who only move themselves through their self interests, who do not accept their mistakes and always use self-justification, or who want to please the world or their masters, rarely can be reborn in this life.

Only when all is experienced as really being God—including the self, brothers, sisters, and nature—will a great good fortune come and never leave us again! A love is born that does not inspire fear, and that, in its turn, fears nothing. From this point on we no longer need to fear interferences. As Padrinho stated, "the superior self seated on the throne, watching everything."

When I opened my eyes and realized how much time had passed, we were in Boca do Acre. The large group accompanying Padrinho Sebastião moved into the waiting canoes and kept on going. When the canoes arrived at Mapiá, practically everyone from the village was on the pier to receive Padrinho, returning with a healthy glow in his cheeks. Soon though, the day-to-day routine started bringing hard realities to the surface again. The old man, contradicting all medical orders, was already getting involved with everyday issues, putting the lazy ones to work, calling from his window to reprimand the children for taking dangerous jumps from the new bridge— in other words, everything was back to normal. In some ways the return of our routine made everyone breathe a sigh of relief, but Padrinho's involvement with everything only accelerated the stress on the old patriarch's heart.

In many special moments of my spiritual search I had the impulse to look for Padrinho and tell him about a moment of ecstasy that inspired a deeper understanding about the superior self. In other moments, I would repent from such an impulse, feeling the ground opening under my feet and searching for but not finding the self, much less a good explanation for its sudden disappearance. Sometimes the old man's presence precipitated this shift, and he would laugh at my embarrassment. But he never stopped teaching that we should each believe in ourselves, at the same time that we "carefully give proof." Pompous declarations of spiritual gifts received and eloquent tales of heroic deeds performed in the miração can lead one to delusions.

The problem of rebirth is basically a question of realization, which connects us with the center of our being, the self. The meaning of any authentic religious practice has this internal reconnection, so that this imprisoned soul is reborn a totally free spirit, conscious of earth and of Heaven. I wish I had the gift of explaining all these transcendental issues with the simplicity of Padrinho Sebastião.

A few days after our arrival, a great circle of people was gathered on the steps of his big house. I confess that I nurtured the hope and expectation that the old man would gift us with wisdom on the same themes that I had been mulling over. It was not an unusual expectation, because he referred to the need for spiritual rebirth in almost all of his talks. We were all getting comfortable, and he soon digressed from his impressions of the south to spiritual teachings.

"It was as in the time of Babylon. Also in the city that burned, how was it named?"

"Is it Sodom that you are talking about?" I asked.

"Sodom and Gomorrah burned and fell into the ocean. I was not there, I only know how to tell the story. Many were warned to leave the city because it was prophesied to burn due to the sexual customs they had of man with man and woman with woman. They did not want any other way. Lot and Sarah were transformed into two pillars of salt. It was because of the derangement that happened. I had nothing to do with it!"

"Why are you talking about that, Padrinho?"

"Because in Rio de Janeiro there seems to be a lot of confusion about love, a lot of fights between husband and wife, and pornography. It is on the television all the time. But through the Santo Daime, many have already escaped it! I know because many came to me to tell what they had overcome. The most important thing is to discover your whole story, who you were in past incarnations, and what you did. Who used to usurp the place of the self through their own excuses."

"All of this has a spiritual reason, does it not, Padrinho?"

"Nobody wants to know what they did or who they were. In the spiritual reality they want to know who arrived, who found truth, and who resisted. It is like this:

> *Everything that has already happened*
> *Thus it was because God wanted*
> *If we are not more united*
> *Never happy we shall be.*[3]

"Let's unite ourselves. What has passed is gone. He or she has become already a different person, is it not true? They become different people, and all that was disturbing leaves them. I myself do want to know the results, because it is as the hymn says: before he and she became they already were. Before being born, the spirit already existed. And thus it is with all of us. Before we are born, we already are. We are born to the flesh, but we still do not know who we are. It is necessary to be born again. To be sure of being of Heaven as well as of earth."

"Is the rebirth simultaneous consciousness?" I asked.

"Yes. If we are here together, receiving the power of knowledge, of lightning! With the sun's strength, with the strength of the moon and stars, earth, water, wind . . . when we are connected with all of them there will be nothing that can harm us."

At that point someone sang Mestre Irineu's hymn.

> *Sun, moon, star*
> *The Earth, the wind, and the sea*
> *It's the light of the firmament*
> *It's only this that I must love.*[4]

The old man continued, "Yes! We are all connected, just like the hymn says. Not like the parrot I have at my house. Ask Rita—the parrot sings the whole hymn, 'The Shine of the Sun.' But this is not the way that I mean, one should sing the Hinário within the power of the miração, conscious of all the Divine Beings that are in the astral. The Hinário tells the story very beautifully. But to penetrate into this study we have to discover who is the 'I am.' The main difficulty is that we deny ourselves the presence of the Divine . . . on earth as is in Heaven. We are there and we have to be here. The body has to be a Divine presence. The women are the presence of the Supreme Virgin, and the men show the face of Christ. Each man that is perfect in Heaven should be also perfect on earth. Everyone has to respect one another and see God's presence in everyone else, because we all are the same presence. I respect all. I am always trusting in who I should, in who holds me, the Divine Power, in the forest's strength, and the wisdom of primitives. Is not 'primitive' the name the doctors give?"

"Primitive is still OK. Some call them savages," I added.

"Yes, but they were the first to discover these plants of knowledge and taught the truth about the spirit."

"We are savages and primitives, aren't we, Padrinho?"

"I was once very hard-headed, but now I have knowledge. I do not speak in vain either, even when I hear someone doing so because I know I am not only a body! Matter is like an empty bag. Have you tried to stand up an empty bag to put rice, beans, or corn in it? When empty it does not stand up no matter what! We have to fold the empty mouth, hold with one hand, and fill with the other, but when it is full there is no problem. It stands up all by itself. We tie the mouth and it is ready. We are also like this. If we do not put our body on the path of knowledge, if we do not become filled with spiritual knowledge of the self, we will continue to be empty, we cannot stand up at all. Without knowledge of the self, nobody arrives at the rebirth. But it is difficult when the time comes to discover the most important things, the body complains and becomes like an old bag that does not want to be filled."

"Why is it that we are so afraid, Padrinho?"

"Because it is really hard. There are times when the Daime calls, calls, and calls us but we do not hurry to answer. We are afraid of falling, vomiting, and so forth. Very well, if you cannot stand up, sit. But the surrender is necessary, because the Daime is trying to tell you something. I call it Daime by habit, but it is wrong because the Daime calls itself a Divine Being. As expressed in the hymn:

> *I live in the forest*
> *I have my teachings*
> *I don't call myself Daime*
> *I am a Divine Being.*

I am a Divine Being
I come here to teach you
The more you pull on me
The more I have to give you.[5]

Padrinho continued, "If the power of the forest and the primitives is true, is it possible that all this beauty is a lie? No, I trust in this power. I am happy, thank God! Like in Alfredo's hymn: 'the more we look for God, the more we see him in front of us.' We all have to remember our other lives before this one, to remember if we were in favor or against, to know that we have to strive to be really what we are and invoke, is this not true? Otherwise we invoke, and instead of surrendering to it we misunderstand and end up regretting and afraid of what we invoked. Can you imagine having to experience the doubts and fears Christ suffered?"

"Have you experienced it Padrinho?" someone asked.

"Did you not see what I went through when the Confen was here?"

From there the conversation changed momentarily to the crescent moon setting in the west. Padrinho threatened to go, with the excuse of being sleepy, but as always, someone else asked a question: how can one differentiate the real self from the illusions?

Padrinho returned to the conversation, saying, "If I feel it is good inside of me, it inspires me to do good things. If it is good, it is because it is true. The proof is inside of us, if the Christ presence is true. Even when we still did not realize He is true and all He represents. One should then understand why He is inside oneself. But if it is no good, then it becomes a different deal: Go away beast! This body is to become a church of Christ and not a lair for beasts anymore, as it has been before this discovery."

"That is why we have to remember who we were."

"So we do not pretend or disguise. Those who pretend will not endure. As they come begging for alms, they enter the church because it is where the 'Man' is with alms in his hand. The ones who arrive asking for help cannot be treated like dogs. Incarnated or disincarnated, each brother or sister is a gift that we must receive, and we are receiving. The way is not to scorn those who seem fallen, calling them all sorts of names. We have the doctrine for them; this is charity. I believe in everything that has been shown to me and the way it should be done, but to believe is not enough, to have an inappropriate faith that wants to believe in everything. We need a living faith. Do I believe in God? Not only do I, but I also know where He lives! It is different, is it not? I am not misleading you nor anyone else. I know where lives the Man who made it all. Do you believe me?"

"I believe," said someone.

"Is belief the only solution left to those who need faith?" I asked.

"If you have faith, it is better. It is what we labor for. To find the people who, when I ask, 'Are you seeing?' will answer, 'It is coming.' And one has to study it all with the eyes well opened, because in spiritual reality there are beings worth seeing and we pretend blindness, looking down."

Padrinho stayed serious and mute for a minute, his expression changing in front of us. He spent some time absorbed while the moon was setting, and when he began to talk again, it was in the rhythm of a prayer.

"Yes, I am what the Creator is. In the beginning was the Word, I am the Word and the Word is God. It was in the beginning in God and in all things done by Him. Without Him, we have nothing, because everything was done by Him. He is life. And life is always continuing in us. Always. It never fails. And we are here to be the testimony of the 'Man' and men deny this. And the women with arms crossed, do they not want to do the work? I want to become and there are others as well like me, is it not true? Let's see through the veil! I was starting a prayer and did not finish, yes?"

"It is fine; you already said many things we needed to hear."

"To discover all of this is difficult, but the veils will begin to fall as we keep on living and seeing it all in accordance with our merit. The oneness with the living God. When Moses arrived where God was, he sensed him and asked, 'Who are you?' God said, 'I am what I am.' This is the way I am. I am what I am. And you?"

"I also only can be what I am," I answered.

"Then let's fly together in the starry firmament, because I am is everywhere and is everything!"

"This is all I want."

"Then the day after tomorrow, let's make this trip together and let's see in what kind of condition this business is. One has to bear one's own burdens."

"So you mean that the journey to the stars is going to be in the Star House?"

"Yes. Here everyone is courageous, but when we arrive at the Star House and we must all unite, everyone cries for help. Everyone thinks we are going to break ribs and pull hearts from the mouth, but this only happens sometimes, to warn the inconsistent people, the unclean. Look, suffering is the best thing that exists to cleanse oneself. We suffer, but when we come out on the other side we say, Thank God! I have climbed a couple more of these hard steps. And so in this way we move forward. Like that old woman in the last works—the more she suffered, the more she gave thanks for the beauty. And the beauty was so strong that she was making sounds like this: Ahhh!"

He imitated the woman in such a way that we did not know if she was really in ecstasy over beauty or suffering. He laughed and continued, "It seems that you are not believing me, but she was this way because she saw the beauty for sure."

"I believe Sônia, Alex's wife, has a hymn that says 'to bear the power of this beauty.'"[6]

"Yes, when she saw the beauty she hugged the others. She was happy. I am also happy and satisfied. It was the forest that gave me the Daime, the jagube and the leaf and other herbs of knowledge that I use. I am sure they gave me these Divine gifts. If people paid more attention, everybody would look and see God, but they are still searching. They bump into Him but do not know who He is; they step over Him and do not recognize Him. Let us try to follow our own self, inside and out, here on earth and in Heaven—this is the thing, no? Do not get lost. Take time, do not fall for the illusion of the flesh, money, and all those sorts of things. Do not indulge in fleshly pleasures. It is very ugly to be an unlit candle. I already told you all of this many times. I hope you come to understand it by and by, so you can recognize it when you see it. OK, you all stay here talking, but I am going to sleep. I am already yawning."

Padrinho got up, walked around the backyard for a couple of minutes, blessed the afilhados and climbed the stairs to his room. I lingered, wondering, at the edge of the forest. I felt some approaching encounter was inevitable.

12

...

Memories of the Past

AS WE ADVANCE further into the spiritual universe of Sebastiáo Mota, the more surprised we become at the originality of his teachings. Mestre Irineu had already drawn inspiration from multiple sources—African, mestizo, and Inca pantheons of deities but it fell upon Padrinho Sebastião to formulate the practice of spiritual discipline that harmonizes the search for the superior self through the development of abilities to perceive all the selves in our nature and the principle of spiritual rebirth. A progressive development of consciousness through the works with Santo Daime prepares the ground for the seed of the new self to germinate. The ego's crust breaks down and with it all sorts of illusory ideas about our spiritual journey.

The negative poles present in us form a gravitational center that attracts many vibrations, thoughts, and disturbed beings that share the same wavelength. Sometimes they get dangerously confused with our own self. These vibrations disturb our desires and attachments to exterior objects, thus clouding the longing for self-knowledge through the Divine.

In this phase of our spiritual initiation, according to Padrinho, the seeker must integrate this negative pole with the positive one that has been developed. Thus, the light that we ignite illuminates equally both the spirit and matter. The new self becomes the chick that pecks at the eggshell; only after it breaks through the shell is it really born. This self requires special nurturance to grow. Sometimes we can find our own image in the special condition that is the miração, but we have not yet the strength to keep it with us for good, because our habitual thoughts and material senses start to dominate us again.

We should focus on discerning the many forms in which our self has already manifested during previous incarnations and on studying the significance of each one.

This plunge into the "memories of the past," as Sebastião Mota called them, is a plunge into a world of images and shadows, emphasizing the need for clarity in the discernment of truth. Through this recollection, we can slowly make the self more at home in its own "house," as if we were applying a coat of lacquer over the original paint to increase the shine of its colors.

These are moments of intimate and deep perception, but it is usually necessary for someone to guide us. Someone who has already found his or her self and is willing to help us to penetrate into authentic self-knowledge without becoming confused by the many projections of what we are not. If someone helps to show us the most appropriate way, we can give proof of what we have chosen to be. In truth, all paths of the spiritual matrix are valid and inspiring, although in our tradition we have chosen Christ as our model and avatar. In him we should find inspiration. Confronting him, our identification with other beings already incarnated becomes only for reference. The praised masters who leave many disciples or the humble sages who incarnated to be instructors of a few are only helpers on our search.

"We should never lose sight of Christ," Padrinho Sebastião would advise. "We should identify in him the immense Christian potential that dwells inside human nature. An authentic pearl of great price is the inner Christ or superior self, and the earthly life of Jesus is the proof of our Father's divinity: he was the Word made flesh, the Logos, author of the universe. Those who are humble and meek will perceive in their search that this pearl can be found within the heart, but maybe we need a special probe to penetrate our deeper layers, subjugating ourselves to great pressures geared to our resistance."

Since the moment I started working with the Daime, I wanted to know myself. I would hear from brothers and sisters about the clarity the Daime gave them concerning their previous incarnations, but I did not know how to start. I would also hear some whispers from my own memory but, as much as I wanted to believe that Padrinho Sebastião was a prophet and that other people were also prophets, to me there was no proof because I did not yet have within me a profound conviction that comes from direct knowledge.

The Day of the Holy Kings, Epiphany, January 6, 1984, something significant happened in the Hinário. At a certain moment, I saw layers of thick, heavy curtains opening in succession. As that happened, they gradually became lighter until they were transparent. Between one and another, there were zones of darkness as if after a penumbra. This went on until a few luminous six-pointed stars appeared. Initially, they were just small flashes but slowly they increased in intensity. The stars, of many colors and sizes, succeeded one another, moving faster and faster. As they disintegrated, they let fall colored drops and granules of powdered gold and silver, which soon aggregated and formed new stars, shinier than before. I was looking at all of that with great emotion but without understanding the meaning. Stars exploding and being reborn! I watched it all as a fireworks spectacle, wondering why these six-pointed stars were exploding all around me.

Until that moment the singing of the Hinário had been one of the most difficult I had yet experienced. This miração took maybe the last ten minutes of the final works. The stars began to disappear, and even with my eyes closed, I saw everything illuminated. In a landscape at the same time unknown and yet familiar, a creature was walking on a ground covered with stones, with some tufts of low vegetation and contorted trees. I then experienced a sensation of fear. I wanted to open my eyes but I could not for a moment. I thought my body had already fallen to the ground. But an internal voice was saying, Awaken! Pay attention! And I looked toward the being who was resolutely crossing what seemed to be a battlefield. I could hear voices and the sound of iron. I could not recognize the man who was walking but at the same time I felt as if he were my own self. The next day I asked Padrinho Sebastião about it. He told me to trust the Daime, trust the vision, and trust myself.

A short time afterward I became sick and felt that my illness was due to a being who was occupying my vibratory field. I tried to establish contact with it by drinking Daime and retreating to my room. In a few minutes the miração arrived strongly, and with it an image of a circus stage and a graceful ballerina balancing on top of a moving horse. I was gyrating on the stage, following the horse and ballerina, but no one was in the audience. Then I became dizzy and fell. I stayed on the ground, aware of everything without anyone perceiving me. All of a sudden many faces appeared in the audience. They came up on the stage, put on clothes and costumes, and took on roles. I recognized many of them, and they approached me and smiled. It was as if all of my incarnations were parading in front of me on that stage, and I experienced this with the certainty of reality.

If this vision still did not provide the key to my past lives, the flash-backs and insights did. Realization can also come in the form of dreams or be induced by special regression techniques. We need to go deeply into the perceptions of the many archaeological layers where we find buried the ruins of our old habitations. Our probe has to penetrate and under-stand each of these layers, without staying in any, because the real goal is to find the source that can give light to it all.

This origin, or spiritual matrix, is the aggregation of qualities and attributes essential to our being through many incarnations. It can have strong patterns exclusive of an individual lifetime. The auspicious moment in which we transcend the limits of the personality and realize our own divinity is always the result of a synthesis, of spiritual alchemy. Many exis-tences meld in the formation of these patterns, and many interchanges are made with the experience of previous incarnations and other spiritual lineages that are indirectly connected to our own.

There is no law on the spiritual plane that gives rights to certain incarnations. The light spectrum of a great spirit and his or her future jurisdiction are a field much vaster than those that incarnated and kept themselves within the present transitory personality. The great spirits of light generate and "father" a whole line of incarnations in which the pin-nacle is the realm of prophets and avatars, but they operate simultaneously and silently in many chains of evolution. This explains why we sometimes recognize ourselves spiritually in other people—as though we were of the same essential matrix or were emanations of the same spirit.

In each incarnation we have also the other selves, the many impurities that get mixed with the golden core: they evolved and aggregated themselves to the self in search of somewhere to incarnate. The great spirits, in their karmic evolution, bring a mission of charity to the many aggregations.

The spiritual prospect concerning the memories of the past is a pro-cess in two directions. The probe reaches in and opens a channel, provid-ing a spring of nectar and fuel for being. We make a choice to identify with the vibrations of that Divine spring and to receive its emanations. Our doings, internal and external, are the best proof of our merit.

This is the mechanism of the game: we choose and are chosen until the harvest when, in the course of a specific emanation, a new rebirth of our consciousness penetrates through all that we have been to the eternal wellspring of all these existences. The ones who reach this realization stay in the fountain. They do not need to return, unless on a mission of charity.

At the moment when our soul transcends, it becomes spirit. And this spirit, even tied to a physical body and to a material consciousness, illuminates itself. A spiritual rebirth happens then and sanctifies even the flesh. A spiritual identity is born. This being can have as many names as the personalities it incarnated, but it has always been the same spirit that operated behind and through them.

When the soul opens its shell, it liberates the fundamental center that is the spirit. And once born, the spirit spreads its wings and flies with all the freedom of love, going to nestle in the heart where resides true Divine love. Love is God in full flight, and it is found inside our own selves. It is the bird coming back to its nest, the spirit returning to its reality, and the creature to the Creator, all coming together in the domain of the One who is and always was.

If we keep this hawk of knowledge perched in the heart, which is its place, then it will take over and unveil all fields of consciousness, material and spiritual. The superior self, seated at its place, operates its *aparelhos* (vessel or medium who receives and manifests the spirit) and they start to cooperate with the Divine plane, becoming players in the Divine game of life.

When our spirit reunites itself with the spiritual world, we can also became part of a matrix or a pattern with our brothers and sisters. It is not heresy to say that only one among the many avatars that came to earth was God's son, but neither is it heresy to affirm that everyone who understands and accepts this fact and unifies his or her spirit with the fountain, becomes a Christ, similar and identical to Him, as He was similar and identical to the Father. In this way, all things are equal in their perfection and fit together.

We all have Christ potential and can awaken the Christ within us through the course of many lives and efforts. With this new sacrament, the Daime, this rebirth can happen here and now. The shortcut is dark and the crossing dangerous, but we need to persevere because time is short. Of this difficulty in finding what we are looking for, Padrinho would say: "The Christian condition is very difficult to capture. It is a sharp edge. If we have fear and doubt, it slips. If we become proud of the gifts, it does not work either. It took time for me to believe. It takes time to develop consciousness, to be reborn before becoming disincarnate. There are many people in 'Heaven above,' but they do not attend to what is going on down here. They have a lot of knowledge of the sublime but of the earth, nothing. They do not know about our inheritance."

"It seems that you are not very inspired by things down here, Padrinho."

"Well, here in the middle of the forest we have a chance to find ourselves. But out there, in the world where I visited, people deceive themselves a lot because of too much inappropriate talking and information broadcast by people they do not even know. Many people think that the physical manifestation is the whole person, but this is not true. The physical manifestation is not the whole person. For what is difficult is each one searching alone. But together we become a big shining star in the astral. We only need knowledge to know which one it is."

"The hymns speak of this," someone commented.

"Yes. The celestial presences are here, and if we pay attention we see a lot of things. There are some that fly around. Someone from earth says, 'It is a satellite.' But it is not. It is a soul. It has light to fly and has already been in existence way before man invented the so-called satellite. Humans are strange creatures. They invent all sorts of things, imitating everything that exits in nature, but now, in our time, man has forgotten that he is of the same stuff as the One who created everything."

"It is necessary for us to have out-of-body consciousness so we can remember what we are spiritually. Is this not so?"

"To see, one has to be awake in spirit. The one who spoke then is the same one speaking now. People just want to be, but spiritual knowledge is not in those who only say, 'Ah! I am rich, I am this and that.' This is silliness! Better to be quiet and not judge or be proud of oneself. Our knowledge and faith are such that wherever this Divine Being manifests, there is light illuminating all."

"What does really go on in our works? Through the communion with the Being of the Daime, does this inner spiritual being of ours, the one you speak of, awaken? Is the incarnated self remembering the other true self?" I asked.

"Without effort, people can never fully become themselves because, unearned, the knowledge of who they really are never arrives to them. In a way, their inner being seems true but it is not. It is an illusion, a lie. What is your planet? Where do you live? Is it on earth or in Heaven? We have to reach for the consciousness that we are here and there at the same time. I already am tired of talking about this. It is what I call to be born again. Here we are body and spirit. At the works, when we partake of the Daime, everyone feels it and comes in deeper contact with this spiritual being. There are times when we are happy and others a bit sad. One time laughing, another crying."

"In this way Padrinho, the doctrine of the Daime is similar to other spiritual lineages that seek this connection."

"I do not know my friend. I tried many things, searched many doctrines, but I did not fit well in any of them. I did not leave because of disagreements, but I felt they were not for me. Until I started to work with the spirits. Then after many struggles I found myself. And I want you all and others to be like me: poor, innocent, without too much ostentation but having knowledge. But what is mine I do not give to anyone, OK? I do not take my burdens and throw the weight on the shoulders of others, and I would like to see everyone making the same effort for themselves. In spite of not learning much, I always learn something. All we learn will serve for something. It is in this way we arrive at it!"

"This is the most difficult learning, isn't it, Padrinho? It is easy to know many other things, but to know oneself, it is necessary to have a lot of calmness and courage. It takes time."

"Everything is in our hands. We are the guilty ones if we do not discover our own authentic self with the same facility that we discover other things. In the same way that men and women learn so many other things, they can also discover themselves. Do they not seek petroleum inside the earth as well as in the depths of the ocean? They will dig up and down for anything, but they do not know where to look for the true self. That is why we drink the Daime. When each of us takes the cup to our mouth, we have already invoked the Being. This invoked Being goes inside us, and when it arrives at the Divine chamber, finds others in it who, not working, lie about vainly, only wanting to be beautiful."

He continued, "Here we are a church. Here in the physical world we can put on the face of good and evil. Evil only exists because everyone produces it. The dark is where evil proliferates, is it not? Thus, we should generate light by balancing the negative, which is evil, with the positive, which is good. The light illuminates everything, clears the self and our entire being. While one is in the darkness, the usurpers are there to have fun. When everything clears, the party is over! We get out of the woods, out of the shadows. Darkness is no more. It has been a long time that we have been drinking Daime, and it is already possible to illuminate further. Isn't it, friend?"

"When you say it like that it sounds easy. Is this the basis of true healing, Padrinho?" I asked.

"For us to be healthy it is necessary to have a disciplined mind. It is not for us to be thinking about that illness, this illness; we only should think of abundance."

"And health . . ." I ventured.

"Health is already a form of abundance, OK . . . everything prospering. There is nothing difficult. Also, one should not think we are going to have high fancy dinners in Heaven, us with enormous stomachs. It is better to nourish oneself spiritually."

"And the dreams, Padrinho? Can we also get to know ourselves through dreams and remember?"

"I started with them, and to this day I go around the world with them. We have to be able to leave the body and to acquire spiritual knowledge. The body is asleep but the spirit is living and reliving to be able to communicate the story to the dreamer afterward. Although many people dream and think of this communication, when they awaken they say, 'I dreamed.' They think of it as only a dream. They do not ever think of it as reality."

"It is necessary to awaken to the other reality soon before it is too late, isn't it true?"

"Have you ever tried to light a match in an open gas tank? It will go 'boom,' with everything around catching on fire . . . this is the way everything is here on earth now. To burn the forest, it only takes a fiery flame descending from the sky." Then Padrinho sang:

> *The ocean grows and the earth sinks*
> *In many parts of the universe*

The sons and daughters who live on it
Complain as they leave the earth.[1]

"I hope that we save ourselves," he continued. "I am here with a spiritual mandate. I am waiting for something to happen and hoping we keep improving. Whoever still does not know what spirituality is, come and present yourself! I hope nobody weakens, otherwise the beast will grab hold and hurt them."

Padrinho showed signs of wanting to end the conversation. I still asked him how to distinguish between a present action of our astral body or any other projection in our dreams, memories, recollections, and scenes of our past lives. He thought awhile and said, "All these categories are not very important to the self, because the self encompasses all this knowledge. If it happened in this or that incarnation, there is no difference. It is all in the present and at the same time it is all memory."

That was the way it happened to me! In a short time I was able to intuit certain details of my previous incarnations, and I became better able to track the same route I am on until this day. The important thing is to give less and less attention to the cinematic scenes of our incarnations. Instead, one should not repeat the same mistakes in the here and now, which can increase or perpetuate a bad karma. And on this path, the biggest obstacle is the concealed illusion of the self-condescending will.

Intuition is our best adviser, especially when it is already well established through knowledge and faith. It helps us to decode our miração, to translate it into concrete instructions to be achieved for the development of our spirit and the salvation of our soul. The salvation of the soul and the resurrection of the body is one mystery; the development of the spirit through successive incarnations is the other. Christ came to bring about a synthesis. The deepest spiritual study that the Daime brings to our consciousness is in part the search for the answers to these questions, and the realization of this synthesis. Who has eyes should see. And who has ears should hear. Those who cannot perceive that they are wasting this gift of the earth called life are going to disappear and will have to wait awhile for another chance like the one they have now.

Padrinho Sebastião told us that once, after he had been drinking Daime only a short time, he had an encounter with Saint John the Baptist.

The hymns he composed after this vision echo the profound connection between John the Baptist and Jesus Christ, who were both sacrificed. Sebastião Mota de Melo went to the roots of his being to bring up this story of personal commitment to the truth to the point of physical sacrifice.

Whoever has seen Padrinho working at the healing sessions, transfigured by the Daime's miração, was able to feel the presence of his Divine Being. Likewise, those who lived with him day by day as a canoe craftsman were able to understand his spiritual greatness along with the simplicity of his being. In one way or another, he guided us to never leave a Daime experience without trying to remember the past. He wanted us to aim our "radar" and to track the moment in which Saint John the Baptist and Jesus were incarnated. If we remember our position at that moment in the past, if our Divine memory awakens at that time, rebirth is guaranteed. Even when our karmic debt and our guilt are very big, our repentance and Divine forgiveness will save us.

One time, during a works, Padrinho, in an altered state, revealed many of these mysteries in a lecture. He spoke as though he had been taken by the Holy Spirit.

"Be a Divine man, be a man of love, a true man—without the need to kill others! Because we can kill others even with a deranged thought. Among spiritual truths, man must have perfection. To be perfect is to be with God. Man should not hurt or steal. Stealing is not part of God. The thief denies God and gains nothing. My friends, be like God and trust that God is inside you. If you are not born again, my brothers, you will have nothing in life! You will be an abortion that the earth received. This I say in full consciousness, because for us to become, it is necessary for us to imitate. We have to become because we are. We are sons and daughters of God. We are and should be. This one thing I ask of each of you—I am asking but I have already asked too many times. Be in perfection! In front of our celestial Supreme Father because now is the time of the Holy Spirit, and it even has a name that means to make an oath, Jura. Believe whatever you want to believe, but if you are not born again you will not have eternal life! You have to live and let other people live and stop looking at their lives. Be whole! It is necessary for man and woman to enter into communion with Christ as He did for humanity.

"Another teaching Christ left speaks to us every day: if you are not reborn you will not have eternal life! I am Life, the Way, and the Light. Remember that whoever does not come guided by these three things will never fully realize God. My brothers and sisters, whatever is present here is also in Heaven! And in our hour, we have to show that God is in us. He is Harmony, Love, Truth, and Justice. Hold in your heart where God dwells! Tell everyone and everything that the owner of the house knows what goes on inside it. Because we are the church of God, we are the throne of God. Be a church—each one of us is the church where Christ lives! We now ask the same question asked by the apostles, 'Sir, when is your Kingdom coming?' He answered: 'My Kingdom already is here.' 'And where is it?' 'Inside each one of you!'

"He who walks in the light does not get lost, because of this I hurry up. Men and women have to make a decision and say, I am because God is. And thus by bringing true knowledge here to the earth, they are born again. As long as this does not happen my friends, you should not even bother to talk about it, because it is silly talk, and what is it showing? Polluted thoughts fill your head until you fear it will explode. My friends, let us lower our heads and follow God. Let go of resentment and of gossip about the lives of others. Whoever gossips about anybody is killing them. This is unnecessary. Our material situations should be as we are—sons and daughters of God. We should sanctify man and woman, from the body to the high spirit. The spirit is true! Look and pay attention, because it is the Divine Word that is speaking through the Hinário, and it is for you to prove it. All of us must behave correctly, trying our best to seek perfection and be with God. To have love is to be with God. To have harmony is to be with God. I am very serious. There is no limit to His words. If your words are not true, do not speak, because if you speak and do not manifest truth, then there is no truth.

"We must be with God and listen to God's voice. It was Elias who said that the voice of the desert would come in later times for those who want to hear. Later, Saint John the Baptist was born in the same area. John the Baptist was Elias; and Elias was John the Baptist. Today it is the same, my brothers and sisters: each one who is God's servant is awakening and taking a stand. God is still waiting for each of His children to leave the illusion, to pay attention, and to speak well about everyone. Let us treat each other seriously. Let us prove what we came here to see. I do not wander aimlessly! I am not an orphan; I have a Mother who feels for me.

"Am I not here incarnated? I am an incarnated God! It is the same for me to be here or any other place, in the flesh or without flesh. But for me to bear abuse from brothers and sisters who do not strive to understand what a better life is makes me withdraw. I am not angry at all. I have no complaints but this one. It is a struggle, an enormous struggle, to bring people together until this point, to be sanctified, and I do not feel that my brothers and sisters have the same dedication or interest as I do. If you do not understand, my brothers and sisters, I believe it is because you do not want to. The true Christ said, 'When you vomit, do not be as dogs that go back and eat the same garbage.' And now there are people here in the same condition, vomiting today and tomorrow back in the same place. For whoever comes to a spirit session, it is to receive their superior self and leave here very clean. But some people do not care. If our brothers and sisters knew exactly what they came here to do, they would leave clean because our Father has power. And he will be glorious and victorious in our spiritual journey."

He continued, "Christians who have not yet experienced spiritual revelation by the water of life, please come close. Let go of wrongdoings, resentments, envy, and jealousy. Come to me all those who are sick, oppressed, and tired. Come to me and I will relieve you! These are words from the true Christ himself, who lives in us. Let us embrace this attitude my brothers and sisters!

"This is what I have to ask—from the women as well as from the men—let us treat each other seriously. Let go of the agony. Let us eat less. The less we eat the more advanced in the spiritual life we become. Because instead of the body being busy processing food, it will be moving in the vertical path of spirituality. God made a church using the vine as a format so he could inhabit each pure incarnated being here on earth. Eternally I live with God and God lives with me. He lives in all humanity, and he lives in everything! Whoever does not believe in God does not believe in himself or herself. It has been already announced that humanity will be transformed in the future into something useful within the cosmos. So each person should become knowledgeable of the spirit to better preserve the things of God, to really be able to bring what God wants: perfection here on earth.

"Even here in this community, there are people who are not perceiving anything but who tell me they are seeing marvelous things. Let us open our eyes and pray for ourselves and others. We will be unhappy if we do not have our thoughts connected with all our brothers and sisters in the whole of humanity. Whoever has ears should hear, and whoever has eyes should see. This gift is here for those who want to see! If you do not see, it is because you are still asleep.

"This, my brothers and sisters, is what is necessary for us to work in the spiritual realm: silence. We will develop a broader understanding of life and arrive quickly at our destination. The more you talk, the more you lose your energy. Your energy begins to fade. In a while, you are a man with nothing and will suffer. You did not conserve what God gave to you and that he still to this day asks, be a child to the world and an adult to God! God is very old and at the same time a child. One should not come tarnished into God's presence. Become as God, who is pure essence. You should visualize the Supreme Being without blemish.

"We should be conscious that God really exists and dwells in all beings. Do not forget this. It is necessary to have faith and to be respectful. Take a stand against fear and doubt in your own body, because otherwise Christ will not be resurrected. He remains always on the cross, always hanging on the cross—I am sick of it! My brothers and sisters, let us open our eyes. John the Baptist was killed because he spoke the truth. They caught him because of someone else's dishonesty. They took the life of one who came to light the path. Then came Lord Jesus, who was received without honor and we know what happened. It was not Judas Iscariot alone. Judas was only an instrument who proved how money distorts our lives in this world. Money bought Christ's life, and it is still to this day buying lives. The atmosphere this creates is sad, for it affects not only humans but animals, the whole forest, and even the astral. Let us worry less about our mistakes and more about how we may correct ourselves.

"My brothers and sisters, look at your own dreams as well as imagining the Supreme Virgin's dreams. If you did not see the light before, see it today. Let us have faith so we can have harmony, love, truth, and justice, because they belong to everyone. Harmony is God. Love is God. Truth is God. And justice brings us peace. Because God's justice is peace! It is not the sword, no. If He had wanted to arm for combat, he would have done so and ended everything."

When God closes a cycle, brings about His mysterious purposes, and does His harvesting, great spiritual lineages—positive as well as negative—incarnate all of their fellowship at the same time. This event is a very deep and serious alignment. It is a powerful spiritual task to be a part of God's people on earth, to have a deep faith in and an understanding with our brothers and sisters, whom we should love as we love ourselves.

And as we recognize and realize who we are, we will have greater spiritual strength for whatever comes our way. Because even great men sometimes get afflicted, as Padrinho did, and we with them. They feel for us as their own children, we who have far to go to keep up with what the Time is demanding from us.

The Divine Beings of the Santo Daime are also the sacred plants. They help those willing to sacrifice themselves to find God through a spiritual path and self-knowledge. Nobody can run away from his own consciousness and still accomplish his mission.

On my birthday in October 1988, I had an experience with Padrinho Sebastião that further broadened my understanding of the inner self and memories of the past. I received the gift of singing my own Hinário for the first time at the new church. It was an imposing building dedicated the year before, with a central pole almost twenty meters in height. In contrast to other temples or churches, the new church was hexagonal in shape, constructed with six sections for the *bailado* (a collective dance) around a star-shaped table. An immense spaceship parked in the forest, it invited us to climb in and journey.

The Hinário started at eight o'clock in the morning, and by eleven the church was full. At that time Padrinho Sebastião went to his house for some tea. When he came back, there were still a few hymns left before the first part of the services ended. At that moment, I became aware of a strong presence hovering above the hall. Padrinho Sebastião arrived at the door with his companions, he blessed many people and walked to the end of the men's line, where he began to dance while we were all starting to sing this hymn:

It was in Agarrube
It is also in David
May the time of Juramidam
One day be fulfilled.[2]

As we began to sing, a pleasurable sensation of power and happiness accompanied our celebration. The hymn continued:

I praise our Lord God
In the sovereignty.
I present you my love
To be received with joy.

Who has served the Lord
Now has sworn to the Christ
I returned in his troop
And in the salon made inspection.[3]

In that moment, I clearly felt an enormous force around my being, the miração wanting to close its circuit. For a moment I had the impression that I was going to fall, but I did not leave my place because the hymn was not yet finished. I looked anxiously for Padrinho and saw that he had left the line and was sitting next to the table where the Daime is given. He was vomiting and choking, as if he were encountering a disincarnated being in need of help. Immediately, my nausea and dizziness subsided and the miração arrived. The intense spiritual connection with Padrinho Sebastião continued, and I understood what was happening with him. He had "caught" the being that was around me and whose story was being sung in the hymn. During the next two hymns, the situation continued. When the force began to subside at last, Padrinho Sebastião regained his usual color, the sun shone from behind the clouds, and everything became serene again. It was as if the boat had left turbulent waters and was sailing serenely again. This experience was of great importance to me. The hymn had invoked a being that was saying, "To the commander Saint John / I here present myself."

The next day, I looked for Padrinho, knowing without a doubt that the issue of what had happened in the previous night's works would come up and that he would clarify many things for me. The meeting was in Madrinha Cristina's kitchen, the setting of many of our conversations, between cups of coffee and plates of sweet cakes and fried plantain. The old man was looking at me with a funny face and, judging by his words, the experience had been even more serious for him than for me. He went right to the point.

"Yesterday I almost got in trouble because of you!"

"What do you mean, Padrinho?" I said smiling. "I am the one coming to ask you what happened."

"And didn't you see? I started to feel something strange early this morning. I said to Rita in church that I was going outside because I had a being wanting to communicate with me three times already. I did not drink Daime that day, but the communication with the spirits was open anyway. Then I left to go home and have a quick nap. When I got up and went back, instead of sitting I tried to dance."

"Then did he enter you?" I asked with concern.

"Yes, the being was looking for you but entered me. This is not fair!"

"I felt when you caught him. At that moment I almost fell. I looked behind me and saw you pale."

"Yes, Alex, this time I handled it, but it is possible that he will still try to go to where you live. He knows your address better than I do. He came here to prove it, and I, who had nothing to do with that pain, caught him. It was because I could understand what the being came here to say."

"The name of the hymn he manifested is 'Declaration,'" I confirmed.

"I learned many things I did not know. When I was young, I could work the spirits and handle it. But now, when one of them comes by, I almost die. This being, Alex, was persecuted during Christ's time and had given you his word about something. Then yesterday, he descended to hear the words of your hymn and to see if someone could feel and grasp that suffering. Wow! I was asking God for him to leave. I suffered because he came with the same pain he had endured in this last incarnation."

Madrinha Rita, who was frying manioc, added, "It started in the 'Declaration' hymn and continued through 'Tarumim,' but it was in the 'Cross' that Padrinho had to sit down and work with that visiting spirit." The hymn goes like this:

My God, give me courage
Give me your Love
I want to be your son
Even suffering this pain.

I saw Jesus crucified
Crowned with thorns
So the Master told me
This pain is also mine.

In this time of agony
To cry and have regret
That the Master comes quietly
To revive our efforts.

In this time of terror
Do not complain of bad luck
That the Master sustains us
Gives us life even in death.[4]

The hymn was the synthesis, the pleas and hopes of the being who had manifested. The time was coming for me to develop and deal with this kind of situation and I pondered the ramifications of it all.

13

...

Love Is to Be Shared

MY NEED TO understand the spiritual realms into which I had penetrated was becoming more imperative. True spiritual paths can seem wide at the entrance, but soon they converge, demanding greater attention in order not to get lost. It is almost like the rubber trails. An experienced rubber worker enters and leaves the forest through these paths, guided only by his sense of direction. And although I often walked those paths with extreme caution, observing everything, I sometimes almost got lost.

Once we know the path and know who our guardians are, we come to understand clearly where we are going. The idea that took us there is confronted for the first time by reality and we arrive at a point where we should no longer have illusions or make mistakes in our choices. All our fantasies, caprices, and attachments have to be discarded as we make our choices or we will get lost. Running after the wrong clues will not deliver us to the initiation or to spiritual rebirth.

I already had much understanding about the nature of the Daime-Being, but it was nothing compared to the new revelation I had during the miração at the Daime Feitio in 1988. The miração arrived and the forest became golden. I walked by its edge until I came to a small straw hut that was located just behind the Casa do Feitio. The building had a straw roof supported by three trees in a triangular form. Vertiginous, I first leaned against the biggest of them, and then sat on the roots of another. A strange sensation engulfed me, and I left my body. The images were not clear, but it seemed as if the history of humanity paraded backward in front of me like a movie being rewound. I stopped in a place where my internal voice said, "This is a seraphic office." I saw many big pans there, a preparation for a grand Feitio, with an ocean of plant material and boiling Daime. Archangels and seraphims with their immense wings crossed a sky in which there were many purple suns.

All of a sudden, I returned abruptly to my material body, which was squatting on an old wooden stump. This change of focus was initially painful, but soon I adjusted to feeling these two sensations of form and power simultaneously. In this moment, looking at the ocean of Daime pulp, I understood the knowledge of this Being whose spiritual name is composed of two words: Jura and Midam. I visualized the scene where Padrinho told me, "It is necessary to Jura to be able to be Midam."

Facing the most mystifying and complete inner self and the real significance of this transitory journey through this phenomenological world, we should wake up to true reality, entering it through the umbilical cord called "death," preferably completely awake and without fear. But the ego tries to avoid this encounter by all means, afraid that the triumphant inner self will demand its righteous placement. If we cross this threshold in a somnambulistic state, consciousness recedes into an undifferentiated condition until we awaken. According to Padrinho Sebastião, those who do not achieve their true selfhood while still incarnated cannot add their self to omnific and universal consciousness. Those people literally "die," decomposing in matter. Their energy and consciousness are reabsorbed and reprogrammed by Divine emanations.

My inner self watched me make a commitment to that which had been revealed with a mix of fascination and fear because I could not completely understand its meaning. But I saw that something very significant would happen soon and that those pans represented here on earth a giant Feitio of Divine Creation. I had to mobilize all my courage and love to accept what I was facing.

The vision went through many adjustments. When it changed I saw two steep ravines, one in front of the other. An angelic being landed on the top of the right peak. He seemed to be made of fire and was holding a flaming sword. Between the two peaks I saw many disincarnate beings in the most diverse conditions. I looked into the valley through a stone doorway and it continued beyond, becoming an immense canyon with hawks flying overhead.

"Juramidam!" I thought. This Being whose message echoes in our consciousness through this liquid light, holding us and helping us in the affirmation of this inner commitment that makes us remember our past to better assume our present without fear or doubt of our future. Is it not mentioned in the Apocalypse of John that when he comes back he will have another name?

I felt my consciousness and heart as one. Divinity resides in this double perception, sensitive and intellectual. Divinity is this commitment to the one who created us.

I understood that resistance was the result of the high and low points of my evolution, my karmic ascents and falls, and that we should take a more defined stand against this vague torpor that aims to disguise itself as gentleness but works against our unconditional spiritual surrender.

It is in regions where "knowledge still does not reach that faith needs to sprout." It comes to help the understanding when the latter still is weak, and little by little it illuminates all that is missing. The self is like an inner sun. An inner world illuminated by an inner and secret testimony is a "starry heavens." These things, Padrinho Sebastião said long ago, and only now was I discovering what he meant.

As we near this hour of commitment, of accepting being, it is necessary to have a certain perseverance, to believe in the character of the true reality of these experiences and perceptions. This only happens after we disconnect ourselves from the usual dimension of the senses and exterior focus that accompanies us. In these states of consciousness, we reenact God's creation in dream language. We fly to places where no tangible frontier can compare. There is not any material form capable of outlining or containing the immortal ecstasy, the eternal love, the supreme spiritual reality.

To travel through the starry heavens of our own self, we are less dependent on propulsive rockets than on pure, firm, and integrated thoughts of a higher desire for knowledge, charity, self-abnegation, for love for all people, and for all of life presented to us. But we should take our steps very carefully. Be conscious. Be very awake and aware of the illusions and fantasies projected by the mind onto phenomenological life. Purity of heart and loyalty to Divine laws, discovered through this inner sidereal journey, enable us to reflect the light that crosses the cosmos and arrives at the dense layers of matter where we are incarnated.

The biggest challenge in these states of consciousness is to distinguish between our genuine experience and the many possibilities of illusions. We live the fragile reality of the miração through our etheric body, which confers on us mobility and quickens our process of moving through the layers we encounter. But outside this waveband for dialing the infinite universe, great concentration and devotion are necessary to become atuned. Desire comes from the ego and not from the self. The ego makes our imagination generate a coherent discourse that is at its best a mental game, never a complete perception or a true experience.

This is why purity is necessary. It is the virtue that reaches the truth and permits us to arrive at the condition of those to whom Christ promised the Kingdom of Heaven. Without it, even when we are conscious of our intent, we only arrive at a mirage.

It is common to see many beginners, overzealous in their spiritual perceptions, go through a period in which they frequently confuse their will with the truth. Padrinho always directed us to trust in our discernment as we journey, but he also invited us to give proof through deeds that our connection was real and not illusory. Pride and pretension lead us to pretend we have knowledge that we do not have.

Another difficult part of this struggle for self-knowledge is love. As the hymn says, "I arrive at a point that I can trust / To carry on this battle of love."[1] The road of self-knowledge is the road of love; they are inseparable. To know oneself without knowing love is no good. And love, as in another of Padrinho's hymns "is to be shared / Not feigned / Because it causes pain."[2]

Divine love is our goal. To reach it, we need to understand that all we know about love, from the most bold and voluptuous passions to the most ecstatic and refined flights, is nothing but a phase on the progressive climb to Divine Love. Love's battle is the struggle for the transmutation of dense energy into divine, ethereal, elemental, and angelic energy. The voluptuousness of forms, textures, and touch is substituted by the volatility of subtle emanations in which higher consciousness is contemplated.

Love can become an unending well of obscure desires and karmic redundancies or a supreme realization, a dive to our most profound origins. Because it was love that brought God to manifest creation. And it is for love and only through love that He reveals this secret to consciousness and to the heart.

Padrinho Sebastião believed that the right strategy in this battle was for each one to arrive, through a more or less thorny experience of karma, to the understanding of the possibility in our present life for man to see woman as the presence of the Supreme Virgin and for woman to see man as the image of Christ. And for that there are many pathways. Some can realize this goal in carnal unions that are refined by and by until all polarity is suspended. Others feel more secure on a path of renouncement and celibacy. But one must make this choice with a profound understanding of what karmically, in this life, can transform that sacred union or chosen celibacy into insanity. This is the moment to investigate the motivations of the inferior self. Padrinho Sebastião warned us that every path of love should aim for the encounter with the Divine Lover, giver of grace and consolation.

In his own earthly life, with all genetic, social, and cultural circumstances that enveloped his incarnation, Padrinho opened many paths. He had a long-lasting relationship, married, raised many children, and lived an evermore sanctified life.

Padrinho placed great importance on and gave emphasis to the role of women because we are in the "Age of the Mother." Padrinho Sebastião would often speak of women's roles, advising them to assume the cutting edge of this process, because nothing is better than a mother's love to penetrate and open the capacity for love in the son.

I felt that I had taken an irreversible step in my life after I'd finished the Feitio. I understood the larger meaning of my search, which until then I had only grasped through episodes of intuition and clairvoyance in the midst of what otherwise seemed an arduous desert crossing. I had often been left with the feeling that nothing really spiritual was happening. But the Daime showed me a path and a direction for this life that I was reluctant to accept for a long time.

After we see and limit the dense vibrations emitted by the so-called fornicating spirits (when making love is divorced from soul and spiritual life), the struggle generalizes. It no longer becomes a struggle for the satisfactions of the body. The mind becomes the main land-scape of this struggle where very dark archaic impulses need to be worked out, and we have to bring the light to bear on this trans-mutation. Our relationships, which until then were a goal in and of themselves, stop being objects of seduction and become proof of our understanding. We can then express our new gifts and attributes from this new Divine Love without falsehoods, conditions, or status interests.

On that starry night, as was my habit, I left the window open and was lying in my hammock. The stars shimmered like fireflies. All the landscape induced in me perceptions about my past lives, about the many karmic links of my encounters and missed encounters in this long battle of love. I put on a tape of a talk Padrinho Sebastião had given two years earlier about this subject. His voice was clear and seemed to answer all my questions.

"Woman, if you want to see your own spiritual Mother, you have to consider yourself equal to Her, because it is not with meanness of spirit that you will see the Supreme Virgin. Not with resentment, jealousy, envy, conquest, or acting without consciousness! Why use such a sacred thing as womanhood to do wrong? She is justice. She is a Saint, a Pure Banner that I am here to raise and carry.

"My brothers and sisters, treat time more seriously: 'Because time does not deceive / Neither has it compassion for this body!' Let us be righteous with Our Lady. If you are speaking about the Supreme Virgin, pay much attention to what I say. It was what the spirit of truth taught me: honor each one of the ladies who come here seeking. Honor and tell them to honor themselves, so they will become God's people. As you and me, so they will take on our attitude and soon we will be united as one!

"Each one of us who is connected directly to our Superior Self, who is God, does not gossip, has no jealousy, or envy. Here there are none of these. Jealousy sets back one's life and is a destroyer of families; if it is here, there is false love among us. It is not the perfect love of God. Whoever feels jealousy has evil eating at them. It is evil that wastes our mind and casts our body into a pit.

"My brothers and sisters, there is one other thing of which I have to admonish you. All brothers, be they married or single, please return to your dear Mother. Anyone who does not return to our dear Mother and ask for forgiveness will not have eternal life. A man may grow to a point where the knowledge he has learned is used to suppress women, turning them into slaves, real slaves! Poor things, in this way their value was slowly taken from them. But God invites us to return value to woman. God is the one who bestows value to all ladies to encourage men to recognize what Christ recognized in the Virgin and Supreme Mother.

"Go back! You can return to your dear Mother. Whoever has a wife, be conscious. You both should become aware of the divinity in each other. If She is the Supreme Virgin, She is not only a body or your puppet, She is your mirror. Let us see the presence of the Mother in all women! Those who prefer to live in the profane world will tumble through it, but for whoever wants to pass to an eternal life, do not let your gaze dwell on Babylon. Look instead to women and the great value they embody. In many ways they are more developed than men. God's son was gestated in the Virgin Mother so we could bear witness to Her blessings. All of this bears meaning for today, when yesterday is also here again. But if you did not awake then, if you do not awake now, it is finished.

"If we came to give testimony, we are going to find the synthesis. You will remember how your own mother suffered for you. Suffered! She spent many nights awake, changed your diapers, and is still kissing your face. Thank God she is a permanent figure, on earth as in Heaven!"

I woke up with Padrinho's lecture about women in my mind and approached him early the following day to discuss the topic. Hot coffee was already on the table. My questions focused on my vision from the day before, about the name Juramidam and the themes connected with love, women, and Holy Mary. Padrinho was playful and full of energy.

"Yes, my son, the mystery is also in the name. We have to decipher the name, to look for a close connection between Jura and Midam. Those who understand shine all the lights on."

"Yesterday I listened to a tape of one of your talks," I answered. "You exalted the woman, but what about men. . . .''

"We have to learn to love ourselves a lot. It is not enough yet. We have to love to be loved. As we truly love one another, more love we will find, and others will start to love us, too. It is what we need! But women seem more advanced in this regard."

"Why, Padrinho?" I interrupted.

"Because today, as in the past, women seem more capable of spiritual growth. Christ understood this so well that his best disciples may have been women. They are the ones who feel more deeply the true essence of Christ. And today it continues the same way: women are more advanced than men because women's intent is the search for love, is it not? The love she has for the son only she knows—even for the silly husband. He may be bad, but she bears everything by his side. It evokes pity sometimes, but she stays there, loyal in that love."

All of a sudden Padrinho asked, "Was it not recently that a new Gospel was found?"

"The Dead Sea Scrolls, is that what you mean? Maybe around forty years ago."

"Yes. In it is a story about a woman, a very heavy story."

"Which one?" I asked.

"Peter was somewhat suspicious of women. He did not let even the Supreme Virgin come close because she was a woman. This caused stories to spring up that the apostles believed that women could not achieve spiritual rebirth and therefore had no chance for salvation. Then one day Christ said something like this, 'All of those who make men of themselves will enter into my Father's Kingdom.' This started a controversy as yet unsolved. How do we interpret this idea of making a man out of ourselves? What is it to be a man? It is to live in the spirit eternally. Your Superior Self never leaves you; it is with you all the time."

"Is it when we do not doubt our Divine condition and our destination?" I risked.

"It is for you to do your work but to know that you are not only flesh. It is to be conscious of this Being that has the gift of being present in you and me. Each of us came here to do something."

"But I still do not really understand the story about the women," I confessed.

"All flowers give some kind of seed, don't they? So it is with women. One of a woman's gifts is the gestation of a being. Her fruits are men and women. Through her fruits a woman becomes a man and achieves salvation."

"It is a beautiful interpretation Padrinho, and women without a doubt must like it."

"I try to consider and examine everything so that when I talk, I am rooted in reality. The Voice of the Desert told me a story about all women being liberated because they have never had freedom and were always subjugated to men. From now on they are going to be free. But when I told them this, there was a woman in Rio Branco who wanted right away to live together with two men, and that created quite a tumult!"

"This one took too seriously or misunderstood the emancipation you talked about, didn't she?"

"In the time of Mestre Irineu it was said that the way to relate to women should be hard. But I am telling you that all born into this world comes from her. Doesn't she give of her fruit willingly? I have no doubt about women! To me all women are equal. It is not about a body, my friend. What is important is eternal and lives in everything. She is everything! Thus the hymn says:

> To love and to have love
> One must know
> God in your mind
> God is your knowledge.
>
> To love and to have love
> One must understand
> To love all beings
> Equally as yourself.[3]

"It is difficult," he proceeded. "One does not know who to love. But if a person does not love his or her own self, how can they love the other? People can say to you, 'I love you.' But if they don't love themselves, it is a lie. If I do not love myself I cannot love my brothers and sisters either."

To steer the conversation back to the role of women I asked, "Do you mean to say that a woman, the flower, becomes man by means of her fruit, which is Divine?"

"Yes! Try to grasp the spiritual meaning of this metamorphosis. In the Lord's Prayer does it not say 'on earth as it is in Heaven'? Because we all are the presence of the Perfect Man who was called Jesus. Jesus was the body for Christ and to this day we have the same opportunity. So should a woman consider herself, even if she is not a virgin anymore. Look well to the example of the woman called Mary Magdalene."

"Saint Magdalene?"

"She became a saint later. When she first saw Jesus she wanted to flirt with Him because she was a prostitute. But He called her by the righteous name promptly, 'Come here Miriam!' When she saw and recognized him she changed her tone; she transformed herself and made her commitment. Is she not today called Saint Magdalene? All of this serves to show that she who is courageous has a chance to enter into my Father's Kingdom. She became perfect and God lives in her. We inhabit God, and his presence generates love. It is a dance with the Divine. God in Heaven and God on earth flowing into love, respect, and kindness toward all things. To me, lack of respect is the worst thing! People do wrong things thinking that the Divine Being is not seeing, and then later they complain about punishment."

I left Padrinho's meditating on love and the importance of its practice. The struggle to love was truly without a doubt the one that had provoked among us the lowest points.

It seemed clear to me that the synthesis proposed by the doctrine is much wider than one envisioned in the beginning. When Daime started to expand to large urban centers, it also brought its teachings to a wide diversity of people and to lifestyles with behavior patterns that science and ethics are making an effort to sanction as "normal." Our liberal position should not invite perversions and sexual obsessions. The Western mind is very conditioned to a sensual/sensorial discourse, and makes the confrontation with materialism the first issue in the spiritual battle for self-knowledge.

Many people come to the Daime with the supposition that their caprices and fancies of mind are the truth. Once they really see the truth and their degree of deviation from it, they have to bear the shock of repentance. When, instead of repenting we just feel guilty, we do not face the truth. Guilt sinks in its claws and a weakness is established, spreading doubt and fear, opening the way for illness, insanity, and death.

All of us—having arrived at this point, trying to justify ourselves in the face of outrageous truth—try to escape by one of two extreme and equally dangerous routes: failing to recognize our errors or giving excessive importance to them. Padrinho often lectured about the psychology of desire.

"Let us leave this gluttony! Let us end all maleficent desires that do not help the manifestation of good. A desire has to be fulfilled or abandoned. The right thing is to put good desires into practice and to transform our impulses. The body belongs to God, and God speaks through us. A body without God does not really say anything. God is life, and a body with life speaks. Whoever dwells without God is like a broken radio speaking nonsense. The speaker may talk his or her whole life, but the connection to a meaning is severed. Nobody will hear a thing.

"Spiritual reality clarifies the secret meaning of each desire. If your karma draws you to certain past experiences, what is important now is to understand the present moment, having as a goal the perfection of the issues raised by that experience. 'What is wrong becomes right,' Padrinho Corrente used to say. Our errors, once recognized, can become a kind of trampoline for the truth. Nothing is either extremely important or without significance. Many consider their fantasies or sexual practices as the most important options for them: whatever gratifies their poor notion of identity. Some hide from the responsibility of their desires, while others brag about their free thinking but wallow in stereotypes and prejudice. In a nutshell, they all suffer from the pursuit of pleasure, because they have not reached the understanding of true love, one that frees, heals, and saves.

"It is common when facing oneself and the Divine Power that the ego feels threatened. Many times I meet people who deny themselves spiritual surrender with the excuse of the fear of 'losing their freedom.' As if it were such a great thing to keep a 'freedom' that one has the constant fear of losing. This in and of itself is a dangerous obsession!

"People who cannot transcend their sensorial attachments maintain themselves in the 'oral' stage of their spiritual development. Those who use their psychic powers or spiritual status to satisfy their appetites and desires, sooner or later, will become part of a great transformational crisis that may well be their last call. True seekers transform each experience as it comes, focusing on the search for true love, but false ones will pretend to be who they are not.

"Unbalance and the incapacity for love or misdirected love are the main reasons for the spiritual illnesses of humanity. When families are created without love, catastrophies result: overpopulation, destitution, and delinquency. The pleasure impulse suffocates the most elementary responsibility to feelings, our own and others. There is no sense in love that is not nurtured by way of a spiritual complicity, a search for knowledge together, and a harmonic conviviality.

"The doctrine beckons to us with its wisdom! After conquering themselves, the main challenge for humans is to keep harmony and peace in their families and to provide for their children and educate them in the truth, helping them to prepare for the confrontations of these new times to come. Whoever can find harmony in the microcosms of the family and the self has the key for harmony with all things."

When he wanted to stress the ideal of a Christian family, Padrinho always sang for us the hymn that is sung in our marriage ceremony, "The Symbol of Truth." For a long time I did not grasp the meaning of this hymn. I have since come to realize that love embodies truth, and the family is the practical manifestation of that love. Where there is truth, love shines. The hymn asserts:

> *The symbol of truth*
> *Must be consecrated*
> *To receive with firmness*
> *What our Father gives us.*
>
> *The symbol of truth*
> *Brings us harmony*
> *Notice what's missing*
> *In you and in your family.*
>
> *The symbol of truth*
> *Always brings joy*
> *Look well at your house*
> *Behold the symbol of the Virgin Mary.*[4]

14

•••

New World, New Life

A COMMUNITY CAN represent many things and be directed toward a definite goal, but community itself is the focus of a spiritual science that inspires universality. Day-to-day living in a community fosters a very practical concept of existence. Community life represents the frontier between the macro and micro in terms of human organization, making it possible to experience all levels of human existence. The community is, therefore, a vast landscape for a material realization whenever each person enters into contact with the gifts, virtues, and the shortcomings of its members. It is also the immense spiritual and psychic laboratory that enables our spirits to develop.

The concept of a community is one of Sebastião Mota's main contributions to the doctrine of Raimundo Irineu Serra. Padrinho understood that there was present in Mestre Irineu's teaching an ideal of the common organization of brothers and sisters that is dependent upon the self-realization of each person. The community should be organized in the material realm with all perfection possible. The human capacity to live in peace, harmony, truth, justice, and love with oneself and with one's brothers and sisters continues to be the ideal for many saintly men and women. Through it all, a spiritual dimension is woven within everyday life. When the infinite fits into the mundane and each day partakes of infinity, a spiritual potential is brought into fulfillment, attaining Christ's spiritual utopia.

Each day in a community is one big lesson. Spiritual paths and doctrines that do not preoccupy themselves with this test called community cannot survive the turbulence of the coming purification. The spiritual community is the only one that can give a conclusive answer to some important questions. Is there any hope for material reality? Does salvation depend on faith and personal virtues? Or can it also be reached by a people united and guided by a legitimate prophetic inspiration?

The ideal community, which we all hope can be realized in our era, is one that amplifies the ideals of brotherhood and sisterhood, cooperation, solidarity, and the development of fellowship where men and women integrate themselves in a relationship with Heaven and earth. The community then becomes a constant challenge that proves or disproves the possibilities of its informing ideals and structure. Does it invite the construction of the Kingdom of Heaven on earth? Day-to-day life can be brought into the infinite, and we need only two or three to believe and to work with this goal in mind.

Without a coherent spiritual path in such a chaotic world, we become reduced to an endless repetition of the same sad scenerios. A world in this state has already exhausted other options: political, social, judicial, and ethical. And any solution that does not include a spiritual option is destined to fail, as has happened with the many predecessors. But we need to protect ourselves from approaches that, although spiritual, do not foretell of the material hardships at the end of time. The ideal of community continues to be the great utopia to be reached as the key to this challenge.

The challenges of the world have not been solved by any of the alternatives presented because the development of community is a global spiritual science, wherein it is necessary to bring together the teachings of the higher planes with the goal of realizing more harmony in each human life. If this challenge is overcome successfully and the people unite themselves in understanding and love, a great thing will have happened for humanity.

Communities today cannot be merely schools for the ecstatic, meditation centers, or convents administered by cloister rules. They have to be living institutions, creative laboratories for living, eating, thinking, loving, educating, and surviving the difficult birth of the new era in the world. The communities that organize themselves only according to secular social structures and economics, without preparing for self-sufficiency, will have few resources with which to alleviate the chaos of the future. True communities will be those capable of enacting a viable model of possible continuity of the human adventure within Divine Creation.

True brotherhood and sisterhood bring about an intimacy of sharing a bond of spiritual understanding, accepting one protocol, with the superior self as common reference for all. Community ties amplify the feeling of being brothers and sisters. Well-defined rules about all aspects of life can be experimented with to increase the inner wholeness and well-being of each member of the community. With brothers and sisters, we ascend spiritually and materially to a new level of initiation that gives us a greater opportunity to improve as individuals and nourishes the community as well. Community is the landscape for the more practical dialogue between the Divine and humanity. It is the ocean always gently roughed by the wind over which the human vessel of cooperation sets forth on its journeys. Do not think that anything is easy in the everyday life of this community, but spiritual communities seem to me the only viable models for transcending the chaos to come. They are the hospital, church, school, office, and laboratory of new interconnections that will rule the physical, astral, and etheric bodies of humans.

All of this was expressed simply in Mestre Irineu's hymns, and he chose Padrinho Sebastião to raise the community that the doctrine was demanding. When Mestre Irineu indicated to Padrinho that his final destiny was to gather a people together in the state of Amazonas, in Padrinho Alfredo's words, "to realize all knowledge about the Daime," Mestre Irineu was anticipating the contemporary epoch that started in Rio do Ouro and to this day endures in the community of Céu do Mapiá.

This is an epoch whose story is not yet told because the difficulties have been many. And if in the external world we can perceive advancements, from within there is always the sensation that we have not yet realized everything. Apart from being aware of the weaknesses that loomed so large, every time I stood in the yard of the new church at Mapiá and contemplated our village, surrounded by the forest, I could hardly contain the great emotion that welled up in me. It seemed that there, at Céu do Mapiá, was being written the first page of a great book, a story of which the beauty and seriousness were not yet glimpsed by its contemporaries.

At the end of the 1980s, questions concerning the communities were very present in my mind. It was a hard struggle to affirm a material base for the Daime centers and communities that were growing in Brazil and beyond. It was equally difficult to initiate a transitional process so that all of these points would come to structure themselves during the following decade, the last of the millennium, into a wider community organized and united around the teachings of Mestre Irineu and following the prophetic words of Sebastião Mota de Melo.

In the last days of his life, Padrinho's intimates, who had long followed him, had an opportunity to attest to his knowledge and his beautiful simplicity. They would join him in his involvement and concerns with community issues such as the education of the children and improvement of the soil quality. He sought more fruitful land for the future when the whole brotherhood and sisterhood would be gathered in the same community. He would speak of difficult times, the possibility that we might live through new periods of trials: hunger, war, and epidemics. But nothing worried him more than the lack of unity, distrust, and laziness. He tenaciously fought against all illusion and negligence because time is now short.

The karma of prophets is to involve themselves profoundly with their people, to awaken the spiritual force and faith inside their consciousness that realize miracles and move mountains. This force of will and faith is able to create a community of Divine Love. It is not only with the salvation of souls or with the pursuit of the right spiritual direction that prophets involve themselves. The prophet is at the same time a king and a high priest, herald and messenger of the instructions and prophecies received by him from God. But he needs to be supported by the strength and union of a community of equals, to realize his prophetic goal.

The importance Padrinho gave to the spiritual work of the everyday was lived by his own example. When his health permitted, at five o'clock in the morning he was already in the yard waiting for the sun to rise and for his work companions to arrive. In addition to his well-known gift as a spiritual leader, Padrinho Sebastião was a master canoe builder. With his small team, he spent days in the forest directing the work and exerting himself in spite of his doctor's prohibitions. While he walked from one place to another, watching over the making of two or three canoes at the same time, Padrinho always embellished his technical explanations and instructions with precious spiritual detours and commentaries, which completely charmed his visitors.

The Daime's hymns frequently speak of Noah's ark. This archetypal old story of the righteous facing the flood and the salvation of the faithful is encountered in the archaic layers of human history. Sebastião Mota de Melo, the visionary but illiterate rubber tapper, was also the builder of an ark, although his biggest canoes were nothing like Noah's ark. But when I see the line following Padrinho, my heart expands and I see the village of Mapiá as being an immense ark, spaceship, and laboratory.

One day, as we reached the middle of the forest, we stopped to rest and I asked with a certain double meaning, "Father, what is easier for you to build, canoes or this enormous ark?" And I pointed to the view of Mapiá, visible from where we were standing.

He answered, "This is one of my favorite images: the New Jerusalem. It was the spirit of truth that whispered in my ear the hymn that says, 'In paradise one should tread righteously / Journeying very cleanly / In the presence of my Father.'[1] Here I am giving proof of what the spirit told me to do. The rest is up to all of you. I am old already and sick, I think that on the day of our reunion I will receive you on the other side."

"Did the master give you this mission?"

"Thank God, I received this power and now I know what I am doing. Because everything for me is truth and certainty, everything I go through, I know why. And thanks I give to my Supreme Lord, who brought to me sufficient knowledge to undo the false and the strength to carve the path to world fellowship."

As he said this, Padrinho's eyes shone with flames from a great depth. While he spoke of these themes, it was as if he visualized through clairvoyance certain dimensions and secrets that were still inaccessible to us. After a small pause, he continued, "I myself did not know if I wanted to prepare a people here in this place, but I am not really here because of what I want. And neither did I leave Colônia 5,000 because I wanted to. I left because it was shown to me. I saw the whole world and knew that I should gather those belonging to God and wait in the center of the forest for the right time. It is because I believe in God that I am here and have true and living faith in the doctrine of Raimundo Irineu Serra. Because of this I am here inside this forest, moaning and crying, but then there are times that we receive consolation."

> *I feel pain, I feel pain*
> *And feel pleasure in my heart*
> *To be reunited*
> *Here with my brothers.*[2]

"What did Mestre Irineu say about the future?" I asked.

"He told me to trust in the Superior Power and assured me that there would be a good time for a few for a little while but that those who do not prepare and gain spiritual knowledge will be sorry."

"And is community the solution, Padrinho? Or is there a chance at this point of someone saving himself or herself alone?"

"My son," he gave a long exhalation and began to answer. "We have to continue developing our consciousness. The greatest school for this is the relationship with others; together we can achieve many things. The will, when it is not manipulated by the lie, when it finds the direction of truth and unites with others who are searching for the same thing, has great power. We should not fear the peace of Christ, in spite of knowing that it is a powerful cleanser that unites the power of the sun, moon, stars, ocean, forest, and earth. Mother Earth offers us everything, and we respond by assaulting her. Some are like beasts and try to grab, take advantage of, sell, and kill others. They envy each other's land when actually everything belongs to God. Each one by his or her own doing is self-destructing and yet seems not to care. This egotism suffocates the world and shortens its chances.

"It seems that the time of the great kings is over, when one person had the charisma and the strength to sustain a great empire. It is better to unite with others as equals. With all intent on doing their part, unity is achieved, and we realize what is missing in each person's understanding."

"Isn't that what it's all about?" I said, trying to rejoin the conversation.

"It is a very fine test and a very big responsibility as well. This union is what I would most like to see, and we have not yet reached it. It seems that I will not see it. A pure brotherhood and sisterhood, one so pure that anyone who comes against us changes his mind and seeks our help. And whoever is not with us lives among the illusions and miseries of the big cities, which seem to have no expectation of the purification that will come to this world."

Padrinho then sang one of his hymns, which was usually how he emphasized a point or ended the conversation temporarily.

> *Whoever comes against me*
> *Get ready to suffer*
> *I have with me the Queen*
> *And my Master to defend me.*[3]

He finished singing his verse and continued. "That is what I want, to have a tranquil people, pure, with consciousness of having fought before without winning. Now our chance to win has increased! Christ is already sick of remaining nailed to the cross. He is now coming to be victorious, for the harvest. To me, it seems that the world will not remain as it is. We are the Divine creation! If we make beasts of ourselves, it is because we desire that. Let us awaken promptly, brothers and sisters, to see if we can realize this united community, united people so that everyone who hears about the Daime and the Juramidam's people should find only reasons to respect us. We live a different politic, no tricks. This world is so very well made and we are playing here as idiots, not taking advantage. We hope the time is ending when some can gain power at the expense of others. Do you want power? Show your worth, back up what you say, and be a beacon to your brothers and sisters! Let's finish the false power of pretension and ignorance. Now it is necessary to be in the time of the real greatness."

"It is here and now, isn't it?" I added to the flux of Padrinho's words.

"This boasting should be stopped! Finished! I have the faith in what is of God. We should live like the forest, where all the trees are the same, from the smallest until the biggest. One tree falls as the other breaks but not one is complaining. They are all happy. All of this we need to learn to live within our community, following the peaceful teaching that Divine nature gives us. Observe how the world is made and how it can be improved. Be a good friend to your brother and sister, because without him or her it is more difficult. Nobody alone moved such a heavy thing as the world, but love, when it is proven in brotherhood and sisterhood, can be a lever that transforms the world."

All of this he told us and other things that I do not remember, but the joy of that moment and the love that his presence inspired in me stays permanently inside my heart. He expected from us the understanding of the big picture, of what was at stake, but he always advised us to steer toward simplicity. The one who cannot be a simple and humble worker of the Lord will not pass untouched by the changes.

Padrinho got up, shook the dust from his pants, and concluded, "I am already a bit old. I may want to pass on before the final days arrive, so I can also be in spirit among the ones who stay on this side. I hope that soon people will be living consciously, without so much silliness, so much gossip. It is time for us to step forward and assume the image and likeness of the true human."

We were at the edge of the forest. Padrinho finished our dialogue and entered a path followed by all of us in single file. The line was so big that it snaked through the forest. It was a wide and pleasant path that took us to the Igarapé Quinanzinho. After about ten minutes of walking, we arrived at the place where canoes were built. A great noble tree had been felled, and from the main trunk the shell of a canoe was being carved, and finished with an axe and a chain saw. It was turned upside down and supported on big movable props. On that day workers were opening the shell. Padrinho explained, "We build a fire under the tree until the wood becomes black and softens. Then we turn it right side up and use those clamps over there, do you see?" He pointed in the direction of two giant clamps.

After the fire had been burning for a while under the canoe, at Padrinho's orders, it was turned right side up with the shell on the ground. Two men, one from each end of the canoe, started putting the clamp on the edge and pulling outward with all their body weight, forcing the wood, softened by the fire, to open itself lengthwise without cracking. As the men opened the canoe with clamps, another man nailed pieces of wood in its interior so it would hold the correct shape at that point. Now it was missing only the finishings: the prow, the stern, ropes, benches, a place to put the motor, and so forth. The old man was happy that the canoe came out without cracking.

We walked a little farther in the forest to another canoe yard where two other men were sawing the two sides of another trunk for a canoe eight meters long. Up to a certain point, each canoe was shaped with a chain saw. After that, work was done with an axe and smaller tools, which demanded a lot of patience and expertise.

The old man sometimes showed irritation with the slowness of his apprentices. He would tell stories about the old days when canoes were made in half the time and only with machetes and axes. With a dyed thread they marked the lines for the cuts. And with a small piece of vine for measuring, which they handled between the fingers dexterously, they marked the trunk with the precision of a measuring tape. Once the shell was cut, marking the canoe's plumb line was the most delicate part. He liked to make that mark himself and preferred to be present for the final phase of the opening.

The work was being concluded. We took a break to drink coffee and eat boiled manioc. Attracted by our sweat, the bees were not giving us a break. At the end of the afternoon we found that the path to the river was crossed by many round long logs where we had to push the canoes. Inside myself, I felt the conviction that I had been in this scene in another time with Padrinho and those people pushing canoes through other forests. In front strode the patriarch with the long white beard. Already almost back in the village, we made a circle and stood in silence for a couple of minutes. Padrinho began:

"I am here looking inside and outside. It is meaningless to try to pretend to be beautiful because I can see the uncleanness from inside. Let us love and respect, my brothers and sisters, otherwise there is no way! Do you want me to pass for a liar? Do you not believe in my word? Then let us realize it. I suffer because I see many who still are children and others who are asleep. It is necessary for all to sanctify their lives, sanctify their thoughts, so we can all live in peace and harmony, acquiring the knowledge without which we can never be happy. I am saying this to you because my self is not blind and he sees far. They already did all sorts of things to me in other incarnations and it continues to this day. But everyone follows the realized man nevertheless, isn't it true?"

"The truth is Christ," someone answered.

"He has been the only one who saved me until now," Padrinho

continued, turning to me. "Hold yourselves, my sons and daughters, who are missing the mountains of Mauá. It is still possible for you to stay where you are, learning and becoming steady. It is necessary to stop being a crybaby. Those from Rio de Janeiro, Minas Gerais, from here and there, everybody be firm! But if you see a crisis bubbling up, the hour has come. Mestre Irineu said we have a chance to escape."

"One has to pay attention not to miss the last plane," I joked.

"We are already accomplishing our mission with respect and tranquillity because we are at peace. But also it is not to lower the head for any bandit, no, I am following the Voice of the Desert, the voice that clamors in the desert! And I am already somewhat tired of calling those who do not hear!"

The old man got up and ended the conversation. Walking through the forest, the people followed snakelike on the path through the field under a sun that was still hot. We stopped to take photos and tape a video shot. Again, I saw myself as if I were in front of Noah and his ark. The community was this ark, and the doctrine was the renewal of the alliance.

The opening of the canoe by the fire symbolized the spiritual widening that is necessary for our rebirth, the sacred plants, taking on the role of clamps, stretching our consciousness and our hearts. I imagined the size of the original ark mentioned in the Scriptures. What a colossal effort it was to burn, turn, and open such a giant. This is what this village growing in the forest also represented. The headquarters for the collective effort of constructing "the ark" was the immense church on top of the hill just in front of us. This new ark sails the waters of the astral, and God knows where it transports us. The community is the new ark, the only one able to sail in the waves of the announced purification.

Padrinho looked at me as if he could see inside my vision and said to me, "To Noah was given the task of caring for all kinds of God's creatures, was it not so? Now let us see what we still can save. In our union, in the new community, we need to save at least our brothers and sisters. Each one who arrives is a gift whom we are receiving. Only united, one to another, will we be able to survive the purification."

The rest of the day I spent meditating about the expansion of the individual and collective consciousness. The strength of the fire purifies our minds, making them malleable to the consciousness expanders. God's clamps pull men's ears. As I was thinking this, I saw the tall figure of Padrinho Sebastião crossing the bridge to his big house. I looked at his figure, slender and full of energy, Sebastião Mota de Melo, canoe craftsman, builder of the "new ark" in a tropical New Jerusalem at the edge of the Igarapé Mapiá, the River Jordan of a new world.

Until evening I thought a lot about the theme of community, especially about everything we needed to get to the ideal of our good Padrinho. That night we gathered at the Star House to discuss some organizational issues. Padrinho Alfredo, with his practical sense, opened the conversation by explaining his ideal work structure.

"I cannot tell if we are sages or something else, but we need to have a solid material base, so we can work with a tranquil spirit. When this material base is missing, equality is missing, and where equality is missing, happiness is missing. We need an organization in which nobody weighs on the others. Let us stretch ourselves, knowing that above us is the sun, the moon, the stars, the infinitude of all! In the material world all is represented, and one has to be calm and have patience with all kinds of minds. Sometimes people walk in with a lot of imbalance in their lives, and we have to help, in addition to bearing our own situation. What we spend and gain with all of this is patience, is it not?

"We must always study the movement of the body, focusing on the weak points and helping the body and spirit to be strong in the current. This is the hope that Padrinho told us. We must grow in unity with less fussing and keep on preparing our corner here in the Amazon as our Lord told us through Father. After we look at the outside world, we give value to the Amazon. It is as a patch of grass in a desert, is it not?"

Padrinho, who was sitting silently, added, "Yes, and soon we will be all together. I have a living hope that all of a sudden when we are not even thinking about it, we will see our unity. And at this hour we will be propelled forward even further."

"And how are we going to know the hour?" I asked.

"It is not necessary to have doubt or be desperate or think about it all the time. When the time to return here comes, we will know that the hour has arrived."

"If we are attentive, does the spirit warn us?" I questioned.

"That it is time to get out he warns. But the voice of truth speaks very softly, do not forget," answered Padrinho. "Meanwhile, let us try to be closer, better the situation where we are, and then come here to where all are destined to gather. Let us perfect our knowledge. We have the need to be together to know ourselves, to be brothers and sisters, to be able to forgive and unite. But we still see a lot of fights and deceits, do we not? It is because we are all in a pot of purification. The community is this pot, a constant Feitio, is it not, Alfredo?"

"Yes, Father," answered the son and successor. "Our greatest richness is to be united with the Virgin Mother. In union nothing is missing and richness follows. We should not even need to worry about food or clothing."

"The Daime takes us until it says, 'Here is your place!' My greatest happiness is to live inside the forest, waiting for what Raimundo Irineu Serra said: that the Amazon would be the place to prepare for the purification. It is said that in the purification of another era there was a submerged city."

"Atlantis?" I ventured.

"Nobody knows where, do they? Perhaps it will now rise along with the realm of the Incas. It is enough discussion for today, is it not, my son?"

The meeting was finished, but some continued their conversation under a mango tree next to the Star House. Padrinho said goodnight and I started to return home. Without a doubt we were living a modern epoch of God's people, something like an era of the Essenes. We were continuing the old messianic search to make the splendor of the infinite fit inside our everyday lives.

15
• • •
The End of Time:
The New Beginning

HARMONY, LOVE, TRUTH, and justice are the necessary prerequisites for life to continue on this planet according to Padrinho Sebastião. During his life, he applied his energy to the creation of a great symbolic ark, a message to prepare men, women, and especially young people for the coming demands of spiritual life.

There are two very different ways to relate to prophetic revelations. When we do not anticipate their fulfillment during our own lifetime, we do not need to become directly involved with the problems predicted. A contemporary of Nostradamus would not have worried much about the catastrophe predicted for the year 2000, but those living in 1992 consider the issue differently. But in a very personal way, generation after generation, incarnation after incarnation, we all confront our own inexorable apocalypse. In the hour of our departure, we will be obliged to show a certain level of knowledge and a lot of serenity. Our situation on the other side may not be unlike what we experience on this side of incarnation. We will still need all our faith and trust in God.

Padrinho Sebastião insisted that this magical process of spiritual rebirth will become more urgent as we are invited to participate in the transformation of the whole planet; could it be at the advent of the millennium? Some people affirm this with certainty, while others doubt it. Some people pray for it to be so, while others ask God to grant more time to this material world so we can heal old wounds and again become worthy of hope. There are traditions that do not care to practice charity or

217

work for general salvation. They limit themselves to asking God to save only their group, those who on Judgment Day can show a "salvation identification card." But we must remember that the passage from this side of life to the other is the final level of everyone's initiation. And our biggest challenge is to verify our spiritual knowledge whether we encounter this trial alone in a bed or as part of some collective karmic enactment.

The date of the "event" is not so important if we consider that throughout the ages prophets have shown that reality is essentially atemporal. In Sufism prophets are called "doctors of the heart" and are believed to apprehend God's plan and present their diagnosis and prescription at the same time. Our world has already lived through many prophecies, so let those who ignore them suffer grave consequences.

The Semitic, Sumerian, and Babylonian sources tell of a flood that almost washed away all life on earth. Around the last glacial period, many tribes simply disappeared, while others migrated to warmer lands. The earth was repopulated, and many cultures with common roots completely lost contact with each other. All of this still does not explain the nature of the prophetic event of the end of time. The Christian tradition bases itself on a tradition preceding the people of Israel, found among the Essenes, who were waiting for the end of time and the advent of the Messiah. Their leader was called the Master of Justice, and they awaited His return. The writings and interpretations of the Essenes could be seen as the missing link between the Old and New Testaments. Saint John the Baptist was the prototype of an Essene prophet. Many seekers of the truth, be they scholars or intuitives, speculate about the connections that Jesus may have had in his formative years with the Essene community of Omra, at the edge of the Dead Sea.

As is well known, Jesus was not quite the Messiah that the Pharisees and Saduceus had expected. The Essenes could not hold within the limits of their community the magnitude and universality of the incarnation of Christ.

Jesus, when initiated by the Essenes, came to understand the mission for which He was destined. As explained by the Santo Daime tradition, Christ's spiritual rebirth coincides with His physical birth. When He arrived at this knowledge, He found within Himself the inner nature of the whole of humanity, bearing as it were the spiritual evolution of the planet up to that point. He recognized himself as being the avatar and savior so long awaited, He who broadens possibility of our understanding love and knowledge. His presence was a manifestation of Love and Divine Mercy. The Power of the Sun incarnated. Is not this fact a prophetic sign of a postponement of the end of time?

It seems to be so. It would have been unreasonable for a being of such magnitude, the Hebrew Yahweh, to incarnate his Son with the mission destined to save humanity and then have him perish right away. The power that averted this sentence was the Power of Love, embodied in the mystery of the Resurrection. Christ is the expression of the superior self present in the consciousness of all men and women. He is a symbol of spiritual rebirth and self-renewal, so that His followers may partake in His Passion and believe in the Resurrection.

The Passion and the Resurrection of the Prince of Light were keys left for those who seek to understand in themselves charity and faith. After His departure, the apostles closest to Christ began to speak of the end of time and of the fulfillment of the prophecy of His return to judge the living and the dead. Other more symbolic interpretations were also suggested about the term in which the prophecies would be fulfilled. It was said that unenlightened forces would gain power once again and seize the physical world until the final advent. This is the apocalyptic tradition that is attributed to John, and it can be read in many ways, but in truth there are many indications that evil has been very active during this past two thousand years. The End of Time and the Last Judgment have been awaited in the past, an enigma that remains present in all beings who returned to earth in search of their definitive rebirth.

Two thousand years is often cited as the time when the cycle will be closed and an inventory of the human experience will be conducted. It would be an end for some and a new beginning for others. But we should be examining what other prophets have to say. As in other times when a date was scheduled, the apocalyptic possibility of a sudden settling of accounts is always accompanied by the opportunity for a new postponement. It is understandable to resist the possibility of being precisely the generation that will see with our own eyes the Divine Judgment, but one way or the other, we all are going to pass through this transition to spiritual consciousness after the extinction of our physical bodies.

Padrinho Sebastião did not speak openly about this theme. Sometimes, when he wanted to emphasize the urgency of our transformation, he would remind us that according to the Julian calendar, 2000 would arrive four years earlier. Another time he referred to other dates, such as 2014. For Padrinho Sebastião, this decisive day was already here, and the question was how many angels were still missing to play their trumpets and, as he said, "to pour the contents of their cups over us." He did not hide; he was awaiting a very strong purification. Part of what he knew came directly from Mestre Irineu, and the rest was spiritual confirmation obtained in his own miraçãos through the years. From these he knew that the people of the New Covenant—the ark chosen for this new alliance—should be prepared at any time. We also should be studying the hymns that speak of a night of great transformation and of a gathering. There is a difference between expecting an end that comes gradually through old age and a sudden harvest by the Creator.

The extinction of the material world as a solution to a worn-out biological process is a comfortable idea for some of us. The alarm that was set at the beginning of time sounds, and we transfer our dematerialized consciousness to other planes, to which we gained access through hard work for self-knowledge. But the idea of a sudden change that puts in question the viability of human civilization on the planet as a whole is a challenge that only can be understood on a spiritual level.

Although matter on its more dense level is in question, it means the end of a world of illusion, not the real world. The "real" and practical solutions for this transition are eminently inner and spiritual. They depend upon a mutual surrender between the mind and the heart and consciousness and feeling, until we have found a safe place and the certainty of the permanence of our Christian flame. In the face of this certainty, all other questions are secondary.

If the final decipherment of the riddle of existence is a deeper issue of the self, which can only be resolved inwardly, why then build cities, communities, villages, or even ashrams in a material world? I have witnessed great confusion in many brothers and sisters about this issue. On the one hand, pessimism about the end of time can make us extremely negligent, disbelieving in the value of any material realization. On the other hand, some people make the dangerous presumption that nothing bad can happen. This induces in them a certain spiritual indolence, as we observe today in religions without any mystical content or passion to present to their followers.

I went to a scheduled meeting with Padrinho in hope of asking him to answer some of these questions. I wanted to have hope—hope in a new life and in the new world that I had heard so much about from him. I hoped for a new vision of Divine Justice and Mercy.

I found Padrinho up and about on the front porch. He was attending to a group while other people were waiting around for the opportunity to talk to him. After waiting we went to the kitchen for a coffee break and from there in search of shade where we could sit together. He started to speak:

"Each one of us should be connected directly with his or her superior self, so we can receive the communications from the spirit of truth. Those who are attentive and vigilant, as our Lord Jesus Christ asked, will know the right time and will be prepared, but those who take it as a joke and pursue their own silliness, never can discover their higher purpose. It is also necessary to have perseverance to discover whence we came and what we are doing here on this earth."

"Not everybody has courage," I retorted.

"Those who do not want to see it, do not seek it; but those who search may see it. There is a hymn that teaches:

> My brothers the book is open
> Everyone must read it
> It's by reading that we learn
> And by learning that we perceive.[1]

"Isn't it true?" He paused and repeated, "Isn't it true?" The question was so penetrating that nobody dared to say a thing. He continued, "Let us consider this a good and righteous lesson. I cannot call him 'brother' or call her 'sister.' If I call someone 'brother' or 'sister' and tomorrow I put them down, they are not my brother or sister! Whoever acts like that does not have consciousness. Whoever puts others down also receives the same energy because those who with iron wound, with iron will be wounded. This has been said before, and I am saying it now."

I questioned Padrinho Sebastião again, asking "It is difficult, is it not? Even yesterday, I was asking myself how today will become today. We think that in the present nothing happens, that everything belongs to the past. Only the past was once the present, wasn't it?"

"The thing is that everyone has to awaken. Nobody excluding anyone or gossiping about the ugly things that they hear about others! For what? If it is about foolishness, save it, because it is not worth anything. Ugly words and thoughts are unhealthy. The less we feed ourselves in this chain, the greater will be our healing power. Let us all give value one to the other here on earth. There is always a vagabond spirit wandering aimlessly through life and wanting only personal gain. This is not possible anymore. Whoever partakes of this condition should remember that he has one foot in the other world as well. Otherwise keep on going! Do not come here to disturb us. We live with the Daime and Santa Maria, the Divine plants, powerful medicines passing through our being, receiving the light and helping our brothers and sisters. This is it. Right now, it seems that nobody knows what will happen, but I believe by 2014 the new world will be completed!"

I asked with all the sincerity I could muster, when and what will happen.

"This is a secret. Very few know. Mestre Irineu knew."

"They say he told three people," I prodded.

"They say he received the revelation in that little marching hymn that ended up without words because the words told the secret, and he preferred to save it. Now nobody knows what is going to happen. I have the feeling it will arrive in the blink of an eye. A strong transformation, as strong as the one I passed another day, do you remember Alex?"

Padrinho Sebastião would always mention passages of great significance for me, such as the one that happened during my Hinário. He was righteously indignant about what Mestre Irineu called the correio da má noticia. As long as we cannot break away from that chain that lurks around us, from our most formal relationships to our intimate circles, no spiritual progress can be reached. A hymn I recently received says, "Correio da má noticia / It is what will bring us to the end of time."[2] What a strange compulsion people have to spread what is bad—and they perpetuate it, making judgments and holding values that do not arise from their own experience. Could this be one of the fundamental causes for insanity in the world? We remained silent, concentrating for a couple of minutes, and then Padrinho continued with his energetic voice.

"I have pure faith in our Juramidam, in all that Christ said is going to happen, and the teachings of Christ the Savior will not again be demolished in any way. We are holding tight, giving proof so that it can happen now. A new world is waiting to be born, vibrating with new vibrations. Our being also illuminates itself in these Divine vibrations. Imagine an entire people in the same attunement and vibration. We say together, 'This is how it is!' Faith moves mountains."

"Can we make a choice in the critical hour, a kind of 'I want to go' or 'I want to stay?'" I asked.

"If we have faith and certainty, trust in the Master and in ourselves, our power is total. Even to actualize God's word will be in our reach. It is a choice then, as you are saying. If we go to the other side, at least those who remain can read our conversation in the book you are going to write."

"Many will be called, but few chosen," someone said.

At this moment, Padrinho Alfredo, who until then had been silent, spoke up. "The transition is an abnormal feeling that the spirit feels in relation to its own flesh and that can lead to a conscious discarding of it."

His words echoed deep inside me. They described with precision moments I had already experienced under strong miração, the sensation of crossing the entrance in a way similar to what we will experience at our passage. Sometimes without being able to escape certain fears, I felt something very close to this "abnormal" sensation in relation to the body, with the desire to fly like a "tenacious bird," to use Sebastião Mota's expression. In these moments, we seem to have the power of choice, and we are not limited by the body. We can visualize the power of a community of united minds purified in love and with an ardent desire for truth. What can't we achieve in a high miração state?

Certainly an intense faith and a trust in the Divine promise can facilitate the precipitation of a formidable power, able to transform the world. Maybe the fulfillment of this goal is where the biggest secret lies, the fountain of all the power Padrinho Sebastião would like to see shine.

I remembered that I had received a hymn that said, "One day we will be harvested in the middle of a miração."

Padrinho Alfredo went on, "Then we are at the end of times! All the spirits are preparing themselves, purifying and repurifying, dying and being reborn. The best in the spiritual realm and the worthless in the material world are attuning themselves for a solution."

"This is what determines that a time is really final, the end of the line, isn't it?" I observed.

"Exactly," answered Padrinho Alfredo, "when types like Hitler and other antichrists incarnate, it is because of the proximity of the last battle. I have said that a prophet, like this old man here, passes this test. And the people, do they attest to the word of their prophet or do they let him speak alone?"

"Will I be a voice that cries alone in the wilderness?" wondered Padrinho. "To cry alone in the desert until one is disgusted by not being heard, isn't that what it's like? It is exactly like the story of the 'day and hour.' Everyone wants to know. There has been a lot published about what is going to happen, but I do not know how many really know. It has been two thousand years, and people have imagined in a thousand ways how God will once again assume his form as the true Christ. In past times there were worldwide wars, the catastrophe coming, and people screaming, but still no one listening . . . the greatest war is in the human heart. If we win the battle, we understand what comes. It requires a great effort, but we understand. If we lose, we remain in the preparatory phase and do not pass to prejudgment phase. In this way we do not arrive for the final audience."

Alfredo added, "It is a struggle against our own ghosts. They are the plagues and epidemics that can reach enormous proportions. Here, thank God, we are safe. It is more the beginning that is our concern. Whoever remains only in the material realms, in the illusion with a wandering mind, will have heavy suffering to endure."

Padrinho added, "God said to leave the cities because they will become a den of lions. He said for everyone to be born again. This is the story I was shown. . . . I am like Job and Lot, enduring the same trials to see if I am connected to God. I am connected with everything material and spiritual, fighting all kinds of doubt. Do not be deluded by the flesh and money. To merely pleasure the body does not further anyone. The body demands real worthiness from those who inhabit it."

Everyone was feeling uplifted. Padrinho Sebastião's magnetism was leading us to new and unexplored realms.

Padrinho Alfredo offered, "Many run because it is not easy to prepare the way for the spirit, and they continue to suffer because they did not prepare. In accordance with the story of Juramidam, He is the final judge of all that exists. He wants to gather all the sons and daughters because the Virgin Mother requested it. And the process is this one about which I was speaking. First, the spirit illuminates itself to be called, but even then there is the risk of not being gathered. Maybe from thousands a hundred will be taken. We have to gather the people who were together before this lifetime. Each one arrives and receives what is his or hers, remaining within the faith with certainty. They do the best to affirm themselves. Then we leave the bad behind us."

"And this is already the prediction of victory," I said, completing his thought.

After a pause, Padrinho resumed, "This is the story now: mother against daughter, daughter against mother, father against son, son against father, daughter-in-law against father-in-law. All of this is happening, and long ago it was said that this would be a sign of the end of time. God does not worry at all about this, so why should we be worried? Are we really capable of denying what we are? Is it lack of knowledge? Or are we innocent? But when we know that all is Divine, then we will not deny Christ anywhere! Consider this: where is the Midam? After that it is good to apply ourselves in the present. We are still somewhat spread out and do not know the direction in which everything will go, which makes it difficult, but one day we will unite. This is the story of God's people; this we know. The meaning of which is to always go toward a greater perfection and that together we will be even more so!"

"This mission is very serious, isn't it Padrinho?"

"Yes. It is necessary to be in tune with the sun, the moon, and the stars as the universal rulers. Present in the 'I am,' we cannot stay in denial. We should be the same in Heaven as on earth."

I looked at the setting sun. The moment was grave and majestic. I felt again that sensation of reliving a scene from the past, from another time when we waited together for this glorious event. We are again reunited to wait for it. As in a vision I had. We were all younger and we were silently gathered to investigate God's designs in the stars. I detached from my body and felt my spirit soar, wandering over these memories. I floated on the wind, like the time I drank Daime and became a condor. I flew above valleys and deserts. From there I saw us in ancient times, all covered by fur skins and witnessing a ceremony in which a similar drink to the Daime left us in trance. Soma of the gods, Soma of all human knowledge, a powerful, mysterious, and improbable Being who granted me this flight, soaring in the winds!

I flew over a city in the Andes' icy heights, maybe Machu Picchu. I looked at the terraces planted with quinoa, coca, and flowers and saw the stone aqueducts and stone staircases. There I saw us again, at sunrise, drinking the Daime in ceramic cups. We were all searching to understand the meaning of time and invoking God's oracle.

As I sat there next to them, a great quietness and serenity overcame me, and the image of the condor stayed with me. The shadows of evening had crept through the forest. We were in my small jungle hut, behind the Casa do Feitio. Above the altar, the jar of brown-yellow ayahuasca, Santo Daime, vine of souls, vine of the spirits. If my hour had come then, separating from my body would have been easy. I felt unafraid in my heart for the first time. Far from being the end of anything, it was a true beginning. A new hope was being born in me, awakening after a long, long sleep.

Paulo Amaringo
14.04.02

16

...

The Future of New Jerusalem

I WENT TO say good-bye to Padrinho Sebastião in May 1989. It was the day before I was to leave and I did not realize then that it would be my last time to see him healthy—totally lucid, active, and playful. We had made plans for me to stop at his house and to go together to the site in the forest on which I wanted to build my own house. I walked with Padrinho Sebastião and Padrinho Corrente along the path to the site. Arriving there, Padrinho Sebastião indicated the ideal site for the construction, near the merging of two small igarapés.

At that time, he was excited about some land above the Inauini River. His restless spirit still would not settle in a definite place. He considered the land around Mapiá weak for complete self-sufficiency in times of need. He felt that the future gathering of the Daime people was going to be big and that new locations for settlements would be necessary. He spoke more and more about the subject and referred to his visions of a high-placed land with small ravines near the juncture of two igarapés as being the definitive place for our community. Padrinho Corrente embraced the idea enthusiastically.

"You have to see Ramiro's land, which is located near Arama. It is just like the vision you are describing. You are still going to see it, right?"

"I would like to," Padrinho confirmed. "If I can make it, I will still climb with Alfredo and Waldette to look at this place."

Since this idea began to take hold of him, he was always saying that he would go "in a little while" to Inauini. In the beginning we laughed, thinking it was a joke, but with his constant references to it, the possibility of yet another exodus became less and less unlikely. I do not believe that he thought it would happen soon, but nevertheless, he visualized ahead new places and communities springing up nearby, and we would be called on to develop this project with great responsibility.

In the presence of Padrinho Corrente, a longtime friend, Padrinho Sebastião told me many things that day. Most of it I would not have remembered if not for the testimony of the faithful Padrinho Corrente who, as time went by, refreshed my memory with more details from his recollections.

Sitting there, near the edge of the path, the old man told me I should prepare myself to really follow him. "If you have really decided to follow me, trust in me and do not look back. Do as Lot did. You are going to go through many difficult things and feel them deeply. Do not listen to small talk, but go forth always trusting in me, because I am going to be with you. Find a way to study and learn from these situations. Have courage because they will pass."

"Are you going away?" I asked.

These words were full of double meaning, as if my intention in talking about his upcoming trip to Inauini could signify also his departure to the astral. He thought a bit before answering, and when he did, he was ambiguous.

"I am not leaving completely, but it is good for you to start getting used to the idea. Here it is, the city of the Daime. Here it is, the church. This will never end. It is not the same as when we left Rio do Ouro, but we are running out of space. There are a lot of people yet to be involved. That is why we are going to open new places to receive those who are still coming. The movement has grown a lot. In the name of the Holy Virgin! There were so many new faces when I went to Rio and Mauá that I do not know everyone's name in this great big family."

"Master Irineu's mission is expanding."

"I have had the satisfaction of accomplishing this with the help of all of you. But I am not deceiving anyone. You are not being deceived my son, are you?"

"I think not, Padrinho," I stuttered.

"I am not calling people to the forest with the promise it will be effortless, that it will be just taking it easy."

His tone, which had been serious, acquired a sudden playful tone, "I am inviting you to join me in God's plan for us. Though we go hungry at times, we are at the same time happy and satisfied. Be with me always so that I may always be with you."

He also explained the special mission that would be mine there in the forest. I had only God and Padrinho Corrente as my witness. I began to understand the meaning of my work within the Santo Daime and the effort I would need to make to deserve that placement I was receiving. This was the way that the transmission of the teachings, instructions, and degrees in the tradition of the Daime took place. Each receives his or her role and tries to achieve it one day. As in Alfredo's hymn: "Firm yourself and change yourself to be worthy."[1] Padrinho advised me about the times to come.

"Do not be shy. Go and return, more than once. Bring your family slowly so they can adapt. Little by little, people begin to overcome the difficulties, doubts, and disunity. It is always like this when we start, and it is not very easy to put your foot here in Céu do Mapiá. But slowly you can start to place people from here to Mr. Padrinho's land."

There at the edge of the forest, where I would one year later build my house, I definitely sealed my surrender to that man, my spiritual master and guide on this hard road of self-knowledge. It was then that I asked Padrinho to baptize me.

We walked to the edge of the path where a clear creek ran. I kneeled with Padrinho Sebastião, and he sprinkled water over my head while saying in a low humming voice, "I baptize you with this water, so that the gift of the Holy Spirit opens your mind and your heart to understand evermore the Divine mysteries." For a moment it seemed that the archives of all our history opened to me. I felt the thunderbird vibrate the air and heard his acute whistle. I heard a chorus of voices singing, "The one who baptizes here / Baptized in the Jordan River."[2]

A few days after that important encounter, I prepared myself to return home and to travel abroad. Upon my return, I felt tension in the air, but the news was that Padrinho seemed in good health. There had been a healing works before Father's Day in which he had strong *atuação* for many hours, speaking in another language. On that day, Saint Michael and Christ expressed their suffering through his mouth in a stirring manner. Some other entities gave warning to the people and announced that Padrinho would make his passage soon.

Padrinho had also gone to a healer from Boca do Acre, who material-
ized many objects that were inside his body. With the intent to rest and
continue his healing, he retired to a small farm called Anajas, which was
near the Purus River. However, on his return journey to Mapiá, Padrinho
exceeded his limits. Of an active and restless nature, he exerted himself
physically far beyond limits set by his doctors, pushing his canoe alone
through many segments as well as walking long distances through the
forest. Because of this physical effort, his condition took a turn for the
worse. And it was not long before we had news of a new crisis: cardiac
insufficiency.

When I arrived in the first days of October 1989, he had gone to a
small old hut on the other side of the Igarapé Repartição. He had left his
house at the center of the village and had not been able to feed himself
normally for a couple of days.

Two days before his birthday, his condition worsened dramatically.
The crisis continued through the early hours of the morning, and many
thought he would make the passage that day. Healers and mediums praying by his bedside created a strong healing current. His cardiologist was
brought in a hurry, and he warned us how delicate the situation was. On
his advice, the family made a decision to remove him by helicopter to
Boca do Acre and then hospitalize him in Rio de Janeiro.

This time his illness had serious consequences. When he arrived at
the church in Rio we could feel the difference as he talked with us. His
gaze would become empty for a few moments and a small stroke had
caused difficulties in articulating words. Even so, there were still moments
in which we felt the spark and vivaciousness of the old Padrinho we had
always known.

The hospital attempted to restrict access to his close family, but
Padrinho continued to receive everyone who desired to be with him. In
his simple but profound talks he kept encouraging his sons and daughters
to become true human beings. "To break the eggshell" was his favorite
image of spiritual rebirth. He reiterated his advice for us in many different ways, assuring us that death would no longer have power over us once
we let our light shine. After this understanding he prescribed community
life for a commitment to love each other with respect and trust.

During a recent works I thought about Padrinho's words when he had said, "We are here in this school, our Centro Eclético da Fluente Luz Universal (Eclectic Center of the Flowing Universal Light) here in Mapiá. We come here, one more time, to deepen our silence or meditation and to listen to the lessons embedded in Sebastião Mota's hymns. They are very important lessons, for those who are alive as well as for those who are here in spirit. Everything being said in the Hinário applies to everyday life, and love is an important theme. Let us try to discover how to love. We do not prove this love by speaking badly of one another. Much more eloquent is the testimony of the animal and vegetable worlds. I do not know of any confusion and neither have I heard of any complaints being registered by them. Indeed, every day shows us everything, plain and true. The great spiritual lesson for our community life is to perfect our doings, actions, and thoughts in our everyday life."

I was overtaken by the conviction that I had little time left with this man who played such an important role in my life. Each time I visited him he looked more like a shriveled bird, and an enormous love and gratitude would well up in me. It was only after the passing of many years that I came to better understand how much I owed him. Thanks to his understanding and charitable spirit, I succeeded in reclaiming everything that was positive in my previous incarnations and escaped an imminent fall in this life. If I had not been rescued by the Daime, I could have fallen.

Little by little, all of us from his inner circle were becoming accustomed to the idea of carrying on the path opened and cleared by Padrinho without his physical presence, but no one spoke openly about it because we always hoped for a miracle. Padrinho himself behaved in a normal, human way as he faced his serious illness and the ultimate consequences. He had a strong instinct for self-preservation, and he linked his hope of self-healing to the healing of humanity. He believed that with faith and true confidence in the Daime, the healing of the fellowship and of his own tired body was possible. He gave very little importance to the "shell," as he would refer to the physical body. He did not judge himself to be the owner of it. As his last hour came closer, he gladly participated in every attempt and proposal to heal him. Although in truth Padrinho's supposed healers were the ones benefitting by contact with the "patient."

For the works on the night of Saint Sebastian in 1990, Padrinho Alfredo, many members of his family, along with the committee that had accompanied Padrinho Sebastião to the south, visited our community in Mauá. Padrinho Sebastião stayed in Rio de Janeiro and was stable. During a break in the Hinário we went to a small dwelling at the end of the church. The Daime force was still strong with all of us. Alfredo sang hymns and we evoked many episodes from Padrinho's life with great emotion.

We went back in after a short break and continued the Hinário. Often, with the first rays of the sun, all brothers and sisters enjoy an inexpressible spiritual happiness. The feelings of solidarity produce a vigorous impulse of love that closes old wounds, heals, and transforms. But on that January 20, daybreak brought a heavier atmosphere, even though the works were strong and beautiful. When the mountains took on the rose of dawn, my heart did not become happy as usual. At the end of the works, a messenger arrived from Rio de Janeiro with the news of the passing of Sebastião Mota de Melo to the spiritual plane. Trying to maintain serenity, I approached his son and successor, Padrinho Alfredo, to tell him the news. The look on my face preceded my voice and he understood before I spoke.

"Your father made the passage." After a pause I added, "Do you want to say anything at this time?"

He shook his head to say no. I swallowed dryly and communicated the sad news to those present. A great emotion overcame all of us. I asked to sing a hymn that I dedicated in 1983 to Padrinho Alfredo. We sang with emotion:

> *Padrinho is Bastion*
> *Gives light in all places*
> *Padrinho in the forest*
> *Saint John in the astral.*
>
> *We should not have fear*
> *If he goes*
> *Because there is his son*
> *Who in the same Master dwells.*[3]

On that unforgettable night of Saint Sebastian, *o Bastião* (the Bastion), as Madrinha Rita liked to call her husband, our bastion of light, detached from his body and flew away from his beloved forest. On that night, all the centers, churches, and communities affiliated with Padrinho sang his Hinário. Padrinho's last hymn, "I Am the Shine of Sun," with which we always close our spiritual works, from that day on had a much deeper meaning. It was his last message in which he left signs so we could always find him.

> *I am the shine of sun*
> *I am the shine of moon*
> *I give shine to the stars*
> *Because they all follow me.*
>
> *I am the shine of sea*
> *I live in the wind*
> *I shine in the forest*
> *Because it belongs to me.*[4]

From now on we would have to develop a new way of communion with the universe, looking where he always declared knowledge was located: in the shine of the sun and stars, in the ocean and wind. By remembering these eternal things, we can keep love in the memory of our hearts. Love perpetuates itself and is the only channel to the infinite. On the day of his passing, a refrain occupied my mind: "What leaves a more permanent legacy than love?"

We drove down to Rio de Janeiro where a funeral Mass was to be held over Padrinho's remains. In the car, curving through the mountains, we were grave yet serene. After the Mass, we again sang Padrinho's Hinário spacing out each hymn with an Our Father and a Hail Mary. Two days later, the body was transported to Rio Branco. In the airport there we held a small ceremony before the helicopter's departure to Céu do Mapiá.

At the moment of the body's arrival in Mapiá, everyone was dressed in white, singing Padrinho Sebastião's Hinário, and a group of fardados then deposited the saint's remains in a newly built chapel. Thus ended the physical life of this guide and benevolent father who was born and lived in the interior of a great forest, where he taught his many sons and daughters to be true men and women of knowledge and prepared them for the new world.

I reflected on the meaning of his passage for the next few days. There was a clear feeling of emptiness, an orphaned state inviting me to meditate about our lack of capacity to carry forward the legacy of this prophet. It seemed to me that the requirement for the continuing incarnation of a prophet is the existence of a people who follow him. Without doubt, many of his visions had already been realized. As Padrinho himself affirmed one day, "I started with my dreams and visions and, thank God, I realized them all and they were for me a fountain of truth."

His relic had been laid in the earth: the man whose spirit had been the yeast that leavened the unformed dough. Undoubtedly, much remained to be done to realize Padrinho's vision. But in a certain sense a prophet is a natural leader. His knowledge and charisma persuade the great masses, stimulating the people to prove their faith. The prophet prepares the future paths that God reserves for His elect. The elect are those who fulfill His will.

Even when the prophet has already obtained the spiritual realization of inner divinity, his ability to realize the prophecies still depends on his capacity to move the elected people to the fulfillment of their destiny. Those elected are not genetically privileged or predestined. We choose ourselves for a destiny determined by the prophets we follow. Padrinho, therefore, had to live between the happiness of seeing a large part of his dreams realized and his apprehension over the inertia in realizing the deeper essence of his teachings.

It was difficult in moments of deep reflection not to feel an accusation in our hearts. We could not avoid the implication of our own weaknesses and errors in the early departure of Padrinho. I believe that, in any place in the world and at any time, disciples have to go through the same feelings when their guru leaves. In spite of the inescapability of the destiny, when Padrinho's body arrived that day in a helicopter, each one of us asked: Could we have done things differently and have had him stay longer among us?

No external admonition could be more eloquent than this one. It was in this way that we awakened to the hard reality of the decade of the 1990s, the last decade needed to complete the second millennium, since the coming of Christ in this corner of the universe. We now felt this great responsibility of being the people who reaffirm in our hymns His return for harvest. We felt orphaned, but this was balanced by signs of the spiritual presence of Sebastião Mota among us, soothing us while instructing and exhorting us to continue his work.

At the closing of these reminiscences, I feel the necessity of summoning some images to emphasize and enrich the meaning of this story. The message of Padrinho, the wisdom from the ancient forest, full of peace and hope, has much to tell the neurotic inhabitants of an urbanized and polluted planet. Our world is facing a great purification, but the use of Santo Daime in the service of acquiring self-knowledge facilitates access to deeper levels of consciousness and awareness. This is presented to us by the miração. In the miração we are obliged to understand in the astral, in direct contact, the basic laws governing our health and many other aspects of our lives.

Even when we are not prepared to walk the path of the sacred plants, there remains an urgency in our time for all to awaken, so they can be finally reborn, assuming and recognizing their role and mission in the great transformation. Padrinho Sebastião said that it could happen suddenly, making the idea of leaving any spiritual task for tomorrow nonsensical. A spiritual warrior should be prepared for departure at all times. If he or she is really a warrior, the return to the physical must be of secondary or of no importance each time one is confronted with the "reckoning." What is important is the quality of love and the mastering of ourselves, so we can face the power in humility and loyalty.

This is the healing that Padrinho Sebastião proposed to all of us through what he called "remembrance of the past." Remembering increases our faith. And by believing in eternal life we are reborn into it until we are intensely alive on the physical plane but have no fear of abandoning it. The key that he proposed to us was not new: it was the recognition of the same Divine Being who dwelt among us two thousand years ago, saying these same things.

Padrinho Alfredo, the man to whom was entrusted the task of continuing his father's mission, ably summarized these teachings while at my house in Mauá in 1992. He began, "What happened proves what is written in the Scriptures. We are in the squeeze of the end of time and the return of Christ. We should be firm and tranquil in understanding and accomplishing what my father left us. Each vessel should feel that the life that dwells in him- or herself is the same as in others, an understanding necessary so we can live together as a community. Then we will remove the martyrdom and suffering from among us. This weighed heavily on the departure of the head of our spiritual household. His words were like Christ's words: be clean within and without! But some still were fascinated by mundane trinkets. That is why for us healing is in the doctrine. Give up your ignorance and find more patience and calmness to understand this teaching of Christ, now being offered through this drink, the Daime, or in some other way if this is better for you. It depends on us to bring faith to our understanding. We will only be healed when we consider everyone equal. The first announcement was given in Isaiah's prophecy, more than six hundred years before Christ was born, and nobody understood what he announced or who would arrive."

"They waited for another powerful king who never came," I said.

"Exactly. He spoke in a way that at the time nobody understood. Then Christ arrived, and initially only a few believed."

I had a thought that everything indicated that prophets of today are perhaps subject to the same incredulity. Then I asked, "How did Padrinho Sebastião understand the process of individual healing?"

"He said that what most often got in the way were unworthy thoughts and negative feelings. But the Daime helps to burn our karma. Sometimes we have to go through the eye of the needle experience, but when we acquire knowledge, we stop our negative feeling and thinking."

"So the knowledge releases us from wanting or possessing something more than ourselves," I affirmed. "It is not only to take Daime. Padrinho Sebastião said in his hymn that, 'Even better than knowledge is the ability to correct oneself.'"

"Yes," said Alfredo, "and that is why I say that all of us who take the Daime regularly should clean our minds until these difficulties come to an end. The struggle for equality can also be difficult. Everyone has his or her place and should be satisfied. My father's plan, which is now mine, is to realize something that is hidden inside this doctrine. There is a great power in our story. In the hour in which we will be reunited with God in the world, we will need this power."

"Material and spiritual power," I added.

"Freely we give what we freely receive. The doctrine is going to receive a lot because it gives so freely. We need to navigate with a clean mind, without giving extra work to others. To live while making work for others, in and out of the Daime, to stay stuck in our opinions, to bring sadness and exhaustion to meetings or wherever we may go. . . . This is not advisable. It is necessary to finish with this attitude quickly."

As he spoke I kept looking through the half-opened door of my office. The hummingbirds were flying over the beds of dahlias and returning to their nests at the top of the cypress trees. We rested a bit in the office, still recuperating from the emotions brought up by discussing the passage of Padrinho Sebastião of more than two years earlier.

In the days preceding the celebration of Saint Sebastian, I had a strong omen concerning his passage. I was seated in the old armchair that I'd inherited from my father when I had a clear vision of Padrinho descending the stairs of my small wooden tower. He had on a checkered flannel shirt and gave me a beautiful smile. At the time I felt that he would still see my house finished. We had planned this moment two years before, dangerously perched on the scaffolding of the construction. Whenever the idea of his departure would pass through my head, I would hold on to the hope of this visit. Really, every time I was with Padrinho during his recovery time in Rio de Janeiro, he promised to soon be well enough to visit us in the mountains. In my vision of Padrinho descending the stairs, smiling, it seemed to me for a moment as if his visit was happening. It was his spiritual presence that was manifesting itself two years later.

I asked Alfredo, "My friend Padrinho Sebastião had no fear of anything, did he? His words inspired us to have great courage. I think it is why we miss his physical presence so much."

"His example was one of humility. I now feel the responsibility he had felt through his whole life—all these people working in the Daime, only God can hold all this together. But a secret exists in this story of Mestre Irineu and Sebastião Mota that, though serious, gives great pleasure and lifts us up. Our tradition aims very high—up there where the sun is. From here on earth we try to see and understand everything, but that is not possible. I mean, spirituality is a page we know to have another side, but we have not yet turned it."

"And what side is that? Is it the one we customarily call death?"

"There are many things on that side. We glimpse them only as shadows. . . ."

"That are ours."

"That are our phantoms also. According to Father, if they appeared to us at once we would wet our pants from fear. Do you understand? Because they manifest in our feelings as well as our vision. You feel in the flesh as well. The flesh trembles. This is the crucial moment of the revelation of knowledge. Some seconds or minutes in this place can be the glimpsed reward of a lifetime of striving."

I agreed, "It is incredible that the Daime can give us this in such a clear form and still there are those who doubt."

"Isn't it true? Even we sometimes doubt this internal knowledge of everything that Creative nature manifested. It manifests its power in everything. That is why the Daime is a very serious study. It clears, it gives, it can inspire, but it is necessary to deserve the knowledge: at the right hour the doctrine will ask you to confront this knowledge."

"That is the 'rebirth' as the old Mota called it," I said.

"It is. Without this knowledge, it is impossible to be firm. And if you cannot be firm, then there is no advantage in spending years cultivating something with no future for you. So this future is in each one of us. If we pay attention and enter through this angle, we arrive at this authentic spiritual healing," concluded Padrinho Alfredo.

I continued thinking how it was hard to affirm and to give proof of all the things that Padrinho affirmed and proved. I remembered how he suffered to obtain all this knowledge, including his combat with Tranca-Rua. I asked then, "But everything that Padrinho did was in full consciousness, was it not?" The son then made an expression that reminded me of the father and answered, "With a lot of consciousness as well as tranquillity. Father felt that he had all the knowledge of the other side. When Father entered into this story, he had visions and only when he fulfilled all of them could he reconcile with everything. When we arrived at Céu do Mapiá, his healing was concluded, and he recovered from the contact with Satan and his legion of darkness and received the vision of the New Jerusalem. He said that not even he had seen clearly what was inside New Jerusalem. He wanted the people to penetrate into it with the Daime—and they will like what they see!"

"He spoke of a transformation. Was it the new world, as he liked to call it?"

"It was. He repeated many times that he was waiting for this old world of dirt and ambition to pass and for the arrival of the new world, for a new generation, a new system, a new life. The hymns speak of a new life to be found through Christ and Holy Mary, don't they? But they also speak of how much care we must have from now on because he said that in a blink all can be transformed. This experience will be difficult to bear for those who have no practice. The Daime revealed some things about it to me also."

"What?" I asked anxiously.

"Suddenly material life becomes abnormal because everyone has already begun to sense a spiritual life. There are already signs of it. My father also said that 2000 is the mark, a crisis will come, but he thought it could come earlier as well. A global audience is going to manifest. Now I do not know from which angle it will come. What I call an audience is also a great purification; we will experience lessons and gain a lot of knowledge. Every day this presence is growing. Now the world itself and its people are in distress. But they are not yet at the 'audience,' do you understand?"

"Do you mean that they are not conscious of the intent of the purification and of the lesson they are learning?"

"Yes! Those who do not seek the answer will fall under Divine Justice. Father affirmed it to be a justice that manifests itself in the astral. And around the year 2000 he expected us to have the opportunity to make a choice."

"A choice?"

"I do not know what he meant by it." He became silent.

Many times when Padrinho was still alive, I approached with this question. He would all of a sudden become evasive, as if he intended to say that we should forever do battle to obtain the answers. Because of this he insisted: There will be a choice to stay on the material plane or not.

Alfredo added, "It will be through a world purification that the choice will occur, but maybe only those firm and with conviction will be able to bear the event."

"To stand the force of this spiritual encounter," I added.

"Yes, the old man would say that. And that he would be on the other side. He was already preparing us for the fact that he would not be with us forever in the physical plane. Always saying, 'There is a people to form, there is a people to affirm.' He started with one, then two, today there are more than a thousand, I do not know how many . . . but still there will be a fine sifter to find out who is going, isn't it true?"

I added meditatively, "So it is in this encounter that a new people will be formed, a new world. I remember Padrinho saying that in this moment matter could also become eternal."

"Yes, he said that but what he really affirmed was that from the year 2000 on we will be with the spirit. 'But Father,' I said, 'what about our bodies?' He answered, 'They are not worth anything.' And I continued, 'But you look so handsome with this long beard. If you purify a bit more will it be impossible for you to stay here throughout?' And he would even make faces, 'The physical body? It has its place—in the hole! Our final true value is found in the spirit. Everything is in the spirit. From 2000 on, those who are not in the spirit will die again.' And he would warn me, 'Be careful not to die because those who die now, die forever; there is no more time to reincarnate. They will die and be completely dead, do you understand?' Thus he would speak, 'It was fascinating but hard to bear the weight of the possibility of being the generation to witness all this transition.'"

We fell silent for a moment, reflecting on the twilight. Then I asked, "And ahead of all of this, what is the message of hope that Padrinho Sebastião left and what can you reaffirm to give us the hope that everyone is searching for, with or without Daime?"

"The message is to work for justice, to promote things more or less straight and just and always be on guard. We have to be mindful of what he told us. It is necessary to remember what he said and to awaken as he has asked us to. Otherwise, even working in the doctrine we can be lost. If we do not have the conviction that our deeds are for God's sake, it is of no use. To have this certainty, it is necessary to make an effort to be evermore humble. Those who remain unattached to material things will not cry from the loss of them. Those are the ones who will be able to survive the transformation of this world."

"What else do we need to do?"

"Fulfill God's will. We must really respect nature, even while we

respect God. Father's last hymns have many lessons. If we do not manifest the lessons of the New Jerusalem, then it is not there! Let us consider
ourselves all brothers and sisters, living according to the doctrine, sons
and daughters of God. Do not let nonsense enter in, do not let money
dominate us, having passion for what we gain and feeling sorrow when we
lose. But I do not know . . . there is not much to do in this world! After
the person finds him- or herself . . . what is left?"

I added, "Life with discernment and abundance, as Padrinho used to
say."

"It is necessary to be calm and to have clarity, because everything is a
mission. What Father taught most at the end was about unity."

"Padrinho often spoke of a later vision in which he flew over the
burning forest. How was it?" I asked.

"It was already after he had received his last hymn, 'I Am the Shine
of Sun.' That day he had a miração inside the church in Mapiá. When he
came back from his inner journey, he said that it was a strong miração.
He saw the whole forest burning and many people had fallen in ashes,
including me, his son. He saw me in a pit of ashes and it was a great struggle for him to descend into that great fire to get me. The miração was
so strong that he would sit down, stand up, and moan. He said, 'I saw
everything in flames, even people, but it was impossible to save the whole
world, but when I saw you rolling inside the ashes, I went to get you.'"
Alfredo beamed with joy at the thought of his father's tender attention
in the miração.

We sat for a while in silence, then Alfredo spoke again, "You asked
before about hope, didn't you?"

"I did."

"The image that comes to me now is of the day Father said, 'My son,
we should be well prepared and conscious of what can happen from one
moment to the next around the year 2000. But even knowing the date,
just in case, shouldn't we till the soil and water our plants?'"

In the moment Padrinho was making his passage my thoughts traveled to the break at the works of Saint Sebastian. I interrupted, "Friend,
do you remember the hymn you sang for us in which there is a verse he
did not want to publish? Why was that?"

"He considered it to be a very strong revelation. And although he did not want it published, we all know and use the whole hymn. Maybe we are already in the time when the verse is to be sung. In the change of the name to Juramidam a new understanding is in the rising."

Alfredo found the right note and sang for us the hymn with the unpublished verse, while we pondered over the fulfillment of our humanness and the reconnection of our bodies to soul and spirit.

My Master is with me
In the world of illusion
I hail the Eternal Father
Jesus Christ and Saint Joseph.

Here I'm singing
Paying attention
I hail all beings
And the Virgin of Conception.

The Master who teaches me
He's in my heart
I work with love
To receive salvation.

The name has changed
So as not to have confusion
Changed from Jesus Christ
Now to Juramidam.

The brilliance that thou hast
Is where the beauty is
I hail our Mother
Who is the Mother of the Savior.[5]

Notes

• • •

FOREWORD

1. Charles Tart, *Altered States of Consciousness* (New York: John Wiley and Sons, 1969), pp. 161–67.
2. The author worked with Joseph Campbell for many years, hearing him lecture and having personal conversations with him. This "largest building" was often referred to by Campbell.
3. John Humphrey Noyes, *Strange Cults and Utopias in Nineteenth Century America* (New York: Dover Publications, 1966).
4. See *Emanuel Swedenborg: A Continuing Vision,* Robin Larsen, ed. (available, as are other works by this remarkable man, from the Swedenborg Foundation, 32 N. Church Street, West Chester, PA, 1938).

CHAPTER 2. THE PROPHET OF THE AMAZON

1. I Take This Drink—Mestre Irineu n:124
2. Shading Tree—Maria Damião n:16
3. I Live in the Forest—Padrinho Sebastião n:6
4. Flower of Jagube—Mestre Irineu n:38

CHAPTER 3. THE DIVINE GARDENER

1. I Came to Justify—Padrinho Sebastião n:116
2. My Father Did Tell Me—Padrinho Sebastião n:84
3. My Father Is the Key of Harmony—Padrinho Sebastião n:155

4. To Say That You Are with God—Padrinho Sebastião n:14
5. Concerning the Virtues—Mestre Irineu n:78
6. This Was the Pleasure—João Pereira n:6
7. Remembering—Padrinho Alfredo n:24

CHAPTER 4.
ZEN CANOEING IN THE IGARAPÉ

1. My Brothers and My Sisters—Padrinho Sebastião n:14

CHAPTER 6.
PADRINHO SEBASTIÃO AND MESTRE IRINEU

1. I Was in a Palace—Padrinho Sebastião n:1
2. I Was in a Palace—Padrinho Sebastião n:1
3. I Was in a Palace—Padrinho Sebastião n:1
4. I Was So Joyful—Padrinho Sebastião n:15
5. I Am—Padrinho Sebastião n:28
6. I Am—Padrinho Sebastião n:28
7. Fine Silver—Padrinho Sebastião n:65
8. It Is in the Sun and in the Moon—Padrinho Sebastião n:66
9. I Came from Afar—Padrinho Sebastião n:69
10. When My Master Arrives—Padrinho Sebastião n:73
11. I Present My Truth—Padrinho Sebastião n:74
12. I Came to Gather—Padrinho Sebastião n:82
13. Here I Am Going to Reveal—Padrinho Sebastião n:15
14. I Lift Up My Flag—Padrinho Sebastião n:89
15. The Lecture—Antônio Gomes n:2
16. In the Sun, the Moon, the Earth, and the Ocean—Padrinho Sebastião n:91
17. Night Dew—Padrinho Sebastião n:111
18. I Went on a Journey—Padrinho Sebastião n:126

CHAPTER 7. I RAISE THIS BANNER

1. This Is How I Want to Be—Padrinho Sebastião n:127
2. I Was in a Palace—Padrinho Sebastião n:1
3. I Am within the Truth—Padrinho Sebastião n:37
4. To Say That You Are with God—Padrinho Sebastião n:14

5. What Are You Going to Do?—Padrinho Sebastião n:21
6. The Children Seek for the Father—Padrinho Sebastião n:129
7. My Father I Want Your Love—Padrinho Sebastião n:149
8. I Ask My Brothers—Padrinho Sebastião n:16
9. Here I Am Going to Reveal—Padrinho Sebastião n:15
10. God Is for Everyone—Padrinho Sebastião n:115
11. New Annunciation—Alex Polari n:65
12. I Already Said and Am Going to Say—Padrinho Sebastião n:95

CHAPTER 8.
THE DUEL WITH THE SORCERER

1. New Annunciation—Alex Polari n:65

CHAPTER 9. I LIGHT MY CANDLESTICKS

1. My Brothers and My Sisters—Padrinho Sebastião n:14
2. Voice in the Desert—Padrinho Sebastião—New Jerusalem n:9
3. God Is Your Knowledge—Padrinho Sebastião—New Jerusalem n:25
4. My Candlesticks—Padrinho Sebastião—New Jerusalem n:8
5. I Gave You a House—Padrinho Sebastião n:143
6. Hail Mary—Padrinho Alfredo n:95

CHAPTER 10.
FEITIO: GOD'S WILL, HUMAN ACTION

1. Three Noble Springs—João Pereira n:27
2. The Daime is the Daime—Padrinho Alfredo n:84
3. I Shake—Mestre Irineu n:46
4. The Queen of the Fire—Alex Polari n:67

CHAPTER 11. THE SPIRITUAL REBIRTH

1. My Brothers and My Sisters—Padrinho Sebastião n:14
2. I Sung Alone on the Bar—Mestre Irineu n:74
3. Lecture—Antônio Gomes n:2
4. Sun, Moon, Star—Mestre Irineu n:29
5. I Live in the Forest—Padrinho Sebastião n:6
6. Divine Moment—Sônia Palhares n:3

CHAPTER 12. MEMORIES OF THE PAST

1. The Ocean Rises—Germano Guilherme n:36
2. Declaration—Alex Polari n:1.3
3. Declaration—Alex Polari n:1.3
4. The Cross—Alex Polari n:61

CHAPTER 13. LOVE IS TO BE SHARED

1. Battle of Love—Padrinho Alfredo n:132
2. Love—Padrinho Sebastião n:147
3. God Is Your Knowledge—Padrinho Sebastião—New Jerusalem n:25
4. The Symbol of Truth—Padrinho Sebastião n:142

CHAPTER 14. NEW WORLD, NEW LIFE

1. Voice in the Desert—Padrinho Sebastião—New Jerusalem n:9
2. The Little Boat—Padrinho Sebastião n:1
3. I Came and Was Called—Padrinho Sebastião n:17

CHAPTER 15.
THE END OF TIME: THE NEW BEGINNING

1. The Book Is Open—Padrinho Sebastião n:124
2. Between Death and Insanity—Alex Polari n:14

CHAPTER 16.
THE FUTURE OF NEW JERUSALEM

1. Very Quiet—Padrinho Alfredo n:152
2. I Ask That You Hear Me—Padrinho Sebastião n:145
3. My Padrinho—Alex Polari n:7
4. I Am the Shine of Sun—Padrinho Sebastião—New Jerusalem n:26
5. My Master Is with Me—Padrinho Sebastião n:39

Glossary

• • •

Afilhado   A spiritual protégé. In the Santo Daime tradition, when some-one has chosen a more experienced member of the community to be his or her Padrinho or Madrinha, that person becomes their afilhado, transform-ing the relationship to that of master and disciple.

Agarrube   An entity quoted by Mestre Irineu in his hymns. One of the three Kings of the Forest, he is also identified as one of the Three Holy Kings, together with Titango and Tintuma.

Alto Santo   A place near the city of Rio Branco where Mestre Irineu formed his first congregation.

Aparelho   The vessel, or medium, who receives and manifests the spirit in the mind and body.

Apuração   The point in the process of the cooking of the sacred plants when the mixture becomes the Daime, the entheogenic drink. It is also used similarly, when in the works our interior journey becomes intense, even hard sometimes, demanding transformation, and purification.

Apuro   Short for apuração.

Atuação   A form of spirit manifestation in which, through a medium, spirits are called to manifest both in the mind and in the physical body (especially the latter).

Atuar   To manifest the spirit in the body and mind.

Bailado   Collective dance performed during the ritual that is rhythmically marked by the maracas as the hymns are sung. The dancing is choreographed to generate an energy field and a spiritual current.

Bailar   To dance the bailado.

Bailava, Bailavam   Singular past tense and plural past tense of bailar.

Balançar   To shake, to tremble.

Balanço   The strong trembling or shaking that precedes purification.

Banca Espirita or Banca de Trabalho   Popular healing-spirit work in rural Brazil deeply influenced by the Yoruba culture in Brazil.

Batedor   An enchanted being of Amazonian folklore that lives in the water of the igarapé. The "batedor" produces a loud clapping sound, hence its name (one who pounds or beats).

Caapi   The name chosen by the English ethnobotanist Richard Spruce, in the 19th century to designate the type of *Banisteriopsis* with which the natives of Amazon prepare the entheogenic drink called *ayahuasca* or *Daime*.

Caboclo   The more evolved entities of the Yoruba spiritual tradition who are related to the spirit of the natives of the forest.

Caravaca Cross   Also known as the Saint Andre Cross. Traditionally from Northern Spain, it was introduced into the Santo Daime by Mestre Irineu. This cross symbolically acknowledges the Second Coming of Christ with a second horizontal cross beam.

Casa da Bateção   The room in the Casa do Feitio where the vine is macerated to the rhythms of the hymns.

Casa do Feitio   The building where the Daime, the sacred entheogenic drink that is used in the rituals, is prepared. The Feitio is one of the most important celebrations of the calendar.

Céu do Mapiá   The Daime community where reside the original church and its people. With a population of about six hundred people, it is characterized by great beauty, cleanliness, education, and a balanced relationship with the surrounding environment. It was founded by Padrinho Sebastião in the 1980s.

Chacrona   One of the names used for *Psychotria viridis,* an indispensable plant in the preparation of Santo Daime.

Colônia 5,000   The place where Padrinho Sebastião created his first congregation after leaving Alto Santo and where the seeds of the community were planted.

Compadre   A term of friendship used in the interior of Brazil.

Concentração   Meditation works with the use of the Santo Daime. The Concentração occurs twice each month on the 15th and the 30th.

Correio de má notícia   "The Bad News Post Office," the name given by Mestre Irineu to the circulation of gossip and things said and passed from one to another without knowledge of their source. According to him, this is responsible for many illnesses and afflictions that disturb the world.

Daimista   A practitioner of the Santo Daime religion.

Dimed   The branch of government that regulates controlled substance.

Dono   Popular title for married women; Mrs.

Encosto   The influence of a spirit entity in the aura of a living person. It usually refers to a presence that is not benign.

Estado Maior   Word borrowed from the army to define the body of "fardados," who have many responsibilities during the works.

Fardado   Those who have officially entered the Santo Daime church, and wear the uniform during ceremonies.

Feitio   The ritual celebration to make the Santo Daime, the sacred drink.

Fiscal   A church member officially designated to see that all rules of the works are complied with, and to help brothers and sisters when needed.

Hinário   The works that represent the apex celebration of the official calendar, where the sacred drink is ingested, and the hymns are sung and danced to, from dusk to dawn. Also the book of sacred, channeled hymns received by members of the Santo Daime that are sung at every Daime works.

Hymn   Songs received by the initiated direct from the spiritual world, each carrying a teaching. They are sung during the works and belong to the whole community.

Igarapé   Small river in the Amazon forest.

INCRA   Instituto Nacional de Reforma Agrária. The government agency in charge of administrating and distributing infertile land to rural workers.

Jagube   The name used for *Banisteriopsis caapi*.

Jura   Third person present tense of Jurar.

Juramidam   The name given by Mestre Irineu to the Divine Being who lives in the spiritual drink. Juramidam presides over the spiritual lineage of the Santo Daime. The hymns speak of Juramidam as being the new manifestation of Christ in the forest.

Jurar   To make an oath, a commitment.

Macumbeire   Black maguan.

Madrinha   Literally "grandmother," also the name for the female spiritual leaders in the Santo Daime tradition.

Mestre   Master.

Miração   The ecstactic visionary state characteristic of the Santo Daime, wherein each person becomes protagonist of his or her shamanic flight.

Mirando   First person singular past tense of "mirar."

Mirar   To have a miração.

Mirou   Third person singular past tense of "mirar."

Mutuca   Ferocious mosquitos.

Mysterium tremendum   The inexplicable mystery of the universe and life's existence.

Ogum Beira Mar   The Yoruba deity of war and iron, and in this case also related to the edge of the ocean.

Padrinho   The male spiritual leaders in the Santo Daime tradition. Literally it means "godfather."

Passagem   The special moment within the spiritual work, when each person needs to overcome quickly what is being crystallized to attain transformation. Depending on the resistance to the surrender asked by the Daime, the "passagem" is made with some effort and suffering.

Rainha   Short for "Rainha da Floresta" (Forest Queen,) guardian of the Daime doctrine. *Psychotria viridis* is also referred to as "Rainha."

Raspação   A step in the process of making the Daime. Literally it means "to scrape."

Santo Maria   *Canabis sativa*

Seu   Popular title for married men; Mr.

Star House   House where the healing works are performed.

Star-works   Healing works that are a part of the mission of charity of the Santo Daime doctrine.

Tarumim   Spirit entity related to fresh water, waterfalls, and springs. Brought to the Santo Daime through one of Mestre Irineu's hymns.

Tintuma   *See* Agarrube.

Titango   *See* Agarrube.

Trabalho   Literally "works"; it is the name for the ritual in the Santo Daime tradition in which the Daime is offered as Eucharist.

Tranca-Rua   Entity from the Afro-Brazilian diaspora. As a messenger between gods and men, they can therefore do good and evil.

Yagé   Another common name for ayahuasca or Santo Daime.

União do Vegetal   One of the main groups in Brazil using the ayahuasca in their rituals.

Unio Mystica   Communion with the mysterium tremendum.

Works   *See* trabalhos.

BOOKS OF RELATED INTEREST

Sacred Vine of Spirits: Ayahuasca
Edited by Ralph Metzner

Ayahuasca
The Visionary and Healing Powers of the Vine of the Soul
by Joan Parisi Wilcox

Iboga
The Visionary Root of African Shamanism
by Vincent Ravalec, Mallendi, and Agnès Paicheler

DMT: The Spirit Molecule
A Doctor's Revolutionary Research into the Biology of
Near-Death and Mystical Experiences
by Rick Strassman, M.D.

Plants of the Gods
Their Sacred, Healing, and Hallucinogenic Powers
by Richard Evans Schultes,
Albert Hofmann, and Christian Rätsch

The Shamanic Wisdom of the Huichol
Medicine Teachings for Modern Times
by Tom Soloway Pinkson, Ph.D.

Salvia Divinorum
Doorway to Thought-Free Awareness
by J. D. Arthur

The Encyclopedia of Psychoactive Plants
Ethnopharmacology and Its Applications
by Christian Rätsch

INNER TRADITIONS • BEAR & COMPANY
P.O. Box 388
Rochester, VT 05767
1-800-246-8648
www.InnerTraditions.com

Or contact your local bookseller